THE 7 HABITS

Habit 1: Be Proactive
Being proactive is more than taking initiative. It is accepting responsibility for our own behavior (past, present, and future) and making choices based on principles and values rather than on moods or circumstances. Proactive people are agents of change and choose not to be victims, to be reactive, or to blame others. They do this by developing and using four unique human gifts—self-awareness, conscience, imagination, and independent will—and by taking an Inside-Out Approach to creating change. They resolve to be the creative force in their own lives, which is the most fundamental decision anyone ever makes.

Habit 2: Begin with the End in Mind
All things are created twice—first mentally, second physically. Individuals, families, teams, and organizations shape their own future by creating a mental vision and purpose for any project. They don't just live day to day without a clear purpose in mind. They mentally identify and commit themselves to the principles, values, relationships, and purposes that matter most to them. A mission statement is the highest form of mental creation for an individual, a family, or an organization. It is the primary decision because it governs all other decisions. Creating a culture behind a shared mission, vision, and values is the essence of leadership.

Habit 3: Put First Things First
Putting first things first is the second or physical creation. It is organizing and executing around the mental creation (your purpose, vision, values, and most important priorities). Second things do not come first. First things do not come second. Individuals and organizations focus on what matters most, urgent or not. The main thing is to keep the main thing the main thing.

Habit 4: Think Win-Win
Thinking win-win is a frame of mind and heart that seeks mutual benefit and is based on mutual respect in all interactions. It's about thinking in terms of abundance—an ever-expanding "pie," a cornucopia of opportunity, wealth, and resources—rather than of scarcity and adversarial competition. It's not thinking selfishly (win-lose) or like a martyr (lose-win). In our work and family life, members think interdependently—in terms of "we," not "me." Thinking win-win encourages conflict resolution and helps individuals seek mutually beneficial solutions. It's sharing information, power, recognition, and rewards.

Habit 5: Seek First to Understand, Then to Be Understood
When we listen with the intent to understand others, rather than with the intent to reply, we begin true communication and relationship building. When others feel understood first, they feel affirmed and valued, defenses are lowered, and opportunities to speak openly and to be understood come much more naturally and easily. Seeking to understand takes kindness; seeking to be understood takes courage. Effectiveness lies in balancing the two.

Habit 6: Synergize
Synergy is about producing a third alternative—not my way, not your way, but a third way that is better than either of us would come up with individually. It's the

fruit of mutual respect—of understanding and even celebrating one another's differences in solving problems, seizing opportunities. Synergistic teams and families thrive on individual strengths so that the whole becomes greater than the sum of the parts. Such relationships and teams renounce defensive adversarialism ($1 + 1 = \frac{1}{2}$). They don't settle on compromise ($1 + 1 = 1\frac{1}{2}$)or merely cooperation ($1 + 1 = 2$). They go for creative cooperation ($1 + 1 = 3$ or more).

Habit 7: Sharpen the Saw

Sharpening the saw is about constantly renewing ourselves in the four basic areas of life: physical, social/emotional, mental, and spiritual. It's the Habit that increases our capacity to live all other habits of effectiveness. For an organization, Habit 7 promotes vision, renewal, continuous improvement, safeguards against burnout and entropy, and puts the organization on a new upward growth path. For a family, it increases effectiveness through regular personal and family activities such as establishing traditions that nurture the spirit of family renewal.

Emotional Bank Account

The Emotional Bank Account is a metaphor for the amount of trust in a relationship. Like a financial bank account, it's something we make deposits into and withdrawals from. Actions such as seeking first to understand, being kind, making and keeping promises, and being loyal to the absent increase the balance of trust. Being unkind, breaking promises, and gossiping about someone who is absent decrease or even bankrupt the trust in a relationship.

Paradigm

A paradigm is the way each person sees the world, not necessarily the way it is in reality. It's the map, not the territory. It's our lens, through which we view everything, formed by our upbringing and cumulative experience and choices.

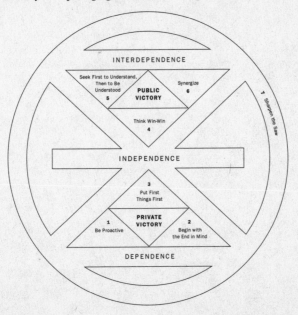

Also from Franklin Covey Co.

The 7 Habits of Highly Effective People

Principle-Centered Leadership

First Things First

Daily Reflections for Highly Effective People

First Things First Every Day

The Breakthrough Factor

*To Do . . . Doing . . . Done! A Creative Approach to Managing
Projects and Effectively Finishing What Matters Most*

The Power Principle

The 10 Natural Laws of Successful Time and Life Management

The 7 Habits of Highly Effective Families

The 7 Habits of Highly Effective Teens

The Nature of Leadership

Franklin Planner

LIVING THE 7 HABITS

The Courage to Change

STEPHEN R. COVEY

A FIRESIDE BOOK
PUBLISHED BY SIMON & SCHUSTER
NEW YORK   LONDON   TORONTO   SYDNEY   SINGAPORE

FIRESIDE
Rockefeller Center
1230 Avenue of the Americas
New York, NY 10020

First Fireside Edition 2000

Manufactured in the United States of America
5   7   9   10   8   6   4

The Library of Congress has cataloged the Simon & Schuster edition as follows:
Covey, Stephen R.
Living the 7 habits : stories of courage and inspiration / Stephen R. Covey.
p.   cm.
1. Success—Psychological aspects—Case studies.   2. Character.
I. Title.   II. Title: Living the seven habits.
BF637.S8C668   1999
158—dc21   99-28061
CIP
ISBN 0-684-84664-0
0-684-85716-2 (Pbk)

To all those who have so abundantly shared their stories—
far beyond those found within the covers of this book

ACKNOWLEDGMENTS

I gratefully acknowledge the hundreds of people who contributed to the creation of this book. I would especially like to thank:

Boyd Craig, for marvelously managing the entire book project. With unfailing good judgment, high standards, and uncommon courtesy and grace, he gave each of us our marching orders. In addition to organizing the book marathon, he ran it himself.

Wes Smith, for his journalistic tenacity and editorial gifts, which resulted in many of the book's major stories.

Tessa Meyer Santiago, for editing stories in a way that preserved the heart, voice, and intent of the storytellers.

Leea Bailey and Annie Oswald, for their extra-mile dedication in coordinating and assisting with all the production activities of this book. They are true factotums—make-it-happen people!

Dave Cole and Ty Jeppesen, the artistic/design team, for providing a visual window into the soul of the book and most every story in it. Their professionalism, artistic ability, and judgment are world class.

Jeanette Sommer, Janeen Bullock, Toni Harris, Pia Jensen, Colleen Covey Brown, Jim Crawley, David Hatch, Lorraine Dieterle, David Harris, and Richard Hammond, for their assistance in interviewing contributors, editing stories, or pulling together key elements of the book.

Janita Andersen, Roice Krueger, Brandon Harding, and Jackie Peterson, for their vision and commitment to bringing inspiring international stories to the book.

Christie Brzezinski and Kerri Sites, transcriptionists extraordinaire, who always came through!

Patti Pallat, Nancy Aldridge, Darla Salin, Kerrie Jenson, and Leea Bailey—my office staff—who, for my work, are the lifting, enabling "wind beneath my wings." As a team, they are a true model of the principles we teach.

Greg Link and Stephen M. R. Covey, for their continuing support and counsel.

Debra Lund, Laura Ellertson, Melissa Adams, and Rhonda Brown—our public relations team—for their devoted publicity work.

Brent Peterson and Tim Bothell, for providing information on measuring the impact of the 7 Habits.

Jenny Sarantis and Ron Thurman, for their legal assistance and support.

Ryan Park and our Copy/Mail Room Team, for cheerfully doing whatever it takes to get the job done.

Dominick Anfuso and the rest of the editorial and production team at Simon & Schuster, our longtime partners in publishing.

Jan Miller, my literary agent, for boundless energy and support.

All my colleagues and associates at Franklin Covey Co., for their dedication, each in his or her own unique and vital way, to helping millions achieve "what matters most."

Finally, and most important, my family, for being an enduring source of light, learning, joy, inspiration, and unfailing support.

Contents

Getting the Most Out of This Book

Living the 7 Habits is a book of stories—stories about people from all walks of life dealing with profound challenges in their businesses, communities, schools, and families, as well as within themselves—showing how they applied the principles of *The 7 Habits of Highly Effective People* to these challenges, and the remarkable things that resulted.

What will these stories do for you? If you're already familiar with *The 7 Habits*, they will likely renew your understanding and commitment to the Habits and, perhaps more important, stir up new insights into other creative ways to apply them to meet your challenges successfully.

If you're not a *7 Habits* reader, these stories will likely renew your faith in your own native abilities and wisdom. I believe these stories will enthrall and inspire you, as they have me, with a sense of excitement and with recognition of your own freedom, potential, and power.

But before I go any further, I should probably make a confession. I've not always been big on the value of stories. My main concern has been that the reader or listener might think I was prescribing the *practice* in the story rather than seeing the practice as an illustration of a *principle*. For more than forty years my wife, Sandra, has heard hundreds of my presentations, and almost inevitably, in giving me feedback, she counsels me to use more stories, to give more examples that illustrate the principles and theories I am teaching. She simply says to me, "Don't be so heavy. Use stories people can relate to." She has always had an intuitive sense for these things and, fortunately, has had absolutely no hesitation to express it!

Experience has taught me that Sandra was right and I was wrong. I've come to realize not only that a picture is worth a thousand words, as the Far Eastern expression goes, but that the picture created in the heart and mind of a person by a story is worth ten thousand.

I cannot fully describe the respect and reverence I have for every person who has contributed a story, for their willingness to share their inward struggles to live by universal and self-evident principles. You can tell that all of them are rich human beings who should be respected for what they represent, for what they are trying to accomplish, and for what they have accomplished. Their stories are splendid illustrations of profound change. I feel humbled by their humanity and profoundly grateful for their sharing.

But this is more than a storybook because there is a framework of thinking that permeates all of these stories. That framework is based upon the 7 Habits, which are in turn based upon universal, timeless, and self-evident principles. By *universal* I mean that the principles apply in any situation, in any culture, that they belong to all six major world religions, that they are found in all societies and institutions that have had truly enduring success. By *timeless* I mean that they never change. They are permanent, natural laws, like gravity. By *self-evident* I mean you can't really argue against them any more than a person can argue that you can build trust without trustworthiness. (A diagram of the 7 Habits and a brief definition of each Habit can be found at the front of this book for easy reference.)

It may sound presumptuous, but I believe that *all* highly effective people live the principles underlying the 7 Habits. In fact, I'm convinced that the 7 Habits are increasingly relevant in today's turbulent, troubled, complex world of change. To live with change, to optimize change, you need principles that don't change. Let me reason with you for a moment.

First, let's define effectiveness as getting the results you want in a way that enables you to get even greater results in the future. In other words, success that endures—sustainable and balanced success.

Second, the Habits are embodied principles, principles that are lived until they become habitual, almost second nature. Principles are simply natural laws that govern our life, whether or not we know them, like them, or agree with them—again, like gravity. I didn't invent the principles. I simply organized them and used language to describe them.

I've often been asked, particularly by the media, for examples and evidence. I've shared both extensively. But I find that the best examples and evidence come when I propose, and even challenge the questioners with, this task: "Think of any successful person or family or project or organization you've come to admire for his/her/its endur-ing success and there is your example and evidence." Whether the admired people are aware of the 7 Habits or not is irrelevant. They're living by proven principles. I've never had anyone seriously argue against one of the underlying principles. They legitimately may not like the language or the description of the Habits. That's okay. They may not relate to the stories at all. In fact, in their situation they may think of an opposite example of the same principle. But the principle of responsibility (Habit 1) is self-evident. So also are having purpose and values (Habit 2) and living by them (Habit 3). So are mutual respect and benefit (Habit 4), mutual understanding (Habit 5), creative cooperation (Habit 6), and the need for renewal and continual improvement (Habit 7). Principles are like the vitamins and minerals found in all kinds of foods. They can be concentrated, combined, time-sequenced, and encapsulated into a food supplement. So it is with the 7 Habits. The basic elements called principles are found in nature and can be expressed in many forms. Millions of people all over the world have found the time-sequenced encapsulation of the balanced set of principles in the 7 Habits useful. The "why" and "how" are shown in some of these stories. Give God or nature the credit for the source nutrients.

My Two Roles

I will try to play two roles throughout this book, guide and teacher. First, guide: If you were a tourist, say, going up the Nile River, you'd probably want a guide to give you an idea of what to look for and of its significance. On the other hand, if you'd been there several times before or had prepared in your own special way for the experience, you might prefer to guide yourself. So it is with these stories. You decide if the guide is helpful or not. If not, ignore the preface.

Second, teacher: There's a short postscript to each story emphasiz-ing a particular point or angle or an entirely new way of thinking that may enhance your understanding and/or your motivation to act in some way. Again, you decide. You may choose to come to your own conclusions or learning and to pass by the postscript. Great.

I've come to believe that repetition is the mother of learning and that if you really want to help people become consciously competent, you should repeat similar words and ideas again and again in fresh ways and from different angles. That's what this book attempts to do. Since it is a book about people trying to live the 7 Habits, the language of the 7 Habits will be found continually throughout the book. The storyteller has often identified the Habit being lived right in the middle of the story. Where he or she hasn't identified it specifically, where it is an important insight, and particularly if I don't mention it in my comments before or after the story, I have occasionally inserted the name of the Habit being practiced in brackets, such as [Habit 1: Be Proactive]. If for some reason this annoys you, just forget it and move on, but I am persuaded that it will help most people, 7 *Habits* familiar or not, become more consciously aware of what principle is operating.

In the postscript I will often mention the Habit again, perhaps with another twist or angle or experience. Remember, the purpose of the book is to help you, the reader, deepen your understanding and commitment to the principles that are embodied in the Habits. Don't allow word symbols to turn you off. The key thing is the principle that exists in nature and governs the consequences of all actions. Remember, also, that these are self-evident principles. I am only using language that identifies some of the truths you already know deep inside. I'm trying to make them explicit so that they affect the way you think and decide and act. Therefore, the very words of the 7 Habits are only symbols of a world of principles. They are like the key that opens a door to meaning.

These are all true stories and, in most cases, in the actual words of the storyteller. In some cases there needed to be some editing, but every effort was made to preserve the original meaning and intent, the tone, and the spirit of the storyteller. Most of the names of people in the stories have been changed to preserve their anonymity. The exceptions are those who are identified by name in the title of the story.

The Inside-Out Struggle

As you read these stories, notice that, most often, the people take an Inside-Out Approach, usually requiring personal struggle and sacrifice of pride and ego, and often a significant alteration of life and work style. The alteration almost always requires painstaking effort, patience, and persistence. All four unique human gifts or endowments—self-awareness, imagination, conscience, and independent will—are usually exercised and magnified. Almost always there's a vision of what's possible and desirable. And almost always, marvelous things result. Trust is restored. Broken relationships are redeemed. Personal moral authority to continue the upward change effort is evident.

You'll identify with some stories more than others. Ponder the visuals. They were carefully selected to reflect the uniqueness of the stories. As you pay the price with each story and come to see the underlying universal principles involved, your confidence will grow in your ability to adapt and apply the 7 Habits framework to any difficult situation or challenge you may face now or in the future. You'll also begin to see an opportunity in your problems so that your creative powers are released. When we solve problems, we get rid of something. When we create, we bring something into existence. Ironically, the creative mind-set solves problems better than the problem-solving mind-set. You'll see this again and again in these stories. Enjoy them, learn from them, reflect on them. They will inspire hope and increase faith in yourself and in your own creative powers.

For a personalized downloadable mission statement builder, go to www.franklincovey.com/ms

1

Individual

"Whatever you can do or dream you can do, begin it!
Boldness has power, magic and genius in it."

—GOETHE

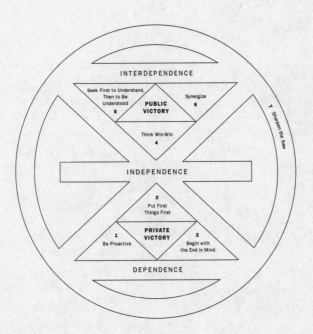

Courage to Change

How Could I Waste My Life?

This grief-filled woman used all four unique human gifts to literally reinvent her life. Notice how she grew in self-awareness, how she consulted her imagination and conscience, and how she exercised tremendous willpower to rediscover and renew her life. What a truly great contribution she is making! What peace of mind resulted.

I was forty-six years old when my husband, Gordon, was diagnosed with cancer. Without hesitation, I took early retirement to be with him. Although his death eighteen months later was expected, my grief consumed me. My first Christmas without him I didn't even decorate the house. I sorrowed over our dreams unfulfilled, over the grandchildren he would never get to hold or touch. I would turn to speak to him, only to be reminded that he wasn't there. Grief filled every corner of my soul. I was only forty-eight and had no reason to live.

My overarching question through my sorrow was "Why did God take Gordon and not me?" I felt Gordon had so much more to offer the world than I did. At this low point in my life, with my body, mind, and spirit fatigued beyond measure, I encountered the 7 Habits. I was led to ask myself, "If I'm here for some reason, what is it supposed to be?" I was motivated to find new meaning in my life.

"Begin with the End in Mind" suggests breaking out the roles of your life. So, I drew a pie chart with my "used to be" roles as they were before Gordon's death. On a second pie chart I left a huge blank where work and wife used to be. That large, blank piece of pie drove home to me that my life was irrevocably different. I drew a big question mark in the slice. It sat there looking at me, asking, "What are your 'going-to-be' roles?"

I grabbed ahold of the idea that all things are created twice—first mentally, and then physically. I had to write a new script. I had to ask myself, "What talents do I have?" So I took an aptitude test, which gave me some clarity on my top three abilities. To create a sense of balance in my life, I focused on the four dimensions: on an intellectual level, I realized that I loved to teach; spiritually and socially, I wanted to continue to support the racial harmony we had endeavored to live through our biracial marriage; emotionally, I knew I needed to give love. When my mother was alive she rocked critically ill babies in the hospital. I wanted to give comfort as she had, continuing her legacy of unconditional love.

I was afraid to fail. I had never done anything in my adult life except work for the Veterans Association. But I told myself it would be okay to try different things, like trying on hats. If I didn't like teaching after a semester, I didn't have to go back. If the racial relations hat didn't fit, it would be okay to take it off and try on something different. I began again by going to graduate school so I could teach at the college level. Graduate school is hard, period, but at age forty-eight, it was really tough. I was so used to passing documents off to my secretary to type that I had to take a semester just to learn how to type my own papers on the computer.

My concentration was still somewhat impaired from the aftermath of Gordon; it was difficult to discipline myself to read what someone else wanted me to read. Turning off the TV and returning the cable box were acts of sheer will. But I knew that I needed to give those things up if I wanted to get where I planned to go [Habit 3: Put First Things First].

I completed graduate school with a 4.0 GPA, and began teaching at a historically black college in Little Rock. I was appointed by the governor to serve on the Martin Luther King Commission to improve racial relations in Arkansas. I rock the crack babies and infants with AIDS who are hooked up to ventilator tubes. However short my time with them is, I know that I'm giving comfort, and I am getting their love in return. It gives me a sense of peace.

Now my life is very good. I can feel my man Gordon smiling at me. He told me time and time again before he died that he wanted me to have a life full of laughter, happy memories, and good things. How could I waste my life, with his directive on my conscience? I don't think I could. I have an obligation to live my life the best I can for the people I love the most—whether they are on this earth or on the other side.

⊛ *This amazing woman not only got ahold of her life, she had the wisdom to mentally create an entirely new one (Habit 2: Begin with the End in Mind). Her inspiring example illustrates the importance of balancing the four dimensions of life embodied in Habit 7: Sharpen the Saw—the physical, the mental, the social, and the spiritual. She faced fear straight on and left her deeply scripted comfort zone of fearing failure. This is no quick-fix story. She was patient, persistent, and paid the price.*

Moving Out to the Country

Many of us feel utterly trapped in our present circumstances. We not only fail to see a way out, we often don't even ask the question, "What else can I do?" This is a story of a valiant couple who chose to do whatever was necessary to fulfill their mission statement to not only keep the family first, but also to secure more enjoyable employment.

I used to work for the federal government in Washington, D.C. I thought my family was happy and just as excited as I was about our situation. I was wrong, but too wrapped up in the urgent, important things at work to notice. My wife and family have followed me all around the world, moving from place to place. Finally my wife said, "Can you make a move this time to somewhere we'll be happy?"

I loved the job, but inner-city D.C. wasn't the best place for my family. In the past, it would have been easy to say, "Honey, come on, be reasonable. I can't just move like that! You know they always control where I go. I just go where they say to go." But when I saw her eyes, I realized this was not just a little request for her. This was, in a way, life or death. She'd had enough. Using my mission statement as a reminder of what I valued [Habit 2: Begin with the End in Mind], I told her, "Okay, I'll see what I can do."

The next day, I went to my boss and said, "Look, I love working here. I'm happy doing the job, but I need to get a balance between work and my family. My wife wants to move out of the city. I think she'll move whether I do or not. If I don't have my family living here with me, I'm not going to be effective for you. I'm not going to be able to do the things you want me to, because I'll always be worried about my family."

He didn't want to let me go, but he could see I was serious. During our conversation, he mentioned an opening in an agency outside the city for which I was qualified. He helped me get the job. When people heard I was moving to the country, they couldn't believe it. "Stan, are you nuts? You're throwing away your chance for senior management. What are you doing?" They were really concerned I was suffering from temporary insanity.

"I don't think I am throwing it all away," I'd reply. "I'm actually picking something else that is better." Most of them just shook their heads and gave me a consoling pat on the shoulder.

I moved my family out of Washington to a small town. I stayed with the agency doing a job I enjoy. I still see my old friends and have opportunities to travel. My children are blossoming and are attending a school where they are able to excel and get the attention they need. My wife is overjoyed with owning our first home. We set aside two nights a week as family nights. We have more time together and love gardening as a family. I never realized how much fun it could be to get dirty in the yard.

There is one sure thing that we directly control—our own behavior. As for the behavior of others, we have only indirect control, which is based upon what method of influence we use. There are also many things over which we have no control—things such as the weather, the economy, our in-laws, our genes. The key to all three challenges (direct control, indirect control, and no control) is always the same— begin by changing yourself—your habits, your methods of influence, or your attitudes. The couple in this story literally picked up and changed their circumstances, which resulted in a more balanced, peaceful, happy personal and family life. They changed their methods of influence with each other by practicing Habit 5: Seek First to Understand, Then to Be Understood. They changed their method of influence with the husband's boss by courageously seeking to be understood (the last half of Habit 5) and by coming up with a win-win synergistic arrangement (Habits 4 and 6: Think Win-Win and Synergize). It is absolutely marvelous to see the freedom people really have when they take responsibility and initiative.

It's Never Too Late to Change

Observe in this story the basic elements of the change process: self-awareness, taking responsibility, authentic expression, group support, and accountability.

I am a teacher of adults. During the introductions of one of the seminars I was leading, when everyone was talking about why they were there, one gentleman stood up and said, "My name is Harry. I am seventy-six years old, and I am here because my wife sent me." Everyone started laughing, but he was very serious. He continued, "My wife told me that this is my last chance. If I don't straighten up, I'm out on my rear. You see, I've been a rascal all my life. Do you think it's too late for me?"

I answered, "It's only too late if you don't start now."

Well, as the workshop progressed, the group took him on as a personal project. Harry is a person that you hated to love, but you loved him anyway. He was just so cute, but he had this little impish way about him. You could see how his wife might have come to the end of her rope with him. The group could see that his wife's Emotional Bank Account was empty. He had made very few deposits and numerous withdrawals over many years. In fact, her Emotional Bank Account was so overdrawn it was close to bankruptcy. Through modeling and mentoring and teaching, he soon began to make deposits. At first his wife didn't believe he was sincere, and that was very frustrating for him. He was just so disappointed that she didn't automatically think, "Well, look how this guy has changed!" He wanted to give up, but the group would not let him. The group said, "Your wife's bank account is so overdrawn, you have got to be consistently doing things."

So Harry started doing little household chores that he had never done before. He took out the trash, cleaned up after himself, took his dishes to the sink, and began to offer to help around the house. And that was a first for him. His wife apparently was so angry that she was thinking, "This is great, but it won't last." So he continued doing little things for her like making sure when she took the car out that he had it washed and filled with gas. If he came home and she was busy, he would ask, "Can I run to the store for you? Can I do errands for you?" and he consistently did this. He started taking her out to lunch, and doing all kinds of things. You could just see that love was being rekindled.

Our group was together two hours a week over an eleven-week period, so we would get a progress report each week. As the weeks went by, she began to trust him and feel like maybe he really was making a change. At the last session Harry walked into the room with a big smile on his face. He came to the front of the room and gave me a great big hug. Well, I kind of held him off at arm's length and I said, "Now Harry, this isn't some of your rascally behavior, is it?" and he said, "Oh no, that hug is from my wife, and she baked cookies for the whole class. She wanted me to tell everyone that I could stay—she said I could stay!"

�֍ *True group support, a lot of genuine expression, and a sense of accountability not only gave this seventy-six-year-old man the power to transform his life, they are elements common to most successful change efforts. One-shot events may begin a change process, but they are usually insufficient. Both a process and systemic reinforcement based on self-evident, universal, timeless principles are needed.*

Many years ago, at the end of one of my semester courses in college, I remember asking a speech professor, "If you were to do your career all over again, what would you do differently?" In addition to teaching, he was also a speaker of international renown. His response to my question was both interesting and instructive, and I am convinced that, among other things, it unconsciously had a marked influence on my life. He said, "I would build an organization." I asked him why. He said, "So there would be follow-through and lasting influence—a process, not just an event." That very principle is what led me to leave a university many years later to start my own organization.

Living for Today

Notice the growth of this young woman's proactive muscles through using all four unique human gifts (self-awareness, imagination, conscience, and independent will). Notice the movement in her mind-set from being a victim to becoming the creative force of her own life. Think also about the statement, "Planning is invaluable, but plans are worthless."

As I sat in the intensive care unit watching over my comatose older brother, Byron, I kept asking myself, "Why? Why did I walk away from the same accident without a scratch or bruise on my body?" His head was wrapped in gauze from the severe brain damage and his eyes were swollen shut. The doctors convinced us that he probably wouldn't survive the night.

They now say that the accident that I miraculously walked away from may very well have been the environmental stress impact in my life that resulted in the onset of a very serious chronic inflammatory disease that affects many of the body's organs. This disease would later bring many more difficult and challenging trials to my life.

I was nine years old at the time of our accident and my dream was to become the next Mary Lou Retton. I survived the setback of the accident but my dreams were shattered one year later when I began experiencing joint pain in my wrists and knees. The doctors diagnosed me with juvenile rheumatoid arthritis but said I would most likely grow out of it. In the meantime, they advised me to quit gymnastics because of the high stress on the body. Tears were shed, but my activities, goals, and dreams only shifted. Academics, basketball, swimming, tennis, skiing, and water skiing became my new loves in life.

During my junior year in high school, I began to feel much more severe joint pains throughout my entire body. I felt the slightest touch or movement of every joint and bone. Rolling over in bed, getting up to use the bathroom, tying my shoes, and brushing my teeth took tremendous effort. The question "Would I ever walk or run again?" ran through my head several times. I remember so clearly my concerned innocent little sister asking my mom in a quiet voice, "Is Elisa going to die?"

More tests were done which determined that I had the incurable systemic lupus erythematosus. Lupus is an autoimmune disease that attacks the body's tissues. I convinced myself that this was my secret. Despite my condition, I would be just like everyone else and this diagnosis was not going to keep me from doing in life what I had always dreamed and hoped for. I grew to learn that a smile on my face and determination in my heart were the only things that would keep my spirits high and give me the strength to move forward [Habit 1: Be Proactive].

I was able to successfully graduate from high school with the help of massive dosages of medication. I knew I would live with this disease for the rest of my life but thought the episode I experienced in high school was my last trial and that I could live with whatever else happened.

Getting a college education was the next goal in my life [Habit 2: Begin with the End in Mind]. I could not wait to move out on my own, cook my own meals, be independent, and live the life of a college student. First semester was difficult making all the necessary adjustments, but I loved the challenges and the memories I was making. I returned home for Christmas to spend the holidays with my family and there I began to experience symptoms I had never experienced before. I began to retain water and soon looked nine months pregnant. What was happening?

Once again I was back in the doctor's office, only this time the lupus was attacking my kidneys. I was determined to be back in school in less than a week, so we needed to cure this quickly. But the doctors informed me that school would not be an option for me that semester. I returned for a week's worth of intense hospital treatments and then four months of intravenous treatments. I was nineteen years old, trying to get a college degree and live my life as actively as anyone else would, but my physical condition was not allowing me to.

After endless days of hospital care, needles, IVs, and tests, I slowly began to shed the water retention. Although once kidney function is lost it is never fully regained, with medication I was able to return to full activity and was back at school for another start. I was a semester behind, but caught up in the spring and summer terms.

My major in communications required all students to do an internship before graduation. Winter semester was my scheduled internship and graduation was to take place in August. I was lucky to get the internship of my dreams and work with some talented people in my field. Two weeks into my internship I began experiencing the same symptoms of water retention and bloating. This couldn't be happening! It couldn't happen right now, not with this internship I had been longing for. I knew exactly what was coming and what I was going to be faced with for the next three to four months. Only this time I was not going to drop out of school. Mentally I convinced myself that I was going to stick it out—school, internship, everything.

Once again I looked nine months pregnant and couldn't wear any of my own clothes. The intense swelling in my legs and feet left scarred stretch marks. The capillaries popped in my face, leaving purple bruises and swelling for months. Friends and classmates who saw me one week looking normal turned quiet and stared as I forced myself to go about my normal day-to-day activities. So many times I wanted to crawl in a hole and hide until it was all over. The smile I learned to paste on my face during my junior year of high school kept me going. I knew there was an end to all this but could not see it at the time. My symptoms varied with each flare-up and I was able to fight this round without extended hospitalization, so I was able, painfully, to move on with my life. Each day I got better and within time I was back to full strength. My goal to graduate was attained and despite my condition I did so in less than four years.

A career was next on my list and I was anxious to apply my education and experience in the workforce. I found a wonderful job and was slowly adjusting to this new lifestyle. I had been through enough trials. Only two months into my new job, and still trying to make a good impression, I had another flare-up. Why? Why? Why?

The treatments continue. Each time my kidneys get weaker and weaker and the treatments get stronger and stronger with more and more side effects. I fight nausea, fatigue, hair loss, bone depletion, bruising, and sun sensitivity as a result of the medications my body daily depends so heavily on. The threat of dialysis or a kidney transplant lingers. It may just be a matter of time; nobody knows.

Living with lupus is living on the edge. I never know when it will attack, what symptoms I will experience, how long recovery will take, and how much debt for medical expenses I will be faced with later. Bearing children is very unlikely and the thought of someone accepting me and my condition is always a concern. I've learned not to ask "Why?" anymore but "What can I learn from this experience?" The goals I set for myself are goals I know I can accomplish but obstacles will be put in my way. I live for today and what I can do today, not in the past nor in the future. Because for me, the future may not be what I have planned.

⊗ *What an amazing person! I would like to make four points:*

First, people who study the characteristics of stress-hardy individuals basically focus upon three attitudes, all of which are manifested by this brave woman: challenge, control, and commitment.

Challenge leads you to learn from experience, whether it's positive or negative, rather than having an entitlement approach to a life of easy comfort and security.

Control basically means keeping your focus on the circle of things you can do something about, however small they may be, so that you don't lapse into victimism, passivity, and powerlessness.

Commitment leads you to stay involved with different tasks and goals, such as completing an education, rather than just hanging back in self-protection.

Second, notice how this woman's questions changed from asking "Why?" to asking, "What can I learn?" While struggling to survive the death camps of Nazi Germany, Viktor Frankl learned to ask himself the question, "What is it that life is asking of me?" instead of "What is it I want from life?" He would also confront others who were in deep depression and experiencing suicidal tendencies with the same questions: "What is life asking of you? What have you got to live for? What meaning can you find?" instead of "What is it you want out of life?" This is why Frankl says that each person's sense of meaning is usually detected rather than invented. When you ask the question, "What is life asking of me?" you are listening to your conscience. Like radar, your conscience scans the horizon of your responsibilities and your situation and then gives you guidance.

Third, the statement that "planning is invaluable, but plans are worthless" has some wisdom in it. While I don't fully agree that plans are worthless, I do think the statement has meaning in changing situations and that it leads to important insights. Take the woman in this story as an example. All of her plans and expectations were repeatedly dashed and she experienced continued disappointment, so she began to define Habit 2: Begin with the End in Mind, in terms of learning, adapting, coping, adjusting, and optimizing.

Fourth, Lloyd C. Douglas wrote a beautiful story called "Precious Jeopardy" which parallels, in some respects, the woman's life's journey in this story. It's when your life is threatened that you really fully appreciate and value life. Life is very precious, but can be constantly jeopardized by forces outside our control. For many years, our family would read "Precious Jeopardy" around Christmas because it had such a sobering, yet exhilarating and inspirational, effect upon us, particularly as we reflected upon the previous year, planned for the next year, and, most importantly, sought to live in the present moment with gratitude.

My Flower Shop

This story is a beautiful illustration of how our mind creates our world. If we hold a vision or a dream deep inside our heart and mind, it will begin to not only influence our attitudes and actions, it will reach out and influence the circumstances of our lives. Notice how all things are created twice—first mentally and then physically (Habit 2: Begin with the End in Mind). This woman planted the mission statement so deeply into her heart that it bridged the gap between her dream and its fulfillment.

I've dreamed about owning a flower shop since high school. In college, I studied horticulture. Slowly the dream died under the pressure of marriage, divorce, and raising a family. Ironically, it was my son's death that resurrected my dream. As I saw those beautiful flowers coming to our door in expression of people's sorrow for our loss, I was moved. As I touched their petals and smelled their fragrance, I thought, "There you are. You're what I've been looking for—your touch, your brave color, your smell. I'd forgotten all about you." I envisioned the florist carefully arranging these beautiful blooms so that this arrangement could brighten our lives at this dark, dark time. I knew I wanted to help in that way.

When I imagined my eightieth birthday as part of developing a Personal Mission Statement, I thought about my flower shop. I imagined all the people I could help: the births, weddings, birthdays, and funerals. On all those days I could help people show they cared. I couldn't imagine a more nurturing and rewarding way to spend my days. When it came time to write my mission statement, I put that I would own a flower shop one day. Just seeing the words on paper somehow made my dream more real.

About a year later I ran into the owners of a flower shop called Ocean Shores. I asked, "How's the flower shop going?" They said, "Oh, we're getting ready to sell it. We haven't got a buyer yet. Would you be interested?"

These words grabbed my heart. Rather than saying, "I can't do it; it's not possible," instead of making excuses, like "Gee, I would really like to, but it's not the right time," or "You know, I have a full-time job, and am a single mother supporting two teenagers," I thought, "This is it. This is it. Here comes my dream."

I set to work to make it happen. I examined their profit-and-loss statements. I hired a business consultant to see if this was financially feasible. I got the financing I needed and was able to buy the store.

Now that I own my own flower shop, all of my business decisions and how I deal with the employees is measured against the dream I had in the first place. My mission statement gave me the courage, and I am actually doing what I've always dreamed. I know owning a flower shop is my own peculiar dream come true. Others want to own the world. I just want to make it more beautiful.

 Imagination is more powerful than memory. Imagination taps into possibilities, into the infinite. Memory is limited by past events and the finite. When this woman used her imagination and her dreams as the criteria to make her decisions, they became self-fulfilling prophecies. The subconscious mind seizes upon experience and opportunity to actualize those imagined dreams. Such dreams also ignite excitement and hope in other people.

My Living Nightmare

The following story is profoundly sobering. Sense the depth of this man's sorrow, and also the exhilarating power of a single idea—that there is space between stimulus and response.

After graduating from college, I became a successful engineer. Then in my late twenties, I felt my inner voice telling me that I could teach single adults. So I quit my career and enrolled in a seminary.

I poured myself into my studies and graduated with the highest honor the seminary faculty and administration awards each year. Just before graduation, my wife and I, together with our newborn son, Seth, moved so I could be involved with a single adults program at a large church. Again, I became successful, and enjoyed a thriving ministry that was making a difference in the lives of people.

Our family flourished in our new situation. We were expecting our second child in two months. Life was good. One night, as my wife lay resting on the couch, I decided to clean my shotgun. As I was cleaning the gun, it discharged and shot my wife. The doctors were unable to save her or our unborn child.

I was devastated. It was a living nightmare. My emotions alternated from denial to anguish to despair and complete emptiness. At age thirty-three, my life came to a screeching halt. I moved in with my parents for a few months after the accident. I couldn't live alone. I continued to minister to my congregation for almost two years. Actually, they ministered to me. But I had to stop because the situation was a painful reminder of my life with Julia. You know, when you're a religious leader, your wife and family are such an integral part of your work. I could hardly walk into the church without feeling a rush of pain and remorse. So I quit this job that had given me so much joy.

I didn't really move on to much either. A friend of mine gave me a job selling large construction equipment. I'd never sold large equipment in my life—didn't even know the names of some of the pieces at first. Although my job wasn't really brain surgery, it was a godsend. All I needed to do was show up, sell some compressors or a few backhoes in the course of a month, and go home. I wasn't intellectually stimulated, I wasn't challenged. I couldn't have been at that point. I was still numb. My brain and mind and heart were still trying to process what had happened. So that kind of job was just what I needed.

For a while my life was on autopilot. I woke up, fed Seth, took him to day care, went to work, picked him up, made dinner, cleaned up, and went to bed. Before the accident, I was a very driven person. I would set goals and accomplish them. For the life of me, I couldn't think of one thing that I wanted to accomplish after the accident. I could do all the little, everyday things that needed to be done, like shopping for milk. But I couldn't bring myself to start doing the important things. I couldn't, for example, start to plan a new future for Seth and myself. I just didn't have it in me to think that far ahead or with that much interest in the future.

I started taking the book *First Things First* to the park and began to read. Just little bits at a time. When I came to the section about stimulus and response, I recognized myself. I knew that I was standing at the edge of the space between stimulus and response. I'd been standing in that space for three years actually. For three years, I had slowly, inch by incremental inch, been moving toward the time that I could respond. Now, finally, three years later, I felt I could respond to my wife's death.

This feeling wasn't an instantaneous kind of experience. Slowly, gradually, I felt capable of more control, more initiative, more action. I can remember talking to one of my best friends, a pastor. I said, "I'm having all these weird sensations again. Something isn't right."

He replied, "Phil, I think what's happening is that you're waking up."

"What do you mean I'm waking up?"

"Well, you're finally ready to leave your cocoon. Your body, your mind, your heart are ready to live again. So, I think you're waking up."

One of the first goals I set was to finish the book. I used to be a voracious reader before my wife's death, but I hadn't read a book all the way through in three years. I probably hadn't even read a magazine either. As I read I became more and more alive. I also felt more equipped to tackle the future and more ready to shape it rather than let it just happen to me.

My second goal was to leave a legacy for my son. I didn't want my legacy to be that my life never got going again. I decided to concentrate on building something he could be proud of. You mustn't think I was gung ho from the beginning. I slowly began to sit up and take notice. I thought long and hard about what was important to me and to Seth. I took as my motto to live each day as if it were my last, so that I would always do the important things first. I examined how I could incorporate this mind-set into my future plans. Then I formulated a mission statement that would help me recover, make a contribution to this world, and develop strong relationships with my loved ones. Slowly, surely, our lives became brighter, livelier, and livable. Ecclesiastes in the Bible talks about a time for everything. When the time was right, I was able to pick myself up and get on with life.

Today I am happily remarried. Seth loves his new mother. I have two beautiful stepdaughters. And my wheels are turning—somewhat slowly, somewhat methodically, but still turning. I began publishing a newsletter for remarried families, I've purchased my own business, and I've accepted many speaking engagements for the upcoming year.

Without a doubt, the most difficult thing I have ever done was forgive myself for the accident. The second was to live through the grieving process. The third was to have the courage to dream again and then begin the process of making those dreams come true.

Please understand, I still have what I call "my blue funks." As John Claypool, an Episcopalian minister, once said after his eight-year-old daughter died of leukemia, "I will walk again, but it will always be with a limp." I might be limping, but I am moving along.

I would like to share a personal exhilarating moment that I recounted previously in my other books. It occurred when I was on sabbatical in Hawaii. I was wandering through some stacks of books in the back of a college library. A particular book drew my interest, and as I flipped through the pages, my eyes fell on a single paragraph that was so compelling, so memorable, so staggering that it has profoundly influenced my thinking and my life.

In that paragraph were three sentences that contained a single powerful idea:

Between stimulus and response, there is a space.
In that space lies our freedom and power to choose our
   response.
In our response lies our growth and our happiness.

*I cannot begin to describe the effect that idea had on me. I was
overwhelmed by it. I reflected on it again and again. I reveled in the
freedom of it. I personalized it. Between whatever happened to me and
my response to it was a space. In that space was my freedom and
power to choose my response. And in my response lay my growth and
happiness.*

*The more I pondered it, the more I realized that I could choose
responses that would affect the stimulus itself. I could become a force
of nature in my own right.*

You're Successful . . . but Are You Happy?

I've often told the story about the person who was climbing the ladder of success and got to the top rung only to find it was leaning against the wrong wall. This story illustrates how Habit 2: Begin with the End in Mind essentially defines the wall you want to put your ladder against.

I was sitting at a restaurant with a young guy who had been with our agency for about five years. He had a large home, a parking place close to the front door, and a brass nameplate on his door. Over lunch, we started talking about the definition of success. I mentioned a Personal Mission Statement. He said he hadn't heard about the concept. To demonstrate to him how to go about creating one, I asked him what was important to him. He started naming all the things he wanted to do. Not one had anything to do with his job.

I was intrigued. "Well, are you happy?" I asked him when he finished.

He said, "Well, no."

I said, "But, you're successful, right?" and laughed a little. He just sat there thinking.

I didn't see him again for a couple of months because we were traveling to different parts of the country. One day, I spotted him in the hallway. Wanting to catch up on his life, I thought I'd walk him to where he was going. "Hey, Christian, wait up. Where you going? I'll walk with you."

"I'm not going anywhere. This is my last day," he said with a grin.

I was shocked. "What?"

"Yeah, I was just in to see the boss. He asked me why I was leaving. I told him it was your fault."

"Oh no. You're kidding me. Why'd you tell him that?"

"Well, I told him about our conversation in El Paso. About how you made me look at my life to see whether I was doing what I wanted to do with my life. And I wasn't. So I quit this job to start doing the things I really love. Thanks, buddy."

I haven't seen him for about two years now. When he quit his job, he and his wife started their own little roofing company. He likes working with wood. He used to be in the telecommunications field;

now he's hammering shingles on roofs and building porches. And guess what? He's happy.

⊗ *The Western world is very action-oriented, the Eastern world more reflective. Habit 2: Begin with the End in Mind, and Habit 3: Put First Things First, attempt to bridge East and West—reflect, and then act on your decision. This story beautifully illustrates the power of choice (Habit 1: Be Proactive), thinking carefully about what matters most (Habit 2: Begin with the End in Mind), and then acting upon it (Habit 3: Put First Things First). This man made a courageous 180-degree shift by putting his success ladder against the wall of happiness. The best way to predict your future is to create it.*

A Prisoner's Story

Study the metamorphosis of this man whose life was shattered, yet while in prison lives triumphantly. Notice the immediate effect upon his mind as he becomes aware of the space that exists between what happens to us and our response to it. Then notice what happens when, instead of denying, blaming, and seeking revenge, he chooses to focus on only those things he can control.

I woke up in the hospital one day with my life in ruins. My wife told me there had been a car accident. I'd been drinking at a party with my friend Frank. He was with me when I wrecked the car after leaving the party. Frank was killed.

I was charged with manslaughter for killing my friend. While awaiting trial, I joined Alcoholics Anonymous. I walked into the meeting on the first night feeling that I had nothing in common with the people there. I walked out feeling as though I'd never belonged somewhere so much in my life.

The twelve-step program of Alcoholics Anonymous was a big help in turning my life around. I needed help with more than my guilt and my grief over the death of my friend. My marriage was in trouble. I was facing a murder trial. The motorcycle dealership I owned, one of the largest in the country, was deeply in debt. My drinking was really only a symptom of far more significant problems. I drank to dull both the highs and lows of my life. Personally and professionally, I was failing.

With the help of AA, I started looking for material to help change my life. I was thirty-four years old when I read the Alcoholics Anonymous book. It was the first book I'd ever read cover to cover. *The 7 Habits* was the second. The part on being proactive versus reactive made a lot of sense to me, particularly because I was probably facing a prison sentence. I'd never been in jail. I also had no idea what would happen to my wife and daughter, my family, or my business if they put me away for thirty years. That was the penalty I faced if found guilty. At times I felt like I wanted to die.

I realized that I had to focus on what I could control [Habit 1: Be Proactive]. At work, I started by focusing on preparing my store managers to handle the business if I went to prison for a long time. I shared with them the principles of the 7 Habits. I also worked with them to reduce the company's debt.

I began to get that aspect of my life in order, but my relationship with my wife was still deteriorating. She was gone a lot during this period, taking care of a sick brother in Florida. I visited her, but it was clear we were growing further and further apart.

One day, I started suffering terrible cramps in my upper body and arms. It turned out that I had a bone spur in my neck from the accident when I had smashed my head on the roof of the car. The spur was cutting into my spinal cord and required eight hours of surgery. I dropped from 240 pounds to 195. But I got through it, in part because I discovered and read *Man's Search for Meaning* by Viktor Frankl. In fact, I read it four times. I learned from that book that I had the power to control my responses to what was happening to me [Habit 1: Be Proactive]. My world was crumbling, but I did not have to fall apart with it.

As I began to change from within, people around me noticed. I received a letter one day from my wife saying that she had come to realize that if she divorced me, she might be divorcing the wrong person. She wanted to come home and try to make our marriage work again.

In our visits during the time we weren't together, I worked hard on seeking first to understand her. I had always tended to think that everything that goes on is about me. It's false pride or ego. When I learned to not react, but to keep gathering information from her, we began to communicate better, and eventually she moved back in with me.

She had only been home three days when the prosecutor's office offered me a plea bargain. Instead of the possible thirty-year sentence I'd faced, they offered me ten years. I accepted it. When they took me off to prison, I went with Viktor Frankl's book in mind, thinking that I was going to make the most out of the experience no matter what happened. I was determined to control what I could control, and to not be affected by those things outside my influence.

There were a couple of times in prison where I almost got into altercations, but I made myself stay proactive and not reactive. I'd focus on the end in mind, which was to stay out of trouble so I could earn time for good behavior and get home early [Habit 2: Begin with the End in Mind].

I earned a job cleaning the front offices inside the prison and I built trust with the administration to the point that when I mentioned a problem or concern to them, they'd listen. One of the things I saw was that when children were brought to visit their fathers, there wasn't anything for them to do while the adults were talking. I put together a proposal to form a children's library for the visit hall. They didn't have the money, so I had my wife pick out books for different age groups and we paid for them. We had guys in the wood shop make cabinets and the library grew into a big thing. Other people donated books and we even got a Spanish language section.

Now you see hundreds of kids sitting with their fathers and reading books instead of just sitting there or falling asleep like they used to.

I also began sharing what I'd learned about changing my life with other inmates who were interested. I ordered more copies of the Frankl book and *The 7 Habits* and passed them around. I invited inmates to my cell to discuss the principles a couple of times a day and encouraged them to discuss these principles with others.

One day, a Muslim inmate came up to me and said, "Out of all of us in this prison, probably no one has lost more by coming here than you. Yet you are the happiest, most positive person in this room. Why is that?"

I told him: "While I have no control over the circumstances of my life right now, which are the consequence of actions I took years ago, the only thing I can change right now is my attitude and my behavior. And that's what I focus on. I can walk around here pissed off, kicking furniture, crying the blues, whining, but that's not going to get me anywhere. It's certainly not going to get me home to my family any faster, and it's not going to make things easier. So I just choose not to be that way, because I might get killed tomorrow, and if I get killed tomorrow, I am not going to waste this entire day, my last day on this earth, being miserable."

One day, I learned that a fire had destroyed our motorcycle store. My parents watched it burn for twenty hours. When my wife arrived on the scene and saw it had burned to the ground, she collapsed. She had been told there was just a small electrical problem. I was so dev-astated when I heard about the fire that I went to a friend in the prison. He sat me down and threw back at me everything I'd taught him. He told me that there is something good and a lesson to be learned in everything that happens to you. He got me to see that this would be an opportunity for my parents to build the store on their own. I built it the first time, and this would allow them to present it to me as a gift when I got out. I've always been bad at taking things from other people, so this fire will allow me to accept something more gracefully. He said it would also give my parents something to focus on other than the fact that their son is still in prison. I felt a lot better after talking it through with my friend. I moved right through the whole experience.

I've tried to give something back here by sharing with inmates what I have learned about how to keep commitments to themselves. Nearly everyone here is reactive. I would have them post commit-ments to exercise or read a book, or write a letter. They found that when they fulfilled a commitment, they felt better about them-selves.

Now I am in a halfway house. They've formed an honors group of about thirty guys and we have our own area to create a more positive environment. It's calmer. The guys are older. A lot of people want to move back here with us. In some ways it's harder than prison because you have to stay focused. You are allowed to leave and go out and work during the day but you have to come back and live within the rules at night or you'll be sent back to prison. You are caught between two worlds here.

Since arriving here I've developed a seminar I call "Think Before You Drink." I go to schools and talk to kids that range from ages eight to eighteen. I share my entire experience with them. It is always very emotional. When I finish, their questions for me often last up to forty-five minutes. In this past year I have spoken to nearly ten thousand kids. My message is always the same: choices, actions, and conse-quences. It helps me deal with killing my friend in my car. From their letters I sense that I'm reaching them.

I keep getting promised that I will be on the next list for release. My wife and daughter have stopped asking when I'm going to get out. It hurt too much to be continually told I hadn't made the list.

Again, these are circumstances that I have to live with which are the result of decisions I made and actions I took in the past. I feel bad that other people have to suffer, too, but again, it's been a growing experience for all of us. My wife is a totally different person than she was four years ago. She's so much healthier now, in all ways: spiritually, mentally, physically. She plans to enter a fitness contest for the first time at thirty-two years old. When I first went to prison, she used to say that there could not be a God because of all that had happened to us. But a year and a half ago, she wrote me a letter. She enclosed the "Serenity Prayer" and wrote me a poem. She closed by saying that she would be honored to walk into eternity with me.

It has been a growing experience for all of us, no doubt about it.

Isn't it fascinating that despite the complications of your past life and present circumstances, by simply becoming proactive in your Circle of Influence, you're put on a totally different road of healing, of recovery, of contribution, of courage, and of peace. That doesn't necessarily mean that all the psychic scars of the past are healed, for those scars may reassert themselves in other ways in the future. But it does mean that if you take responsibility for your response in the present moment, and if that response is based upon a value system of working within your Circle of Influence, that action may mitigate or, through faith, may even erase those psychic scars.

Those who work around prisoners commonly acknowledge that their fundamental problem is that they deny responsibility for their situation. So the concept of taking responsibility—being proactive and working within your Circle of Influence—hits the issue at its very heart. In other words, if there is any space between stimulus and response, no matter what the circumstance—genetics, present pressures, or past emotional or psychological scarring—the most liberating, ennobling, exalting, and freeing thing of all is the awareness of the ability to choose one's response.

This is the essence of the work of Nazi death camp survivor Viktor Frankl. I phoned Mr. Frankl several months prior to his passing to express my tremendous appreciation for his life's work. He said, "Don't write me off yet. I still have two more projects to finish." Meaningful projects were what his life's work was about. He represented a new force in psychotherapy called logotherapy—"logo" standing for the search for meaning, the search to find a purpose, a reason, a goal, a task which carries personal meaning. He said that even though he was blind, his wife was reading to him several hours a day and helping him with these projects. He died the same week that Mother Teresa and Princess Diana died.

Seeking Life Balance

Room 602 of the Oncology Critical Care Unit

This difficult situation of a manager torn between an urgent project, an insecure boss, and a dying mother beautifully illustrates the power of synergy—of coming up with better third alternatives.

I was a single parent rearing two teenagers and professionally I was at a critical juncture in my career. I had been the project manager for a major corporate initiative for two years. The project was nearing completion, and in anticipation of its conclusion, I was beginning to assume some of the responsibilities of my new position in another area. However, the mandate was clear: complete the project as soon as possible.

At the same time, my mother, who lived sixteen hundred miles away in South Texas, was diagnosed with cancer. The prognosis was worse than any of us expected. When the surgeon finished exploratory surgery, he told us, in words that I can still remember to this day, "Resection would not be conducive to life. I can only give her two weeks to three months to live."

Life has a way of teaching us the need for balance in our lives, for determining what is really important. Obviously, my mother's condition was a major focus for me; so was my career. The question was truly one of balance. How could I spend every minute possible with my mother, caring for her, and still complete the project in a professional manner? Convinced that I could not do both because of the distance between the two settings, I concluded that I must turn my back on the project and request family leave to be with my mother.

Having made the private decision, I needed to apply the interpersonal habits—Habits 4, 5, and 6 [Think Win-Win; Seek First to Understand, Then to Be Understood; Synergize]—in working with my employers. Thinking win-win was easy in this case. I really was devoted to my company; I didn't want to leave them in the lurch on this project. I wanted a win for the company but I knew I needed to be close to my mother for those last few weeks. So I thought that turning the project over to somebody else would be in the company's best interests.

I approached my supervisor prepared to seek first to understand. She was new in the company. Her performance was being scrutinized and she needed to make a good impression. She needed this project completed in a timely and effective fashion. She also used Habit 5 to seek first to understand my needs and those of my family. I learned a key lesson that day: when two parties honestly apply Habits 4 and 5, synergy naturally follows. One doesn't *do* synergy. Synergy is a reward for effectively thinking win-win and seeking first to understand.

For the next three months, I continued to complete my responsibilities for the project by laptop from my mother's hospital room. When meetings were necessary, the parties from the office gathered together and I joined them via telephone from my temporary office, Room 602 of the Oncology Critical Care Unit. For the first time in her life, my mother delighted in seeing her daughter at work. She commented on my contributions to meetings and questioned aspects of the project. I provided a good diversion for what had become her routine of shots, medication, doctors, and nurses.

At the end, the project was successfully completed and on time. And I was able to spend precious hours, days, and weeks with my mother.

⊛ *The key moment in this story occurred as this woman courageously approached her supervisor and shared her dilemma. Many people hesitate to do this because they have to confront some fears — particularly the fear of not ending up with the result they desire. Someone put it beautifully: "Courage is the quality of every quality at its highest testing point."*

The key insight that the person acquired was that synergy is the fruit — that Habit 6 always follows the roots, Habit 4: Think Win-Win, and Habit 5: Seek First to Understand, Then to Be Understood. If there is a spirit of true win-win and there is an effort to achieve mutual understanding, almost inevitably new insights and alternatives are created.

Daddy, I Want You to Be Healthy

This remarkable story shows that synergy, where the whole is greater than the sum of the parts, comes from life balance.

I had been working very hard on my career. By the time I was forty-five years old, I was quite successful. I was also about sixty pounds overweight, a compulsive eater during times of stress, and one who didn't have time to exercise regularly because of work. On his fifth birthday, my son, Logan, gave me a book on healthy living. Inside, his mother had helped him write the following words: "Daddy, for my birthday this year, I want you to be healthy. I want you to be around awhile." Talk about a punch in the stomach. Ouch.

That plea from my son changed my perspective on my lifestyle completely. The eating and the lack of regular physical exercise weren't just my individual choice anymore. I saw suddenly that I was creating a very unhealthy legacy for our children. I was modeling for them that one's body was unimportant; that self-control was unimportant; that the only thing worth working hard for in this life was money and prestige. I realized that my stewardship for my children involved more than just providing for their physical, financial, and emotional needs. It also involved providing healthy role models. I had not been doing that.

So I committed myself to being healthy for my children [Habit 1: Be Proactive]. Not to losing weight, but to being healthy. That's the key for me. My commitment had to be to something that held real value for me. I had tried so many diets and exercise programs before. Normally I would be fine until stresses happened in my life. To have losing weight as my inspiring motivation was simply not enough.

But my children *are* significant enough. I care enough about them that I can make healthy decisions. I established as a goal for myself that I wanted to be healthy [Habit 2: Begin with the End in Mind]. I wanted to be vital, to have energy to play with my kids after work, to be able to play in the company softball tournament without getting winded on the way to first base. As a way to reach that goal, I implemented a diet and exercise program. The key here is that the diet and exercise program was not the goal. Being healthy for my children was. I decided to share my goal with somebody else who wanted to be healthy. We now work together on a mutually beneficial exercise program. I made sure I set aside time for me to accomplish my goals. I learned to stop working and pay attention to the needs of my body.

It's been two years since I changed my way of thinking. I don't struggle anymore to get out of bed. Exercising has almost become second nature. I don't talk myself out of my exercise program like I did at the beginning. Sure, there are still days that I don't do too well. I'm tired, I have a headache, it's too hot. Some days, I plain talk myself out of running. But it's so much easier now for me to get back on track [Habit 3: Put First Things First]. Because I have this larger goal, this greater commitment to somebody I love more than myself, I can get right back on course.

A second benefit to this healthful mind-set is that I believe more than ever that I can be proactive. Getting out of bed early every morning, running to the top of the hill, running in my first 5K race. All of these things motivate me. Day after day, as I exercise, I experience private victories. So now I have this sense of faith, of hope, of belief that I am capable of difficult things. In a way, I had a victim's mentality before because I was so discouraged, so stressed out that I couldn't make a difference in the way I lived. Now, I have private victories that buoy me up.

A third benefit to having this larger goal is clearness of mind. I'm getting older. I used to think that getting older meant having to get used to being stiff, sore, tired, achy. But now that I have a much healthier lifestyle, I can see that it wasn't age that made me feel that way, it was the way I was living. I know now that my head is achy because I ate too much sugar, not because I am forty-seven. My body is adjusted to health. I can use its healthy reactions to help me make decisions about how to live. I have learned you can actually trust a healthy body to tell you things. When you pay the price to live by true principles, the reward of vitality and health is discernible. When that clarity of mind is clouded, I know instantly that I need to get back on track with my eating, exercising, and sleep.

Perhaps the greatest lesson I have learned is that my body is intimately connected to the social, mental, and spiritual aspects of my life. That sugar headache I always had didn't allow me to think clearly. Plus, the clarity of mind that comes after exercising is so beneficial. We identify losing weight as being the reward for exercising. I think that mental clarity is the greatest reward I have gained so far. I've never thought so clearly or concisely. Socially, I have benefited as well. Whenever I dieted before, I was always incredibly grumpy, which affected my relationships with my wife, children, and co-workers. I was so grumpy because I had this huge have-to on my list which I didn't have a driving desire to do. Now that I want to be healthy, the decisions to eat correctly and exercise are made more willingly, even joyfully on my part. This lack of internal struggle frees up so much more of my emotional energy to spend on my wife and children.

I never envisioned that a decision to be healthy could have such a dramatic effect on all four areas of my life. I'm not there yet. I'm still working. But I am enjoying the rewards that come from living, exercising, and eating the right way.

⊗ *When this overweight forty-seven-year-old man tapped into deeper emotional and spiritual motivations, including the legacy he was leaving his family, he gained control, perspective, willpower, clarity of mind, profound self-awareness, and personal freedom. Among the many lessons this story contains, it particularly shows the power and the fruits of the private victory. How easy it is to say no when we have a burning yes inside.*

I've come to believe that self-mastery is foundational to maintaining good relationships. Appetite control usually precedes and enables emotional and mental control. We also can't really build strong relationships until we conquer prideful passions. The author of Proverbs taught, "He who rules his own spirit is better than he that taketh a city." Greek wisdom teaches, "Know thyself. Control thyself. Give thyself."

Wednesday Evening: My Time with Mom

Our studies show that most people acknowledge that their lives are really out of balance. People tend to focus so much on work and other pressing activities that the relationships and activities they really treasure most end up getting squeezed and pushed aside. This is a beautiful story of an individual who got caught up in this whirlpool of urgency, and by taking the time to think about roles and goals (Habit 1: Be Proactive and Habit 2: Begin with the End in Mind), and synergizing with his wife (Habit 6: Synergize), he came up with a marvelous solution.

I have always had a special friendship with my mother. Together we endured a series of life events that has created a wonderful relationship. At one time in my life, even though I loved my mother and really enjoyed spending time with her, I got caught up in my commitments to work, the community, and to my own family. My life got so busy, weeks would go by before I would make even a quick phone call just to check in. And when I did manage to squeeze in a visit, we would have just sat down to talk, and it would be time for me to leave. Another meeting to go to, another deadline to meet. My contact with this wonderful woman became mostly hit-and-miss.

My mother never put any pressure on me to visit more often, but I wasn't happy with the situation. I knew my life was out of control if I couldn't consistently spend time with my mother. So, pulling on the First Things First perspective, my wife and I brainstormed for a solution. She suggested scheduling a time each week or so that would work for both our family and my mother. When we looked at the calendar, we saw my wife has choir practice every Wednesday evening. That night became my night to spend with my mom.

Now my mom knows that every week or two I will be coming on a specific night, at a specific time. I won't be running off within the first ten minutes, and there are few interruptions. If she wants to get some exercise, we go for a walk together. Other times she'll cook a meal for me. Sometimes I take her shopping at the mall, which is further away than she feels comfortable driving to. No matter what we do, we always talk—about family, about current events, about our memories.

Every evening I spend with my mother is a peaceful oasis in my busy life. I tell my wife it's one of the best suggestions she's ever given me.

When my father died, I decided I was going to maintain and even increase my very special relationship with my mother because of the new void in her life. I resolved that no matter where I was, I would phone her every day for the rest of her life. Though we lived fifty miles apart, I would also make special efforts to visit her at least every two weeks. She lived for another ten years and I cannot begin to express the depth of my gratitude for her life and for the preciousness of our time together.

I learned that when you regularly communicate with another person, you reach a new level of understanding that almost runs by nuance. I found that the daily phone call was not too unlike our semiweekly visit; we felt as close to each other and as open and authentic with each other as we did when we were together. It was like one continuous conversation. It really didn't make much difference whether it was on the phone or face-to-face, which surprised me, because I'd always thought nothing could replace face-to-face contact. I am sure in another sense that is correct. Because each conversation contains the cumulative effect of the previous conversations there is hardly anything to catch up on. Instead, you can share deep insights and feelings rather than just experiences. Intimate communication means in-to-me-see.

Just like the gentleman in this story, I, too, have had the tremendous benefit of having a very supportive and understanding wife who has the abundance mentality. My wife, Sandra, doesn't see life as a fixed piece of pie where there is only so much time, where time with my mother would mean time away from her. She saw that time with my mother would actually increase the depth of our own relationship.

I Looked in the Mirror and Saw a Control Freak

Notice in this story what happens when work is at the center of our life. Notice also the deep turmoil involved with adding a new center—even when it's one as important as family. Ultimately, we must come to a third alternative—one that embraces and harmonizes all the important areas of our lives—a principle center. When we do, as this man did, it will not only bring the balance we seek, it will cause us to go deep inside and bring order and integrity to our character and emotional makeup. The result is a reduced need to control others and greater productivity and happiness in every area of our life.

I spent my entire adult life focusing on my job. I worked twelve-, fourteen-hour days, six days a week, to get ahead. I was constantly positioning myself so that I could be noticed and rewarded. I took the travel assignments because that gave the impression I was devoted to the agency. We moved to inner-city Chicago so that I could be closer to the head agency. I thought my wife loved living there. I thought she loved the way our life was. I did.

Then my son was born. Suddenly, I wanted to spend more time with him and my wife. So I tried to stretch myself between family and work. I felt like I was on a teeter-totter with my family on one side and work on the other. If I spent time with my family, the work side would shoot up. I'd have to go running over there. That meant I would leave my family. So I would run back to the family side. I felt like I was running between two opposite ends all week. As hard as I tried, I couldn't get them to balance. No matter how fast I ran be-tween the two places, I couldn't keep a balance. I was getting very tired and irritable with the circus act.

When I started learning and thinking seriously about the principle of putting first things first, I realized my priorities weren't straight. I couldn't try to have work and family be my primary focus. If I did, my family would end up taking a back seat again as they had for years. I needed to redefine what was important to me [Habit 2: Begin with the End in Mind]. Then I had to adjust my life so that my actions affirmed my priorities [Habit 3: Put First Things First]. Only then would my life feel calm and purposeful.

When I looked at the way I did my job, I saw a major control freak. I liked to be in the office for every decision. I liked looking over others' shoulders to make sure everything was completed just the way I liked it. I thought nobody else could do it the way I could. Consequently, my life was filled with clutter. Inconsequential reports, briefings, and data sheets filled my days. I felt I had to do them because only I could do them the right way. I was wrong. By not letting go, I set my associates up for failure by not giving them a chance to perform. I began to allow others to participate in those things. My teammates had more of an active role, and I took more of an advisor role on most projects. I found out they felt more fulfilled having a bigger stake in the work.

To my amazement and a little bit of chagrin, those oh-so-important things at work that only I could do were getting done just fine. My boss was still happy and I had less busywork to complete. Which meant, revelation of all revelations, that I had more time to spend on the things I considered important. I started taking a lunch hour regularly, sometimes with my wife and son. I took time to really learn the software we used at the office. My productivity capacity skyrocketed. I thought, with all this free time, I might even go back to school to really learn something after all these years of climbing [Habit 7: Sharpen the Saw].

My family life has changed dramatically. We moved out of Chicago to a small country town (it turned out my wife never enjoyed living in the city). Instead of spending time at the office, I'm with my family. My son and I go to the Saturday matinee. We buy a large popcorn (extra butter flavoring), some red licorice, and enjoy the show. I have a better relationship with my wife than I've had in years. We spend time together. Just time together. To do what we want: walking, exercising, hiking, gardening, and always talking. I am enjoying my life. I've even been known to joke on occasion.

Most importantly, I'm not running between two masters anymore. Life is not as hectic. I know the difference between what work has to be done, what work can be done. Most importantly, I know the work that shouldn't be done. I let that go right on by.

 When we are torn between two opposing values, both good, we usually end up compromising both. Such is the case between the value

of work and the value of family. Yet by focusing on a higher purpose or principle, no compromise needs to be made. You can achieve greater success in both areas and have synergy between the two.

To some, the most interesting aspect of this story would be the paradigm shift that took place when this man's son was born. A paradigm is how you see reality, your view of the world, your map of the territory. The fastest way to change a person's paradigm is to change his or her role. As soon as our role changes from being single to married we see the world differently. As soon as our role changes from husband or wife to parent we see the world differently. Paradigm or perception shifts are more profound than either behavior or attitude shifts. I have always believed that if you want to make a significant improvement, work on your paradigm. If you want to make minor improvements, work on your behavior and attitude. Once you have a correct paradigm of reality, where the map reflects the territory, then go to work on your behavior and attitudes.

The Surprise Visit

When we create a mission statement we identify our purpose, vision, values, and most important relationships in life. There is power in a mission statement, particularly when it explicitly or implicitly deals with all the important roles in one's life. Most people focus on one or two roles, such as immediate family and work, and they often end up neglecting other roles. When the woman in this story focused on her extended family, she got some resistance from her immediate family. But by fulfilling this role within the context of her mission statement (Habit 2: Begin with the End in Mind) and sticking with the plan (Habit 3: Put First Things First), she found a meaningful new dimension of life.

When I wrote my mission statement last year, I said I wanted to be closer to my relatives than I had been in the past. So, when I planned my annual vacation to Tennessee to visit my parents and sister, I decided to schedule a visit to two elderly aunts. I don't think I had seen them in ten years. I felt I needed to spend my time in a way consistent with my mission statement.

When I got down to Tennessee, I told my sister of my plan to visit Aunt Dorothy and Aunt Margaret. She didn't really understand my motive. "Why don't you just give them a call instead of visiting them. I've found these great little antique shops I want to show you. They'll be happy with just a phone call." I don't know why but I really felt drawn to visit these women. "No," I said a little too firmly, "I really want to go see the aunts."

As I drove over to their house, I had cold feet. What would they think of me, popping in to visit after all these years? Why did I think they would be happy to see me? I almost turned the car around.

When I walked into their little living room, they both lit up. We drank iced tea and visited for almost three hours. They told me stories of when I was a little girl, of how they came to visit when I was born. They even told me stories of my grandmother and great-grandfather that I hadn't heard before. It was a delightful afternoon. I was only sorry I hadn't visited sooner. Little did I know I had visited just in the nick of time.

Three months later, Aunt Margaret passed away. When I heard the news, my first thought was, "I'm so glad I didn't go antique shopping that day." In my moment of choice, I had stuck to my plan. I had chosen to build my relationship with the people I loved just as my mission statement said. That afternoon was a priority for me. I don't think it would have happened if I hadn't taken the time to plan and think about the importance of making these relationships first in my life.

Stephanie's Recovery Plan

Notice in this instructive and heartwarming story the synergy that comes from a multidimensional approach to healing.

My wife, Stephanie, and I were scuba diving one day when something strange happened. Every time Stephanie went underwater, she felt like her lungs were filling up with water. In fact, she could even feel air bubbles popping in her lungs. We stopped diving because we thought she had the bends and spent the rest of the vacation on the beach. I didn't think anything more about it.

When we returned home, Stephanie had this nagging cough. So she went to the doctor. He said, "Oh, there's probably nothing wrong, but if you want, I'll send you in to have some X rays taken." We waited a couple of weeks. Her cough never went away. So we went to the hospital for some X rays. Then an MRI. They found a tumor in her chest. A tumor in my beautiful, twenty-eight-year-old wife.

Two weeks later they did a biopsy. The results showed a highly malignant tumor growing rapidly. Stephanie needed to start chemotherapy right away if there was to be any chance of recovery. That week, she started the chemotherapy as well as radiation. Within a month of our vacation we were fully entrenched in a war against Stephanie's cancer.

This life-changing event really forced me to look at myself and how I lived my life. I've always been very career-oriented. When Stephanie's tumor was discovered, I was thirty years old, at the peak of trying to establish myself. I worked long and hard and then longer and harder. My career was central to my life. The tumor came at a time when my family was taking a back seat to my career plans. My paradigm shifted as soon as I found out Stephanie was walking around with a tumor in her chest cavity pushing on her heart and lungs. All I could think about was us, our family, what we needed to do to fight this thing.

Here's what we did.

First, we created a Stephanie Recovery Plan [Habit 2: Begin with the End in Mind]. We had mapped out exactly what Stephanie needed to do physically to beat the cancer and feel reasonably comfortable while she endured the treatments and their effects. After talking to a close friend, however, we added to the physical recovery plan. He said to us, "Don't approach this from just the physical side: approach this challenge from the physical, mental, spiritual, and social-emotional aspects." We knew as soon as we heard that, that he was right. Cancer affects the whole person, body and soul. We needed to take care of and plan for all of Stephanie, not just her body.

Second, we approached this cancer as a family and a community. I had been raised not to bother people with my problems—the macho approach. But this time we felt that the more people who knew about Stephanie, the better. The more we could be in people's minds and prayers, the more successful we would be. Our families, neighbors, and co-workers prayed for us. If they didn't pray, they thought positive thoughts. I'm convinced they helped her get well.

Third, we realized time was precious. Every minute needed to be spent in a worthwhile frame of mind and doing worthwhile things. Our definition of worthwhile first things changed. We questioned activities that we had mindlessly done before: "Is this really where we want to spend our time, in these kinds of activities?" The size of our home, money, even social relationships were not that important anymore. Our conversations changed to discussions of ideas, of relationships that were really important to us.

With these ideas in place, we started living our lives according to the recovery plan. Our lives really did change.

Stephanie was remarkable. She wouldn't allow us to argue for longer than a minute. Arguing was not worth her time anymore. She wouldn't allow the chemo to alter her good mood. Even though she was hooked up to these IVs that were just pumping her full of chemicals, she kept up the banter, making everyone in the room laugh. She was determined that this cancer would not dictate how she lived her life. Every morning, she walked with a group of ladies in the neighborhood. I think that was her time to just get it all out, though I'm not sure. I was never invited. Despite all the radiation and the chemo, she never missed a morning of walking. I really think those early morning walks catered to her emotional, physical, and social needs all at once. They literally forced her out of bed in the mornings because she needed the companionship so much.

We became quite selective about how we spent our time. We chose to be around people who made us laugh. We rented movies that made us laugh. I changed the way I approached my job. For me, our family time became precious. I remember taking a few days off right after she was diagnosed. I spent an afternoon with her, right in the middle of my workday, to watch *Les Misérables*. That would never have happened before.

It wasn't all fun and games. Cancer strikes to the very soul. One particularly heart-wrenching moment came when Stephanie started to lose her hair. She tried to have it cut so that it covered up the bald spots. But she was losing so much, the style didn't really work. One morning, with both of us almost in tears, I took a razor and shaved my wife's head. Just sheared off all her beautiful hair. The memory still makes me ache—her eyes looking at me in the mirror.

Stephanie recovered. She's been cancer-free for five years now. I believe she recovered so much faster because we took the holistic approach. We concentrated on the whole person, and planned for the long term. Our lives have changed completely. Ironically, about two years ago, we found ourselves living just the way we had pre-cancer. We had to shake ourselves awake and say, "Wait, was that lesson for nothing? What did we learn? Why are we forgetting?" The everyday, no-pressure pace of life had fooled us into thinking we could be lackadaisical about our relationship again. So we had to recommit to each other and to that lifestyle.

To make that First Things First commitment real, I am taking off two months this April and May—an unpaid, almost-suicidal-when-you-think-about-it leave of absence. We bought a motor home, are pulling the kids out of school, and going to Baja California to drive the beaches. We've set some goals as a family for the trip [Habit 2: Begin with the End in Mind]:

One, we want to get closer as a family. Two, we want to increase our religious faith. Three, we want to celebrate Stephanie; she's been cancer-free for five years. Four, we want to have the adventure of a lifetime. Five, we want to experience a different culture.

I'm scared, quite frankly. This is a huge risk to take career-wise. It took me about three months to convince my supervisor that this will be good for both me and for the company. I don't think I know of anybody else in this company who's ever done anything like it. But I believe with all my heart that our family is what is most important.

✳ *Anyone who has a serious illness can draw upon six sources of healing: medical, physical, mental, social, emotional, and spiritual.*

Medical *technology has advanced amazingly, but we also recognize that its essential role is to optimize the conditions that enable the body's natural forces to do the ultimate healing. Physically, our bodies have great resiliency and capacity, but we have to use wisdom in making them as strong, healthy, and vital as possible through proper nutrition, exercise, and rest. Mentally, we need to visualize internal bodily forces overcoming the disease—for instance, to literally see the immune system kick in and the white blood cells successfully destroying the disease-spreading cells. We also need to take responsibility for our recovery and to learn as much as possible about what is happening—about the diagnosis and about alternative plans of treatment. Socially, we need to surround ourselves with caring people, particularly loved ones, who bring hope and support to our hearts and minds and with whom we can intimately (into-me-see) communicate. Emotionally, we need to tap into as many positive attitudes on a consistent basis as is possible—such as hope, because it powerfully impacts biology, such as confidence in the recovery process, such as giving love and service, such as having a magnificent attitude in the face of very difficult circumstances, and such as receiving the love and affirmation of others. Spiritually, we need to draw upon our faith, our deep internal belief system, and upon those of our faith who can minister to our spiritual hunger and needs. We can also serve others, if only in maintaining a beautiful attitude in the face of a wasting terminal illness. As Teilhard de Chardin put it, "We are not human beings having a spiritual experience; we are spiritual beings having a human experience."*

2

Family

"Me lift thee and thee lift me, and we'll both ascend together."

—JOHN GREENLEAF WHITTIER

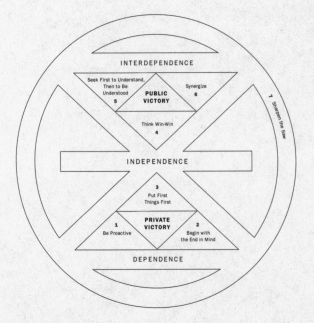

Raising Young Children

Because . . .

In the following story notice how one's awareness expands and deepens through proactive initiative and human interaction. Notice also the amazing wealth produced.

My oldest daughter, Tina, who was about nine at the time, and I were driving to see her grandmother. I remember thinking that with Tina, building an Emotional Bank Account was a key. So I thought, "What can I do in the thirty minutes we have together to make deposits in her bank account?" You know, this took a bit of courage. By the age of nine, a child pretty much has a good idea of the kind of behavior to expect from each parent. I'm not much of a chatterer when we travel. I might comment on the scenery every now and again, but mostly I drive in silence. So I was a bit nervous suggesting the game I came up with.

As we backed out of the driveway, I said, "Honey, why don't we play a game. What we want to do is say 'I feel good about you because . . .' or 'I liked what you did because . . .' The 'because' is important because then we know why the other person likes us. Okay? I'll start."

So I started off. I said something about her. Then she paused and said something about me. After about three or four things, I really had to start thinking. This was quite shocking to me. I love my child so much, but I was having difficulty thinking of specific actions that I loved about her. I was really searching for things to say. Tina found it easier. After about five or six, she started to break through the normal responses. I could tell she was looking at my life, and seeing me and what I did. She was grateful for the work I did, the walks to the park, the basketball in the driveway, the way I woke her up in the mornings. She could see all of me.

I was still struggling. Then, as I looked at this little girl's life, really looked at her and what she did every day in our family, I started to see. I saw her hugs, her little words, her thank-yous. I saw how well she was doing at school and how polite she was. I told her I loved it when she came home from school and gave me a big hug. When we started digging and looking, we couldn't stop. This was only a thirty-minute trip. We got to twenty-two, twenty-three items and then I had to call it off. I couldn't think of anything else.

Frankly, I was stunned by the game. I felt good on one hand but discouraged on the other. Good that Tina could see so much (she wanted to carry on), discouraged that I couldn't find more. More importantly, the rest of the trip we spent chattering to each other. I think the game started a dialogue that I hadn't had with her before.

When we arrived, Tina jumped out of the car and raced into the house, and that's when my heart almost broke. "Grandma, Grandma," she shouted. "My daddy knows so many good things about me. I didn't know he knew so many good things about me."

⊗ *The word "respect" comes from the Latin root* specto, *which means to see—to see another (Habit 5: Seek First to Understand, Then to Be Understood). The more we are self-absorbed, the less we see others as precious individuals with many layers of individuality, and with many facets to each layer. When we get out of ourselves, and truly listen to another, a marvelous journey of discovery begins.*

The Head-Butt

Notice how this mother paused, got control, and waited for things to cool down before getting the two fighting sons to try practicing Habit 5: Seek First to Understand, Then to Be Understood. Notice also how quickly the results came.

"My nose is bleeding! He head-butted me!"

My nine-year-old son, Jet, was hollering, holding his bloodied nose, leaving a trail of blood to the bathroom. My seven-year-old son, Michael, had let him have it, an altercation over control of the TV remote.

My first thought, on this day of extended winter school break, was, "It's eight-thirty in the morning and these two are at it again. I can't go through another day like this."

I sent Michael to his room for a time-out and got Jet cleaned up. Then I called both of them into my bedroom for a talk. I didn't feel angry with them, only disappointed in my leadership of our home; not creating the conditions where they could live in harmony and work out their differences.

I sat between them with an arm around each. "Let's get this figured out. You guys are fighting and hitting a lot and it upsets all of us. Jet, would you tell Michael how you are feeling right now?"

Jet stared straight ahead and shouted, "My nose hurts! You hit me for no reason! You kept pinching me and I told you to stop! The only way to get your attention was to take the remote and then you head-butted me."

Michael was angry, too, and he started his rebuttal: "You always hit me—"

I interrupted Michael and asked him to tell us what he just heard Jet say.

Michael said, "I've always got the remote and nobody likes me."

I prompted Michael: "What else did you hear Jet say?"

"His nose hurts and I was pinching him and he got in the way of my head," Michael said.

"Jet, is that what you said?"

"Yes. He didn't have to smash my nose!"

I said, "How do you see what happened, Michael?"

"Jet always gets to do anything he wants! When I'm watching TV he always turns the channel! When I'm playing with something, he takes it away and says it's his!"

I said, "Jet, what did you hear Michael say?"

"Michael thinks that I take over everything and get to do anything I want."

"Is that right, Michael?"

"Yeah."

We went through a few more rounds of "what did you hear him say and did he get it right?"

The mood in our home changed for the positive literally in a few minutes. The boys started to look at each other, smile, and make jokes. The tension was gone and feelings were understood. It was okay to move to problem solving with my boys.

Then I asked, "The next time you guys disagree on the TV channel or anything else, what can you do besides hit?"

Jet thoughtfully answered, "Go do something else or talk to you or Dad."

Michael added, "Go outside or play PlayStation."

"How about if you look at the TV listings for one or two programs each day and talk with each other ahead of time about what you want to watch?"

"That's a good idea!" They were through talking now; their Rollerblades were calling them.

I was amazed at how understanding each other's feelings and viewpoints raised their self-esteem. They were so pleased with themselves for solving a problem in a new way. I think they saw themselves differently, more capable and in control because of the ideas they came up with. It reminded me of the power of treating people as if they are responsible and then noticing what happens.

⊗ *This is a good story of how relationships in a family or in any other setting can develop an immune system. You simply use the problem, whatever it is, to practice Habits 4, 5, and 6 (Think Win-Win; Seek First to Understand, Then to Be Understood; Synergize). If you can come up with win-win solutions based upon mutual respect and understanding, you gradually cultivate an emotional resiliency inside the relationship so that the next problem that comes along can be* similarly handled. Even if it isn't handled in the same way, people know that they have the ability to handle it. The very awareness of that ability is central to this immune system. It's when people have a feeling of powerlessness, hopelessness, and helplessness that they end up making mountains out of molehills and drowning in puddles. When there is no immune system, small differences are exacerbated through a lack of communication until you see major communication problems and relationship breakdowns.

I Can Choose My Life

*The following story is about the power of deeply affirming another
person's worth and potential. Because positive scripting occurred
early in this boy's life, and because it was so constant and sincere, it
soaked into his soul and became like a freshwater spring to his life.
Circumstances on the surface that might otherwise have been
polluting had no lasting impact.*

I was raised in a wonderful family: never demeaned, abused, or
torn down. I was taught that I was capable, special, destined for great
things. I think those daily affirmations really helped shape me. Because given what happened when I was nine, I could have gone seriously wrong.

I was the youngest of five children when we learned my mother
was suffering from a bleeding abdominal ulcer. Suddenly, early one
morning, she had a heart attack. I remember it was six in the morning
when she died. It was completely unexpected. Suddenly our house
was filled with screaming—screams of utter despair. My family, especially my father, went into shock. But somehow I got sent to school
that day. My mother had just died, my father and sister were devastated, and I got sent to school. I remember one kid yelling at me from
across the playground as I walked in from recess, "Hey Holbrooke, I
heard your mom died." I'll never forget that yell across the playground. Hundreds of kids heard him. I said, "Yeah, she did."

I'll never forget that reply. Because it taught me to recognize what
had happened, to accept it, and to move on. Now that approach probably wouldn't work for everybody. But it worked for me. I learned I
could accept and endure and move on through the hard time.

Things actually only got worse. My dad was an old-time physi-
cian—set bones, delivered babies, and out on call all night, every
night. He had these five young kids with nobody to take care of them.
So he remarried very quickly. She brought with her three children—
two of them close to my own age. So all of a sudden this strange
woman, who really didn't care for me or my siblings, was raising me.
They divorced horribly after about six years of marriage. Let's just
say that from ten to seventeen years of age, I was raised with really
interesting family dynamics.

But those early years of security and positive reinforcement had a tremendous impact on me. I refused to let negative experiences tear me down. Through that terrible second marriage, when I had no mother to love or raise me, I still believed with all my heart that I was special and destined for great things. After all, every night my dad, until I left home, came into my room (when I was young he tucked me into bed, and as I got older, he would just come in to check on me). Every single night, he said to me, "Son, remember, just between you and me and the gatepost, you are an extremely gifted and special young man. There are great things in store for you." At the time, I responded, "Oh yeah, okay, heard this one before." But those words sank into my bones and my soul. They became a part of me.

I'm not really that talented. There are some things I do well, but I'm not a genius or anything. However, I never doubted myself. I have never questioned whether I could accomplish anything, whether I was capable of anything. That is perhaps my father's greatest gift to me: he gave me a belief in myself that is unwavering [Emotional Bank Account]. He gave me a sense of worth and potential independent of my circumstances—that no matter what happened to me, I could still choose my life [Habit 1: Be Proactive].

✳ *I was similarly blessed to have parents who constantly affirmed their belief in me. I knew that they were confident that I would do the right things and that I could make something of my life. Two short experiences to illustrate: One is the memory of being awakened from time to time in the middle of the night to find my mother whispering to me quietly as I slept. It was as if she was trying to speak things to my subconscious mind such as, "You will do excellently on your test tomorrow. You can do anything you make up your mind to do." One night I remember waking up overhearing this talk, and in a startled manner said, "Mom, what are you doing?" She tenderly replied, "I'm just telling you how much I love you and that I believe in you," and left the room. Another experience involved some fraternity brothers in college who used to do some drinking, but who were ashamed to admit it to their families. One time after a trip they had a fifth of whiskey left over, and they gave it to me. I put it on the top of my dresser where it remained for many months. Never once did my parents mention it to me or ask about it. They simply knew that I wouldn't drink. I honestly believe that the most powerful, penetrating, transcendent form of love that a parent can give a child is a constant, repetitive affirmation of that child's essential worth and potential—even when their current behavior would indicate the opposite. Never give up.*

Our Family Poster

*Many times when you discuss Habit 2, Begin with the End in Mind,
in the form of developing a personal, family, or organizational
mission statement, eyes glaze over. Many people have been involved
in vision workshops that never really amounted to anything because
they were rushed, announced in fancy phraseology, and then
forgotten. Done so, they create a lot of cynicism. Here is the story of
a creative father who worked within the frame of reference of his
children in developing a family mission statement.*

I have been trying for years to figure out how to develop a mission
statement with my family. Our four kids are ten, seven, four, and one,
so it's not exactly as if they can sit down and have a serious discussion using all the terminology. Even my wife is a little leery of the the-
oretical discussions. She loves the ideas, but sometimes doesn't really
want me to be the family trainer. We've read the *7 Habits* family book
together, we enjoy the ideas, and then when we sit down to actually
create a mission statement, our four-year-old Jordan ends up doing
somersaults off his brother's head.

Sometimes I'll try coming at it from the side, asking questions like,
"What's special about our family?" or "What sort of family do you
think we should have?" My older kids roll their eyes, and Jordan
shouts, "We should have pizza every night for dinner." I was really
stuck.

Then I decided to try something that was more on the kids' level. I
got poster board, a whole bundle of magazines and catalogues, scis-
sors and glue, and all the kids. I told them we were going to create a
family collage, that we would be finding pictures that looked like
what our family is. They loved it.

Within minutes my daughter found a family walking through the
woods with three kids. "Hey, Dad, remember when we hiked to Silver Lake before Trevor was born? That would be fun to do again."
Then Tanner, our seven-year-old, found a picture of a belt pack filled
with food. "Dad, Dad, look. This is just like the one you wear when
we go skiing." Saturday is our family ski day, and I wear a belt pack
filled with fruit and PowerBars. When we're hungry, we set up our
skis, make seats in the snow, and break out the snacks. I know he was

connecting this very tangible picture with the feelings of closeness and friendship we feel as we ski together. So that picture went onto the poster.

The older two kids easily found their pictures. Jordan struggled a little. He couldn't quite find what he wanted. Then he saw this picture of a polar bear, a wolf, and a deer. Now, he doesn't live anywhere near the North Pole. But the wildlife reminded him of the walks we take together in the evening. We live in a wooded area and sometimes the deer will come out at dusk to feed. So he says, "Dad, Dad, Dad, remember the time that deer came right up to you and he had antlers and he wouldn't move out of the way?" He had found his picture. I could tell that as my kids were looking, deciding, cutting, and pasting they were starting to feel that our family was special, that they belonged to something important. We're not quite finished yet with our collage, but the framework is there. In fact, Tanner got so excited he wants to make his own personal picture of what he wants to be. Can you imagine? A seven-year-old kid with his own mission statement! Of course, he doesn't know that's what he's making. And I'm not about to tell him until he's done. I don't want him to roll his eyes at me.

Everyone has mission statements, but very few are written down. Fewer still are consciously developed. But everyone has mission statements in the form of deeply held values that guide their decisions. Without any question, the most important decision we will ever make is that decision which governs all other decisions. Some call this a mission statement, others a philosophy, a credo, a set of values, or just simply goals. But whatever the name, it basically represents those criteria that consciously or unconsciously guide all decision making.

Such a statement can be put in the form of a poster, a song, an icon, a picture, a few words, or many words. The key is deep, sincere involvement over a sufficient period of time so that harmony between the emotions, values, motivations, desires, hopes, fears, and self-doubts is achieved. The astronauts have an expression for it: all systems go. When such a mission statement has been hammered out and is used on a continuous basis as the central criterion for all decisions, it becomes an enormously powerful source of courage to say no to things that don't fit within it, and yes to those that do.

I'm Not Going to School Ever Again

Deep listening is truly like peeling an onion, one layer after another, until eventually you reach the soft core. The following story illustrates first a sputtering attempt at listening, and then a sincere one. Empathic listening—that is, listening within the frame of reference of another until the power of feeling understood is unleashed—renewed this son's spirit and confidence.

Danny is eight years old. He's my high-energy, everybody-wants-to-be-his-friend child. He loves school, loves his teachers, loves his assignments; has to be the best, do his best. Most of the time he does. Schoolwork comes very easily to him.

I arrived home from work one evening about six-thirty. He was waiting for me in the driveway. Before I could even turn the car off, he yanked open my door:

"Dad, I hate school. I'm not going back—not ever, no way. I'm not going back to school. I hate my classes. My teachers are so dumb. I'm not going to school ever again."

"Hi, Danny, must have had a hard day, huh?"

"Yeah, and I'm not going back to school. It's stupid."

"Oh, you'll have a good day tomorrow, son," I said as I gathered up my briefcase and suit coat. I hadn't really even looked at him yet. I was giving my totally stock responses to an eight-year-old's ranting. As I turned to get out of the car, I saw his face. He was red to bulging. So I switched into "Come on, you know, hunker down, psych it up, make it happen, blah, blah, blah." That sort of settled him down.

Bedtime rolled around and he started up again: "I'm not going to school tomorrow. I'm really not going." I'm clueless. So I talked to him about why he was so upset. Ten or fifteen minutes later, it turned out he hates Mr. Bisset, his art teacher: "I don't like Mr. Bisset. He's so dumb. He's just so dumb."

Okay. So he doesn't like his teacher. But that doesn't mean he shouldn't go to school tomorrow. So I said, "Oh, you'll survive. It'll be better tomorrow."

"I'm not going to school tomorrow. I'm never going back to that stupid place as long as I live." Obviously, I hadn't quite got to the core of what he was trying to tell me by his tears and shouting.

I thought to practice empathic listening. Don't listen to the words; focus on his feelings. Listen with your eyes and heart.

So I tried that:

"You must be really angry, Dan."

"I'm mad. And Mr. Bisset is mean to me."

"Really. That's got to feel terrible when he's mean. What does he do that he's so mean?"

"Well, he makes kids cry. And he gives us all these stupid assignments. And he doesn't teach us anything. And he made Jessica cry yesterday. You got to go see him, Dad, make him stop. You gotta, Dad, otherwise I can't go back to school."

On and on he went. Most of what he said didn't even make sense. But I just listened and reflected his feelings, until we got to the very heart of the matter about fifteen minutes later: Mr. Bisset had given Danny an assignment to be completed in two days. Danny didn't know how to do the assignment.

He had gotten so worked up about his fear of not being able to do the assignment that he almost exploded. After probably twenty minutes of me just listening to him, he was a different kid: "Dad, you probably don't need to go see Mr. Bisset. I'll be okay. He's okay, really. He's kind of a fun teacher, anyway."

You know, I did go see Mr. Bisset, because I promised Danny I would. But the thing I realized is that when my kids are upset, I tend to give them a cheerleader, pump-them-up kind of speech. That's my stock reaction. I probably never recognize eighty percent of the underlying reasons for their emotions when I do that. Just listening to Danny helped me understand his little heart far more than I ever have. I was able to help him because I took the time to listen.

⊗ *I've learned from my own children that if they are expressing a concern, asking some question, or feeling down, there is usually an underlying reason for it. I find that the fastest way to help, though at the time it seems so slow, is to literally stop and listen (Habit 5: Seek First to Understand, Then to Be Understood). It's looking them in the eye, getting yourself into their mind and heart, and listening. Sometimes no words are spoken, but a relationship is established. You're simply present. You're simply there. Perhaps the child is inwardly saying, "Will he still be there if I say nothing? Does he really care? Can I risk being that open and that vulnerable? I'll test it for a minute." And when you hang in there, even when they take you on, the peeling of the onion takes place, and almost inevitably you get to the core. Listening gives such powerful emotional oxygen to everyone involved. When we don't listen, we often give unwanted answers and solutions to problems that do not exist. Most of the time, they're just gasping for air.*

Daddy, I Gotta Go Potty

Notice three things in this wonderful little story: first, the power to change how the end in mind is really defined; second, the instantaneous effect of self-awareness on the father; third, the immediate effect that the father's change in attitude had upon the four-year-old daughter.

One Saturday afternoon, I decided to take my four-year-old daughter, Lauren, skiing. I thought we needed to build her confidence in skiing. An afternoon with Dad was just the thing. My agenda was to have a fun, productive afternoon by skiing down as many runs as possible. While we're standing in line for the lift, she whispers, "Daddy, I gotta go potty."

"Oh, honey, can you just wait a minute? We've been waiting in line so long."

"Yeah, I can wait a minute."

About one minute later she says, "Daddy, I still gotta go potty."

Gritting my teeth in frustration, I took off her skis (you know how long it takes to do that). Then we clumped our way down to the lodge. The lines for the rest rooms snaked out the door and onto the veranda. "Oh, jeez," I thought. "I'm not waiting in line that long. That'll take at least fifteen minutes. We've only got a half-day pass." So we walked all the way across the ski lodge base area to the other side of the ski area, and found another rest room.

When she realized that I intended to take her into the men's room with me, she balked. It took five minutes of me pleading to finally get her into the rest room. Then another five minutes to peel off all those layers of clothing: a parka, a scarf, two sweatshirts, and a pair of long johns. Another five minutes to put all that stuff back on once she was done. Then the hike back to the line—to the back of the line, I might add.

By this time, my agenda was completely ruined. We'd been there about an hour and were still at least thirty minutes away from the top of the slope. So, here's me: "Come on, hustle. We've got to get going. Don't stop. Hustle, Lauren. Let's go." And here's Lauren: "Daddy, don't go so fast. Daddy, I can't walk like you. My feet are hurting me. Daddy, I don't want to ski. I'm tired. Can we go home?" I got stern with her, "Lauren, come on. We're going to have fun. We're going to ski. So stop the complaining and let's get a move on."

I suddenly caught myself and thought, "Wait a minute. Here I have an afternoon to spend with my little girl. She's miserable, I'm miserable. I'm not having any fun because I'm too concerned about having my productive afternoon. What's the purpose of this anyway? Lauren and I are supposed to have fun together. Who cares if we don't get one run in." I completely changed my mind-set in a matter of seconds. I decided no matter how many runs we got in, we would have fun. I immediately started communicating that. You could instantly see the change in Lauren. As soon as she felt that change in me, she perked up. We got on the lift, skied really hard, and we had a great time together. By the end of the day she was skiing all by herself. Plus, we got lots of runs in.

That afternoon was a profound experience for me. Too often we get caught up in the event or the goal; we lose track of the relationship. If you think about it, outings and vacations are often disasters in terms of accomplishing what you set out to do. Parents have all these expectations already formed: what they're going to do, all the sites they're going to take pictures of. We're better off saying, "I'm going for the relationship, and if we get this done, great; if not, fine." Once we decide that, everyone relaxes. The other fascinating thing was Lauren could sense a change in me. When I changed my mind-set, when I stopped being anxious and curt, she responded in kind. Her change of behavior was a by-product of my change of attitude. It's really that simple sometimes.

⊛ *Until age seven or eight, when self-awareness begins to develop, the mind-set of a little child is largely a product of their environment. The attitude and actions of their parents have a particularly strong influence on them. They are kind of like H_2O, which manifests itself as steam, water, or ice, depending upon the temperature and pressure that surrounds it. This young father's experience illustrates how our mental expectations not only govern our behavior, but also our satisfaction. We constantly compare what actually happens to what we expect to happen, and that is what satisfies us or not. We have control over our expectations, but not over our satisfactions, except indirectly through our expectations.*

Off to Bed!

This man pushed the pause button, knelt down at eye level with his son, restrained the physical and cultural impulse to react, and empathically listened (Habit 5: Seek First to Understand, Then to Be Understood). And the magic happened.

I was teaching a seminar in Hong Kong for a multinational corporation, which included a brief module on listening skills. We ended the day with a challenge to the participants, to go home and try implementing the listening. The next day, a Chinese gentleman, probably about forty-five to fifty years old, a senior manager, shared this experience:

> *It was about eight o'clock. I told my son to go to bed. He said, "I don't want to go to bed." I replied, "It's time for you to go to bed. You have school in the morning. So off to bed." He still did not want to go. I tried to use logic with him. He wouldn't listen. Then I found myself moving toward him to just carry him to his room. I was going to physically force him to go to bed.*
>
> *As I walked up to him to grab his arms, I remembered: "This is an emotional experience. I must listen empathically." So I stopped, knelt down, and said to my son, "You seem frustrated about going to bed." My son just looked at me. He continued looking at me. He looked at me as if to say, "What are you doing? Why are you talking to me? What is wrong with you?" I realized that my son did not expect me to talk to him. He expected me to use physical force to get him to obey me.*
>
> *I continued to talk to him and he continued to just look at me, almost suspiciously, as if I wasn't the father he knew. "Let's go to your room. I'll talk with you as you're getting dressed for bed. We can talk about this," I said. He got ready for bed while we talked. It was probably midnight when I left his room. We had talked the whole time, about school, about feelings, about experiences.*
>
> *I left his room feeling for the first time that I really knew my son. He is eleven years old, and only now do I feel like I know my son. I just never listened before.*

The deepest hunger of the human body is air. The deepest hunger of the human heart is to feel understood, valued, and respected. Sincere empathic listening feeds and satisfies that hunger. Remember that with people, on tough issues, fast is slow and slow is fast.

Grandpa's Lap

It's remarkable what happens in the ordinariness of life when a newly and deeply embedded value begins to conflict with an old habit.

My mission statement focuses on building better relationships with my family through spending time with them, listening to them, and engaging in worthwhile activities. Every evening, I go home, read the paper, and listen to the business news. About three months ago, my daughter and her son came to live with us while she started college. Invariably, every night I came home, Connor, my little grandson, would try to climb into my lap. Invariably, I'd respond, "Well, just as soon as I get done reading the paper."

When I was done reading the paper he was already off to bed. He didn't get to climb on his grandpa's lap and play. With my mission statement in mind, I decided a small thing. No matter what I am involved in, whether it's the business news or television, if Connor wants to get on my lap, by gosh, he can climb right up [Habit 3: Put First Things First].

⊗ *One of the most powerful ways to bridge the conscious and subconscious mind is to visualize. It's playing things out in your mind's eye using as many senses as possible—touching, hearing, smelling, and tasting, as well as seeing. Envision yourself living true to a mission statement that was deeply thought through, developed in a very balanced way, and that embraces all the important roles of your life. This story of Grandpa's lap can be duplicated in a thousand different ways.*

The Journal

As you read the following story, try to empathize with this father as he describes his world of hurt. Try to put yourself into that world and sense his desperation, confusion, and fear. Then notice what happens as this father began doing just one thing over which he had control. See if it doesn't begin to affect you in the same way—giving you a sense of power, freedom, and hope.

During the lunch break on the last day of a week-long training program I was leading, this handsome young man in his mid-twenties came up to me. He had listened intently through the whole session. He began sharing his struggles with me: "You know, for the last couple of days, we've been talking about what's important to us, how we want to live our lives. But what if what we want and how we want to live are totally out of our control? What do we do then?"

Through his tears, he said, "I have a three-year-old son. But my wife and I are in the middle of getting a divorce. It's taken eighteen months now and it's just a mess. I've got a lawyer; she's got a lawyer. I mean, she hates me. She even took my son to Chicago so that I would have to fly specially from New Jersey to see him. I write to him and send him things, but I know she doesn't let him see them. I think her whole purpose in life is to make sure that my son doesn't even know I'm his father." He started crying even more. "This is my life. I want to live these principles. I want to be what I've learned about these past few days. But I can't be that. Sometimes I feel like I'm just starting to be this big ball of hate. I hate her, hate her lawyer, hate our marriage. But I want to love my son; I want to be part of his life. And I can't be. What do I do?"

Now, I don't know what led to their divorce, but I could see that he was deeply affected by it. At first, I was like, "Whoa, this is way out of my area of expertise." But then I started thinking: what does one do when there are things in your Circle of Concern that you can do nothing about [Habit 1: Be Proactive]? He couldn't control his wife, or the legal process. He couldn't control his access to his son, and he was paralyzed by his inability to have an influence. He was so focused on what his wife was not allowing him to do that he forgot the things he could still do to have an influence.

Suddenly it came to me, that there was something he could still do to share his love for his son. He could still have a way to influence his son, maybe not right now, but over the years, even after a few years when the child was older. After all, the mother couldn't really squash her child's desire to know his father. When the time came for a closer relationship, this young father would have something to give his son showing that he had loved him all this time.

I shared with him something that I had been doing for my children for some time: I keep a record of my children's lives. In this journal, he could keep a record of the experiences they had together, of the feelings the father has for his son, of his hopes and dreams for him. The best thing he could do right now in his Circle of Influence was to pursue his legal options, but also, while the boy's mother is intercepting the letters and while he can't be there, start capturing his feelings and thoughts about his son.

Even though this is a simple idea, it was liberating for him. When he felt stifled in what he perceived was his only Circle of Concern, he was emotionally paralyzed and blocked and stuck. But when he started to see the possibilities of this journal idea, all of a sudden his energy returned, he was unfrozen, he was excited, he was thrilled, and he started to see, I can do something about this.

This is what I told him about keeping this journal, just some nuts-and-bolts details that make the journal better:

1. *Make sure you date all the entries.*

2. *Share really specific experiences that they will be able to remember.* Your feelings tend to dominate the writing. But that gets pretty general: You're so great, I really love you, I like to be with you. After a while, those tend to just run together. So specific experiences work better.

3. *Set aside a regular time to write in the journal.* I have four kids, so I set aside one Sunday a month to write in each kid's journal. I used to try doing it on the plane but I would get carried away with one child, and soon it would be four or five months until I could complete the cycle.

4. *Start them as soon as you can with each child.* I started our third

son's journal on the day we found out my wife was pregnant with him. So, when I give this to him on his wedding day, he will know he was loved even before he was born. (And also that he made his mother very sick.)

5. *Write all different kinds of stories:* tender, funny, about mishaps, achievements, proud moments.

6. *Use technology* if you have access to it to scan in photographs next to the relevant experiences.

7. *Keep a reminder of the experiences in your planner or some other place.* I jot down funny phrases or moments in my kids' section of my planner. Sometimes it's a couple weeks until I get to that particular journal so the reminder is a good tool to help capture the experience in its entirety.

8. *Keep the journals a secret.* The greatest thing about these journals is that my children don't know I keep them. I am looking forward to the day when they can read them and know my feelings for them.

The young father wrote to me about three months after that session. He said that while things are still not good between him and his wife, they are better. He feels like he is making progress. He keeps his son's journal and feels so much closer to him than he did three months ago. I don't think he thinks of himself as a victim anymore. He's doing what he can in his Circle of Influence, and that makes him feel empowered.

I remember running out of a speech one time to catch a plane when a desperate soul asked if he could ride with me in the cab to the airport. He wanted to tell me of his recent divorce. His wife had won custody over his children and he was feeling hopeless, helpless, and suicidal. So off we went. After listening to his story for just a few minutes we began discussing the idea of focusing on the Circle of Influence (those things in our lives that we can directly influence or control) rather than the Circle of Concern (those things over which we have no control). He gradually came to realize that all of his efforts to reclaim his marriage and children were actually withdrawals from his

Emotional Bank Account with them that had made things even worse. However, he also began to see that there were a number of things he could do within his Circle of Influence that would be perceived as deposits. One of them was to keep a journal, just like the man described in this story.

Journaling is one of the most powerful forms of increasing self-awareness I know of, simply because you observe your own participation in life. I have a daughter who has over seventy journals and has developed an absolutely amazing capacity to reinvent her life at any time and in any way she feels is wise. It inspires me. I am not suggesting that this is the best way for all people. But I am suggesting that it is one powerful way to focus on one's Circle of Influence—of taking the Inside-Out Approach to improving one's life and circumstances.

Raising Teens
(Or Is It Being Raised by Them?)

MY FIRST BROKEN HEART

WRESTLEMANIA

SILENCE IS GOLDEN

THE WORST GAME OF MY LIFE!

SOFT-SPIKED GOLF SHOES

THE DESTRUCTIVE TEEN

THE HEART-TO-HEART TALK I ALMOST MISSED

YOU ALWAYS SAY "NO"!

EVER TRIED COMMUNICATING WITH A SIXTEEN-YEAR-OLD
WHO TALKS IN ONE-WORD SENTENCES?

RAISING BOYS ON LAWNS

YOU'D REALLY DO THAT FOR ME, DAD?

My First Broken Heart

Just as air is the deepest hunger of the human body, to be understood (Habit 5: Seek First to Understand, Then to Be Understood) is the deepest hunger of the human heart. Notice in this story the power of unconditional love, how simply understanding can heal.

When I was seventeen years old, I suffered my first romantic heartbreak. I will never forget the pain of that experience. The girl I had been dating, without warning and without mercy, broke off our relationship and immediately began dating a close friend. In one moment, my world came crashing down. I remember driving my 1952 Willys Jeep out into the hills above my hometown of Redlands, California, determined that I would never, ever go back to school, or life, again. Finally, as evening set, hunger and pain drove me home. I said little, but the look in my eyes must have told my parents what happened. I could not eat, so I went into my bedroom, fell into bed, and began to weep. I sobbed and sobbed. After some time, the door of my bedroom quietly opened, and I sensed the presence of my father standing quietly by my bed. Gently, he pulled back the covers of my bed and climbed in beside me. He wrapped me in his strong, warm arms and held me closer than I have ever been held in my life. He pulled my heart, my body, my spirit into him. I felt his warmth and strength, as I continued to sob. And then, my father began to weep with me. I felt his chest shudder with his own sobs. His face was pressed into the side of mine, and I felt his warm tears leave his eyes and mingle with mine as they ran down my cheek. He said nothing. He just wept. Wept because I was in pain. Wept because he loved me and felt my pain. After long moments, my sobs began to subside and a growing light replaced the pain. My father got up, tucked the blankets around my chin, and rested his hand on my shoulder. He then said, "My son, I promise the sun will come out again. I love you." He then left as quietly as he entered. He was right. The sun did come out. I arose, dressed my best, polished my Jeep, and headed for school.

Life went on, richer than before somehow, for I knew I was loved, unconditionally, by a father who taught me what empathy really means. Recently I quietly closed the lid on my father's casket. Before I did so, I paused, once more, to stroke the whiskers of his chin and re-member that night, long ago.

 Such profound emotional experiences last a lifetime and give powerful scripts to the next generation. My guess is that this person does the same thing with his children as his father did with him.

Wrestlemania

Notice how the tremendous insight this father gained enabled him neither to give up in his effort to negotiate a Win-Win Agreement with his son, nor give in on its conditions once agreement was reached.

I returned from a training session with the phrase "If you do what you have always done, you will get what you have always gotten" ringing in my ears. It wasn't long until I had the opportunity to see whether this was true.

My son, Jake, was about thirteen at the time and really into Wrestlemania. Just before Thanksgiving, he asked my wife, Rebekah, and me whether he could go to a Wrestlemania party at a friend's house the Wednesday before. The party would have finished about eleven o'clock and this kid had a paper route at five in the morning. Plus family was coming over for the Thanksgiving holiday all day the next day. If Jake didn't get at least ten hours of sleep, he wasn't a very pleasant teenager to be around. All these thoughts went through my mind as he asked us whether he could go.

I really wanted him to go, though. I didn't want to be the bad guy. So I decided to start a discussion: "Jake, eleven's pretty late. Let's talk about how we could try to make this happen [Habit 4: Think Win/Win]." He started to raise his voice. I said, "Wait a minute, wait a minute. Why don't we talk about some ground rules for the conversation. I will stay here as long as you want to be able to work out a solution for you to go to this party. I commit to that. But we have to be working together toward a solution. I'll try to understand how you feel about this [Habit 5: Seek First to Understand, Then to Be Understood]. You need to try to understand my perspective. You need to respect my ideas. If you scream and yell, it's going to get very unpleasant in here. We're all trying to find something that works for all of us. Okay? I know it's hard for you to control your temper, yeah, you fly off at the handle, but if you do it three times, then the conversation stops. You won't be able to go and I'll go to bed."

He said, "Okay, I get three warnings." (I think he'll be a union negotiator when he grows up.)

"No, you get two warnings. Third strike, you're out."

"Okay," he conceded with a smile.

So we start. We're trying to build a way for this to happen for him. I suggested that he go to the party, have dinner with his buddies, then about nine-thirty or so, I would come pick him up so that he could get a good night's rest.

"You're kidding me. You would embarrass me like that? You're kiddin' me. You've got to be kiddin' me. Oh man, that is the worst . . ." Off he went screaming.

"Whoa, wait a minute, no screaming, no yelling. We will sit until we work it out. You have my undying commitment that I'm not leaving. I'm not going anywhere. But you will not shout at me. Strike one."

Just then Rebekah clears her throat and asks to see me in the hallway for a second. She's looking at me like I'm a little crazy. So I excuse myself from Jake to meet Rebekah on the stairs. With a strange look still on her face she says, "Dale, I don't know what's made you so different since you came back from that mountain seminar thing. But I cannot handle this. Just tell the kid 'no' and come to bed."

All of a sudden, here come these words out of my mouth: "Rebekah, if we do what we have always done, we are going to get what we always got. I have to try a different way."

She threw up her hands. "I don't understand this. I'm going to bed. This is in your hands. Good luck." With that she handed me the baton and left me alone to finish the race. I went back in and told Jake, "Mom's tired. She's going to bed. But we'll stay here and work on this as long as you want. So, if I understand you correctly, nine-thirty is not really an option. You want to stay there until eleven o'clock?"

"Yup."

"Well, how about you stay there until eleven o'clock? Then I'll pick you up around eleven-fifteen and bring you home. What I need for you to do is to stay in bed in the morning so that you will be pleasant to be around in the afternoon. I'll get up and do your paper route for you. Would that be okay with you?"

Jake looked stunned. "You're going to get up and do my paper route so I can stay in bed?"

I said, "You want to go to this party, right?"

"Yup."

"Then I'll get up and do the paper route for you. Would that be okay? . . . All right, could you get a pencil and paper and just write down what you are contributing to this agreement now." So he starts writing down what he wants to do. Suddenly he's shouting about replays, what if they run replays and he doesn't get to see those because it's after eleven o'clock and I've already picked him up. You can imagine my bewilderment. I thought he had everything in the world he wanted. I said, "Whoa, Jake, that's strike two. Let's back up here. You said you wanted to be there until eleven. I said I'd come pick you up at eleven-fifteen. Isn't that what you wanted? Think about it from my perspective: I'm going to get to bed between eleven-thirty and midnight, then get up at five o'clock so your customers get their paper on time. I'm going to do all this for you so that you can get what you really want. Now you're screaming again? Don't you really have what you want here?"

"Well, yeah," he mumbled. "I really wanted to go until eleven. You're going to come pick me up; you're going to do my paper route; I'm going to sleep in. Yeah, you're right, I really do have what I want." He starts writing it again. He's signing his name, he's literally up to the "e" in Jake and he starts screaming again, "This isn't fair. I want to stay for the replays." About a second after that, he starts crying.

I looked at him and I said, "Jake, why are you crying?"

"Because I just screamed the third time," he wailed.

My response was hard but I had to do it. I said, "That's right. I know it's really hard for you to hear this right now, but you need to go to that phone and call Dan. Tell him you aren't coming to the party. I'm going to bed. I want you to know that I really love you, I tried to do everything I could to deliver what you wanted. Is there anything I can do to help you right now?"

"I suppose you wouldn't consider . . . No, I won't even ask you." He just sat there with his head in his hands.

I got up and went to bed. As I was getting into my pajamas, Rebekah asked, "What happened?" I told her. "Oh," she said. "He must be so mad at you right now." I wasn't so sure.

"Well, I don't know. He might be but I think he's more angry at himself right now. I'm betting that before he goes to bed, he's going to knock on the door and give you and me a big hug."

She laughed. "Dale, you're nuts."

"No really, I can feel it." So we are lying in bed. Fifteen or twenty minutes pass. Then there's a knock on the door. In bounds our five-foot-ten, one-hundred-and-sixty-pound teenager. He jumps into bed between us and says, "I love you guys. I blew it. I called Dan, I'm not going. But Dad, will you still do my paper route so I can sleep in Thursday morning? I'd really like to sleep in Thursday morning."

Yeah, I did his paper route for him. These principles work. Not just in seminars. In real life with real-life teenagers who love Wrestlemania.

⊗ *Most children and teenagers grow up in a world of dichotomies—everything is either/or. You're either nice or you're mean. Either I get my way or you get yours. They are simply not yet aware of the concept of synergy or third alternatives. They are not aware of the concept of win-win on tough emotional issues, particularly in dealing with strong-minded parents whose tendency is to either give in or to arbitrarily take a strong stand and then manipulate everyone to that end. Here the father learns how to go for a win-win third alternative; he resolves to do it, and then does it. When the son violates the negotiation agreement, the father hangs tough, and the son rises to a new level, takes responsibility, and expresses his love.*

Even though I teach this material all the time, I've often found myself in situations with my teenagers where, more often than not, I tended to go for lose-win on fairly secondary issues and win-lose on primary issues. I did so simply because I did not take the time or have the emotional maturity, strength, and wisdom that this father manifested.

My Harvard business school professor Rhand Saxenian gave to me the finest, most practical definition of emotional maturity that I have ever come across. He taught that emotional maturity is the capacity to express your feelings and convictions with courage, balanced with consideration for the feelings and convictions of others without being personally threatened in those expressions. This kind of emotional maturity cannot be faked because of the third element of the definition. A person who is courageous but lacks consideration will go for win-lose. A person who is very considerate but lacks courage will go for lose-win. Or one who fakes both courage and consideration will be torn up inside. The key is the balance.

Silence Is Golden

Notice how the father in this story sincerely empathized with his daughter and, without pressing her or making her feel guilty, reflected her desire to not communicate.

A year or so ago, my daughter, Nell, and I had fallen into a troubling routine.

She would come home after school and I would ask her how she was doing and she would say, "Fine." That was it. I could only get one or two words out of her. It had become a daily routine of noncommunication. By asking her questions each day when she got home it seemed like I was only exacerbating the tension.

I remember reading once that one way to deal with someone who does not want to communicate is to break the routine. So one day when Nell came home I asked her how she was doing. But when she gave me the standard one-word response before heading to her bedroom, I said, "You don't want to talk to me, do you?"

She stopped instantly, gave me a strange look, and said, "No," and went to her room. That was the end of it, but I knew I had touched her feelings.

The next day, I repeated the new routine. This time when I said she didn't want to talk to me, Nell said, "Not right now, Dad."

This went on for a few days before slowly, and on her own terms, Nell began talking more to me. Then one day I was sitting at the kitchen table thinking about something, in a sort of trance, while she was doing the dishes. I was quiet, not talking to her even though she was just a few feet away, and it must have bothered her that I wasn't asking her questions as usual. All of a sudden she started talking about her day and she brought me out of my trance. It struck me that suddenly she was sharing her feelings with me and it was so wonderful I got tears in my eyes.

Sometimes I think the most valuable tool for communication with teenagers is silence.

What would happen if you went into a forest to hunt and began by firing a shot in the air? That's often what asking questions is like; sometimes questions are so autobiographical and controlling that people simply don't want to talk about their deeper or most vulnerable issues. The key is to go in the forest and be quiet; then animals will begin to appear. The same thing happens when you go to a beach.

Walking back and forth you won't see the sand crabs, but if you sit there on the beach quietly, soon they will appear all over the place.

Teenagers want to talk—they really do. They want to open up, but they want to feel that it is safe. They want to do it on their terms and on their time, and parents must simply have the patience to allow this—to be present, to be available, to be accessible, and to be quiet. We have two ears and one mouth and we should use them accordingly. Interestingly, the ears never close, but the mouth can.

In my own life with my teenage children, I have found that if I am simply present, doing no particular thing, but just kind of being attentive and aware, within a few minutes they begin to open up. Silence is truly golden.

The Worst Game of My Life!

Experience in this story the power of focusing on effort and relationship rather than on expectations and results.

I was the junior varsity quarterback at the college I attended. The previous week, we had had a great game. I threw for about five hundred yards, four or five touchdowns, and the newspaper started heralding me as the next great quarterback.

The following week we got set to play one of the best teams in the nation. Their leading defensive lineman was a 275-pound quarterback-wrecking machine.

We were playing at home for this big game. Of course, I wanted to play well in front of the home crowd. And my dad flew back from somewhere just to watch me play. I didn't think he would make it, but there he was just before the whistle blew.

I had the worst game of my life. The monster defensive lineman was all over me. He spent more time in our backfield than I did. My head was slammed into the ground so many times I was leaving divots. I swear I wasn't on my feet after the snap for longer than three seconds. Of course, I didn't throw one touchdown. I did, however, rack up an impressive number of interceptions. We lost by about thirty points.

During the game I must have looked pathetic. After the game I was embarrassed. Nobody would talk to me. You know how it goes when you play terribly? In the locker room, everybody avoids you. So I showered and dressed in silence. When I came out of the locker room, my dad was waiting for me. He took me in his arms, hugged me, looked me right in the eyes and said, "That's the best game I have ever seen you play. Not because you won or threw the most touchdowns. But because I have never seen you be as tough as you had to be out there today. You were getting beat. Yet you kept getting up. I have never been so proud of you." And he meant it.

I felt so good. Good because my dad was proud of me, but also good because what he said affirmed what I had been feeling. In the back of my mind, despite the bruises and the jarring, I had been thinking, "I'm hanging in here. I'm getting back up. I'm playing tough today." My dad was the only person who recognized that in me. For him to tell me that changed my whole perspective on that dreadful game. It was a moment I will never forget and was a great bonding experience for me and my dad.

⊗ *Psychological confirmation takes place when you agree with what the other person is feeling inside. This young man was feeling that he was tough and hanging in there, even though the results were disastrous. When the father confirmed the boy's psychological state, the boy felt understood and appreciated [Habit 5: Seek First to Understand, Then to Be Understood]. The father was not concerned with social expectations, but with the relationship and the intrinsic value of effort.*

I had a similar experience on my son Sean's twenty-second birthday. He had given his all as the starting quarterback during the first half of a major university football game, but it wasn't working and he was pulled in the second half. I had given him an engraved plaque earlier that day for his birthday because I had a premonition something like this might happen. He said it was one of the greatest presents he had received in his life. It was a quote that captures the spirit of the Olympic Creed and reads as follows: "Ask not yourself for victory, but for courage, for if you endure, you bring honor to yourself; and even more, you bring honor to us all."

Soft-Spiked Golf Shoes

This story illustrates how we must listen with our heart and not just with our mind and with our ears; we might call the heart the third ear.

My youngest daughter, Amy, had just taken up golf. She proved such a natural talent that she rose through the ranks until she made the varsity golf team at school even though she was only a freshman with about eighteen months of experience.

One afternoon at work, I received a frantic phone call from her. She was almost breathless as she described what seemed to be a life-and-death situation. "Mom, I just found out that I have to wear soft spikes at the tournament tomorrow. Soft spikes, Mom. I only have hard spikes. They're not going to let me play in hard spikes, Mom. Mom, what am I going to do?" she wailed.

I wanted to put on my tights and cloak and fly off to her rescue. On the other hand, I couldn't understand why she was so upset. So, in I blundered, "You know, honey, we're the same size and I have two pair of soft spikes. You can just borrow mine."

"Oh, Mom, that's not gonna work. That won't work. I can't play in your shoes."

Something about her voice clued me in. I realized there was something more than soft-spiked golf shoes going on here. I had tried to solve the problem before I even knew what the real problem was. So I backtracked and tried again. "Honey, you sound really agitated."

Suddenly she burst into tears, "Mom, it's my first eighteen-hole tournament ever. I'm so scared!" Ah, now the phone call became crystal clear. She was using the golf shoes as the impetus to be able to talk to me about how she was feeling. Luckily, rather than trying to solve her pseudo-problem, I was able to pause and listen. I allowed Amy to share her anxiety in a safe way. And yes, she wore my shoes, did great in the tournament, and is still golfing three years later.

※ *This situation is all too common. So often there is something much deeper going on inside of people than what they initially say. When there is, people often ask questions. If you really listen with your heart you will usually sense a deeper need behind the question (Habit 5:*

Seek First to Understand, Then to Be Understood). If you attempt to reflect that feeling or need as best you can while answering the question, the other person will feel affirmed and validated in such a way that he or she will usually open up. It's like giving someone oxygen.

The Destructive Teen

This marvelous story teaches the power of one-on-one communication with all family members while dealing with the destructive lifestyle of one. As soon as the parents reenthroned the principles of empathy, love, understanding, and respect, and built a strong one-on-one Emotional Bank Account with each child, then they could deal with the destructive teen challenge. Notice also the tremendous power of example.

I am a mother of several children. One of my sons got involved in destructive behavior as a teenager, while we still had two younger children at home. From being a handsome clean-cut kid he turned into a filthy young man, with unkempt long hair that he would leave in thick tangles for weeks without washing. He pierced his ears and body in several places, he came home with tattoos, he hardly ate (probably because he was on drugs), his eyes were bloodshot, his clothes stank of cigarette smoke. Not only did he look dark and scary, but his lifestyle completely changed his personality. He became mean, noncommunicative, and never made eye contact with any of us. He avoided all family functions and never answered us unless it was in a snarl. His younger brother and sister became so upset about his behavior that they often would yell: "Throw him out, we don't want him here, he is ruining everything." His new friends were the same and some were even gang members.

In the beginning we were actually in shock from suddenly having this kind of kid in our home. We analyzed our parental behavior to see if we could find holes in the way we had raised him, we contacted professionals, we talked to other parents to get sympathy and advice, and we tried to talk, plead, and threaten him into change. Nothing helped!

In the meantime we began to have another huge problem on our hands—the two younger children, who were watching our daily confrontations, were obviously being affected. It became evident that they were being hurt by what they watched. Our inconsistent behavior toward their brother (because sometimes we were nice to him when he didn't deserve it) was very confusing to them. They began to say things like, "Well, if Darren can do this and this, and you don't even get mad, then I am going to . . . etc." I remember discussing the possibility of sending Darren away to someone because I could not bear watching him destroy the other two innocent younger children.

Our family was falling apart because of this one boy. All our energy, conversations, and work centered around him. We couldn't even go out to dinner without spending the entire time talking about him. And here we were raising two other children who desperately needed a healthy and happy mom and dad. We knew we had to change our approach.

We then decided to sit down with each of Darren's siblings individually and tell them how much we loved all of our children, including Darren. We reminded them of what a great kid he used to be, and how he was going through a very difficult phase in his life right now, one that he would probably be embarrassed about later. We even got photographs out to remind us all of how Darren used to be.

We asked for their help and a charitable attitude toward him. We told them that things might not appear fair, but that it was necessary for us to show patience, forgiveness, and faith in Darren so he would be able to overcome his problem. We explained to them how drugs completely alter behavior and that what they saw now really wasn't the complete Darren, but just a part of him that had chosen to be very destructive. We talked about all the good things he was missing out on in school and in his social life and what a terrible shame it was. For the first time they actually began to feel a bit sorry for him, instead of just angry or frightened.

Throughout the following year we repeated this kind of one-on-one talk several times with the two younger children, as the need arose. It wasn't easy for them, but they were now able to send little signals to us whenever Darren was in the room and acting up that clearly testified to their understanding of what we all needed to do. When we got far enough in this process of being understanding, forgiving, and nonjudgmental and did special, kind things for Darren (even when he didn't deserve it), the younger two followed right after and did the same.

It totally blew Darren away! Why were we all being so nice, when he was being so rotten? Within the next year he straightened himself out—on his own. We still have repercussions from his bad years. The younger kids will use Darren and his poor behavior when they want something—"We really deserve to get permission to do this and this, we never gave you trouble like Darren did"—but all in all they have survived the three-year ordeal with Darren and have vowed never to put us through what Darren put us through. They actually have much more charitable natures and a greater understanding of people and their problems today. I really don't think there is one thing in our lives that has challenged us and made us grow more than Darren and his tumultuous time.

To top it all off, Darren fell in love with a young lady who herself has serious behavioral problems. She has been through substance abuse and much more. But Darren has been able to see through it all and still love her. And the most comforting thing is that he is using the exact same loving, patient process with her as we used with him. He knows there is a core in there that is good and he is determined to unearth it.

The key to the many is the one. By reaching out to Darren with tough love, empathy, and good example, they reclaimed this boy. In the process they also established a relationship with the other children. They put the problem into perspective and they neither under- nor overreacted. The power lay in the constant effort to communicate through understanding and giving understanding (Habit 5: Seek First to Understand, Then to Be Understood). It was like a lubricant that oiled all interactions. The key is to neither give up nor give in.

Albert Schweitzer was once asked about how you should raise children. His answer was that there are three principles: first, example; second, example; and third, example. What we are communicates far more eloquently than anything we say or even do. The innate essence of who we really are, what our character really is, communicates quietly, silently, and imperceptibly. And children are amazingly sensitive, aware, and alert to all of this. When they are very little and subject to parents and other significant authority figures, they pick it all up in spite of our efforts to conceal, disguise, hide, pretend, or posture.

The Heart-to-Heart Talk I Almost Missed

Notice in this story how one courageous act of prioritizing (Habit 3: Put First Things First) created an unforgettable experience that will reverberate through succeeding generations.

My wife and I raised our children on a ranch. So my son, Cody, and I spent most of our time working together. We'd ride horses, mow hay, brand cows, herd cows, and feed cows. During all of that work, we built quite a good relationship. For Cody and me, our relationship was based on being outdoors, working together, hiking, and other similar activities.

Then we moved to town when I accepted a job with a large company. The move was hard on my son. He went from having the closest neighbors six miles away, with a forty-five-mile ride to a small country school, to having neighbors in every direction as far as he could see. I knew I had pulled my son out of the environment he loved. But I was proud of him for handling the new situation as best he could.

During the summer before he was to leave for college, Cody and I planned a hiking trip together, just the two of us. We decided to go to the Wind River Mountains of Wyoming. My dad and I had hiked into the Wind Rivers about thirty years ago when I was nineteen or twenty. It was fitting I would return with my son on our last hike before he left home. We figured the trip would take about five days: one day to hike in, three days to camp, one day to hike out. We picked a couple five-day weekends that might work.

Since my work involves training educators, summer is my busiest time. We like to teach them when they are not teaching. As I am only paid when I am training, I try to schedule as many conferences as I can during the summer. So when training jobs would come up, I'd take them, and push back the trip.

Suddenly one day I realized with a kind of shock and horror that I had completely scheduled myself out of my weekend with my son. There were only four weekends left and I was scheduled to train on each one of those. I had boxed myself in: either I was going to completely disappoint my son, or I was going to have to take major withdrawals from my work associates to cover for me as well as take the hit on my personal checking account.

In the middle of all my nervous energy about almost ruining the summer plans and trying to fix the scheduling problems at work, I stopped myself short. I heard my own voice running through my head: "I teach this stuff. Why am I not living it?" To make a long story short, I took some massive withdrawals from my fellow employees, rescheduled some of the training jobs, and packed my backpack in preparation for the trip [Habit 3: Put First Things First].

We hiked in and camped in exactly the same spot that my father and I had camped some thirty years earlier. The next morning my son, after the previous day's really strenuous hike, says to his old dad, "Wanna go knock off a peak?" So we climbed this mountain, about eleven thousand feet, way above the tree line. At the top, we happened upon a plateau about the size of three football fields. As we stopped to eat lunch, a herd of about a hundred mountain goats milled around us. I don't think they'd even seen humans before; they certainly weren't scared of us. I've never had a more amazing experience: sitting on top of a mountain plateau in Wyoming with my nineteen-year-old son eating peanut butter sandwiches while shaggy-dog mountain goats grazed between us, around us, in front and in back of us. I'll never forget that moment: blue sky for as far as you can see, mountain peaks stretching on each side of us, my son, those goats.

The next day, after breakfast, Cody wanted to go knock off peak number two. Since I was exhausted and he had had to help me down peak number one, I told him I just wanted to relax that day. I suggested we go fishing in the alpine lake next to our campsite.

What followed was the most wonderful part of the trip, almost bittersweet for me. I'm not sure whether to smile or cry when I think about it. Actually, I do both. You see, we spent the whole day just hanging out and fishing. At some point during the day, Cody started asking me about what my life was like when I grew up. He was really interested in me. That interest touched me so deeply. I started talking about things I hadn't talked about with him before: my childhood, my spiritual dreams and failures, the hopes I still entertained, my fears of the future, my hopes for my children, my dreams for my life ahead. That was the sweet part. The bitter was that I almost lost that opportunity. I had almost let my work consume me. Bitter also because I had left the saying of those things for such a late hour. My time with Cody was almost up. I wish I had said them earlier. There's no way, in four hours of talking, to make up for seventeen years of conversations that haven't been. But I am lucky I said them at all.

Cody left for college—two days after we returned home.

The key to making such unforgettable moments happen is to plan ahead and be strong. The second key is to allow the other to participate in or even totally dominate the agenda, for what is important to the other person must be as important to you as the person is to you. Another key is to have sufficient time for unplanned, unscheduled spontaneity of expression and action. There may be nothing quite so powerful in raising a son or a daughter as having such one-on-one bonding experiences. People can't say they don't have time. They simply have to plan ahead and be strong. The average father spends five minutes a day with a child and two hours in front of the television. It isn't a matter of time, it's a matter of prioritization and commitment. But both prioritization and commitment are based upon first deciding what matters most. Remember that it is easy to say no to the unimportant when you have a burning yes inside you to the important. The main thing is to keep the main thing the main thing.

You *Always* Say "No"!

The critical element in the following relationship-transforming story was when the mother acted on self-awareness and tried to understand. She didn't listen with the intent to reply, she sincerely listened with the intent to understand and that made all the difference (Habit 5: Seek First to Understand, Then to Be Understood).

First a little background before I get to my story: all my family, except my daughter, Alex, moved from Boston to Philadelphia because of my job. Alex stayed behind after high school graduation, went to a little bit of college, and ran herself into a mountain of debt. She had to move back home with Mom and Dad. When she moved in, we laid down some ground rules: you find a job, you pay for your own transportation, you may not apply for credit anywhere, you cannot borrow our cars, you help out around the house.

One day when I came home from work Alex met me at the door. She asked if she could borrow my car to drive to Boston. Well, she knew that the answer to that question always has been, is, and will always be "no." I don't know why she even asked me. Of course, I said "no" without giving my answer a second thought. That "no" upset her more than all my "no's" in the past. Alex became so upset she wouldn't even talk to me. She remained upset for days. Whenever I came into a room, she would get up and walk out. If I asked her something directly, I would get one-word answers. I thought she was mad because I had said "no" about borrowing my car. I thought things would blow over in a few days.

After thinking about it for several days, I finally realized that maybe something wasn't normal. I wondered, "Why is she so upset about a 'no' she's heard so many times before? What's going on here?" I decided that maybe I should apply Habit 5 to try to find out what was bothering Alex.

When I got home, I asked her to come into the kitchen. At first she refused. (She told me later that she thought I was setting her up just to nail her for something she had done wrong.) I went to her room and said, "Alex, please sit down. I want to understand why you are so upset." She still remained silent. After quite a bit of persuasion, I think she sensed I really wanted to understand why she was so upset. Finally she started talking.

Everything came out in a rush, through tears and sobbing:

"Mom, I know I screwed up in Boston. But I've been trying to show you I can change at home. Every time you ask me to do something, I do it. If you want me to get some milk, pick up the dry cleaning, go grocery shopping, I go. I always say yes. Everything you ask me to do, I say yes: clean the fridge, pick up the living room, do the laundry. I do it, Mom. I don't even complain. I just do it for you.

"But when I ask you for something, you always say no. I don't ask you for very much. I feel kind of stupid 'cause I've graduated and I'm still having to live at home. So I don't ask you for very much. But when I do, it's always too late, or you're too comfortable, or it's inconvenient or out of your way. Just once, Mom, I want you to say 'yes' to me. Just once."

She was right. Alex was right. As soon as she started talking, I could see it. She said "yes," I said "no." She was giving me this direct feedback, naming specific instances. I couldn't even begin to deny what she was saying. All I could say at first was, "You're right. Alex, you're absolutely right. I do do that. You're so right." Then I apologized for my insensitivity, for my rudeness. I promised I would make a really conscious effort to say "yes" more often. I thanked her for all the times she had said "yes" to my requests. Even though she still couldn't borrow my car because of our agreement, that conversation changed our whole relationship. We only spoke for about forty-five minutes, but our whole relationship changed. Our lines of communication opened up and our trust increased.

Later, we discussed why that conversation was so life-transforming. Alex said that when she finally realized that I really did want to hear about her feelings and her thoughts, she knew that she wanted to tell me everything. She wanted and needed somebody she could talk to honestly. She needed somebody who could listen and support her, not somebody who would judge and evaluate her. That conversation showed her that I really did value her and wanted to be there for her. From that day to now (about five years) she still comes to me when she needs someone to listen to her.

The human tendency is to judge others by their behavior and ourselves by our motives. The motive behind the daughter's behavior was sincere, well-intentioned, and deserved respect. In receiving no respect the relationship deteriorated. When someone feels genuine empathy it changes their mind-set and allows their desire and capacity to resolve tough issues to surface.

Ever Tried Communicating with a Sixteen-Year-Old Who Talks in One-Word Sentences?

The critical point of this story occurred when the nineteen-year-old son gave feedback to his dad about Caitlin. Notice how this rearranged the father's mental expectations. Then notice the father's willingness to simply be available.

I thought I had a great relationship with my daughter, Caitlin, when she was growing up. Then she hit sixteen. Suddenly I felt like last year's fashion accessories: something that used to have value but just didn't quite cut it anymore. She was sixteen, had her own car, her own job. She paid for gas and her clothes. I had turned into the manager of the Caitlin hotel. Our conversations went something like this:

"How was school today?"

"Fine."

"How's your job going?"

"Good."

"How's that new boy you've been seeing?"

"Dad . . ."

I started to worry that I wouldn't ever be able to talk to her again. So I called my nineteen-year-old son, who was away at college. "Greg, this is Dad," I said. "I'm worried about Caitlin. She won't talk to me."

He started laughing. "Dad, she's sixteen. Nobody wants to talk to their parents when they're sixteen." Then he added, "Don't push her. Just wait. Be there for her. Don't worry, she loves you."

From that week on, I put in my organizer, under my role as father, "Catch a Caitlin moment." I didn't know when the moments would come. I couldn't schedule them, but I had my antenna up for when those moments would come. I just waited.

I travel sometimes up to five days a week. When I'm on the road, I don't usually sleep very well. So when I get home, normally around nine or ten at night, I grab the remote, sink into the recliner in front of the television, and channel surf for an hour. Sometimes, just as I walk in the door I might yell out, "Hi, everyone." But within five minutes, I'm in that chair going through my relax/detox ritual. The next day, after a good night's sleep, I can usually give everybody the attention they need.

I came in one night from the airport feeling like I didn't really want to interact with anybody. Wouldn't you know it, this was the night Caitlin needed me. As I went clomping up the stairs with my bags, she says to me, "Hey, Dad, you got a minute?"

I started thinking, "Well, maybe a minute." Then another thought started rushing through my mind: "Here is the stimulus, now stop and think. What is the most important thing right here? Do I need to go space out? Here is the Caitlin moment I've been waiting for." In a millisecond I said to myself, "Do what is most important" [Habit 3: Put First Things First]. I dropped my bags, sat down at the counter. Caitlin started to talk. I didn't have to say anything. I was just there for the next forty-five minutes, listening and filtering into the conversation now and then.

About three weeks later, a chessboard, all set up to play, appeared mysteriously on the dining room table. Nobody in our family plays chess. So it sat there for a couple of days. One day, I'm walking past the dining room table. I hear this voice from the living room: "Hey, Dad, wanna play chess?"

"Honey, I don't know how to play chess. You'll have to teach me."

"Okay!" she said, and for the next week or so I got a daily lesson in playing chess.

A month or so later crossword puzzles started popping up around the house. One day, I hear, "Hey, Dad, do you know a three-letter word for so-and-so?" We started doing a crossword puzzle over breakfast together. Suddenly Caitlin and I were the crossword twins. Our relationship really started to deepen.

The time I knew my Caitlin moments were paying off happened when I went to visit her at work. Caitlin works in a little café making cappuccinos. It's the cool spot for teenagers to hang out and I love going in on Sunday afternoons to visit her.

One day, Caitlin looked up just as I walked in the door. Spontaneously, she ran around the counter and gave me a big hug. That moment was worth a million dollars to me. Then she made a special cappuccino for me. She's got this way of getting the foam just right: she discards the foam on top of the milk, then scrapes the foam out of the middle with a little spoon. The result is great: I can pour two packets of sugar on top of the foam and it won't crumble. She's the best cappuccino maker I've ever had the pleasure of knowing.

Another day when I was leaving, I stopped between the inner door and the outer door, to check out what was on the bulletin board. I'm sure she thought I'd left and was out of earshot, but I overheard her turn to the person she was working with and say, "That's the best part of my whole Sunday!" My eyes got just a little watery.

It has been over a year since I started writing about catching Caitlin moments in my organizer. In the beginning I had to consciously stop, think, and choose [Habit 1: Be Proactive]; that was hard work for me. Now, after many months, the rewards are so deep, fulfilling, and profound, there's no pause between stimulus and response. Catching Caitlin moments has become habitual.

Our relationship has deepened. Our conversations are usually generated by her. We talk about everything from philosophy and biology to religion, ethics, values, and morals. I have been able to say the most important things that I wanted to say, but what is even more important is that I have gotten to know her. What started out as "Seek First to Understand . . ." has turned into gratitude for understanding another spirit, for being able just to be with my daughter.

⊗ *For years people have talked about the importance of quality time. I suggest that quality time will never take the place of quantity time. Both are needed. Parents simply have to be around and be available. This is a real challenge in today's world where both parents are working and juggling a thousand other balls. The key is to prioritize (decide what matters most—Habit 3: Put First Things First), then schedule unstructured time for spontaneity and availability around the teenagers.*

Raising Boys on Lawns

This mother tried to build a relationship with her stepson but was derailed in her efforts because of the boy's rejection and passivity. Notice then how through self-awareness she became proactive and focused on sincere caring, not on results.

My husband's first wife left him and their three-year-old son, Ty. Most of their relatives said they should be glad to be rid of her. But I don't think a child ever is glad to be rid of their mother. Ty certainly suffered. When I married his father, he was five years old. I'm not sure he could articulate his feelings at the time, but I know he struggled with the whole idea of mothers—natural or step.

It didn't help that his mother wasn't too regular in her visits. She'd disappear for six months. Then one day she'd be on the doorstep: "I want to spend time with Ty. He's my kid, too." I knew the pain she would cause him but he was so excited to see her. What could I do? I think Ty could sense my resentment. He misinterpreted it to think I was trying to replace his mother. I just wanted to protect him. So he pushed me away. For years.

In the beginning, I tried to do all his favorite things to win him over. I'm a teacher. There's not a kid I can't win over in at least six months. But not Ty. He was the only kid I have ever met I couldn't find a way to build a relationship with. We went to the zoo, to ball games. We rented boats to go fishing. All his favorite activities. But nothing. Even though I essentially raised him, we had no relationship.

I had tried so hard in the beginning with no success that I just gave up. I wasn't mean to him. I loved him. I just couldn't get through to him. So I concentrated my efforts elsewhere. I found great success at work and at church. At home, I was civil and polite. I expected him to keep his room clean, do his chores, finish his homework. In return, I cooked his meals, washed his clothes, made sure his bed had clean sheets. That's all I could really bring myself to do.

As a teenager Ty got into a lot of trouble. He drank, did drugs. He spent time in jail. We helped as much as we could. We found a psychiatrist to help him sort through some issues, especially that of his mother leaving him. Our relationship though, if you could call it that, was still strained. To be honest, I didn't spend much time at home. I couldn't deal with the tension when he and I were in the same room.

After sixteen years of marriage and raising this child, whom I really do think of as my son, I heard the story "Green and Clean" in *The 7 Habits*. The light went on. "Oh my gosh," I thought. "That's it. That's it. You've got to raise boys on lawns." I knew that's where I was missing the point. For a while in the story having the lawn green and clean was more important than the boy. In my life, I could see how my demands of Ty—clean your room, pick up your clothes, scrub the bathtub—got in the way. I thought, "Uh-uh, no, I can't do this anymore. He's more important than anything. I've got to try, I've at least got to try."

Ty was twenty-two years old by now. That's when I backed off with the demands and decided to build my relationship with him. First, I decided I wouldn't automatically disagree with the stupid things he said. I would hold my tongue and listen for his intent. Then I would respond in a way that didn't threaten him. Second, I knew I needed to spend more time with him. The problem was he didn't want to spend time with me. He made that very clear in a conversation when I started to broach the topic. "Well," I said, "could you at least go out to dinner with me once a month?" He stopped walking away, turned around, and said, "Yeah, I could probably do that." That was our less than auspicious beginning.

I gave myself six months to make deposits into his Emotional Bank Account. For six months I listened to him intently and carefully. For six months we went out to dinner together once a month. For six months I didn't force him to become what I thought he should be. After six months I realized we were very different people. I actually started to accept that we would always have a different view of life. After six months I could see Ty, the real Ty, so much better than I ever had before. I think he could see me.

It's been four years since I experimented with making those deposits. Ty's moved out on his own now. Only this morning he dropped by to visit for a while. Just dropped by for a chat. I was happy to see him. Our relationship is so much better than I ever dreamed it could or would be. That we have a relationship at all I credit to me finally putting first things first.

When people have had rejection experiences they often pull back into a kind of shell to protect themselves from being rejected again. When we make love a verb, and not just a feeling; when we make it a value to actualize, not just a sentiment; and when we are consistent and sincere, others who have been emotionally beaten up and who have become cynical gradually start to believe again. The tendency of teenagers to reject comes from the fear of being rejected. It is also a self-fulfilling prophecy.

I remember saying one time to my daughter, who had just had a rejection experience, "Honey, stay vulnerable." She said, "But it hurts, Dad." I responded, "Get your security from your integrity to your beliefs and value system, not from how other people treat you; then you can afford to be vulnerable on the surface of your life, because down deep inside you are invulnerable." One of the most lovable things about a person is his or her vulnerability. Others identify with it and are often sufficiently nurtured to expose their own vulnerability. The greatest bonding in relationships takes place when both people overlap their vulnerabilities. That is why the key to staying in love is to share feelings, not just experiences or thoughts.

You'd Really Do That for Me, Dad?

Notice how the father in this story would neither give up on his son nor give in to him. Notice also the tremendous hunger of the son to be valued and his amazement that his father would actually give that value.

I went home one evening to find my then fifteen-year-old son, a sophomore in high school, very upset about having to retake an English writing exam. He was sitting on the kitchen floor, getting angrier and angrier by the minute. He got so angry he started to cry. This wasn't normal behavior for him. I kept saying to myself, "What's going on here? Let me back up. I've really got to listen here. Okay, what are those questions I should be asking him? Now remember, empathic listening is like giving psychological air."

After a little probing and a bit of wading through the tears and anger, it turned out Mike was worried that he was going to take forever to finish the exam. You see, one of his hands was in a cast so he couldn't write as fast as he normally could. In his fear, he had built up this exam until he envisioned himself starting at two in the afternoon and not getting done until midnight. He was so worked up by this time that he just sobbed, "I don't want to do it, Dad. I just don't wanna do it. Don't make me do it, Dad. Write me a note so I don't have to do it."

Because I had been trying to empathize, I could restate his concerns for him. "Mike, you're concerned about taking this exam and how long you'll have to be in there."

"Yeah."

"How about I call your assistant principal tomorrow morning to tell her that you're worried about the length of the exam. Maybe I could ask her to check on you after thirty minutes to see whether you're tired. Then about every fifteen minutes after that. That way you can start the exam. Then just figure it out as you go along. Does that sound okay?"

I could see the blood drain out of his face. He just looked at me. "You'd do that. You'd really do that?"

"I would, if that would help you."

"Well, when you call, can you ask her if I don't have to take it?" He had that begging look in his eyes.

"Mike, you know I can't do that. You've got to take the exam to pass your sophomore year. But are you really concerned about not taking it? Or is it more that you're scared you will feel so tired?" I tried to remind him of what I sensed was really his fear.

"Yeah, yeah, you're right. That's what I'm really scared of," he admitted.

"Okay, so I'll call her in the morning. Then I'll call you and let you know."

Mike couldn't let it go just yet. He tried again. "So, you're going to call her and tell her about my hand. Then she'll say I don't have to take the exam—"

"Nope. What I said was that I'll call her and tell her about your concern with the time. Then she will say she's going to check on you every thirty minutes to make sure you're not too tired to do well."

"But, Dad, I'm going to get hungry. There's no food allowed in there. I can't go without food for six hours. What am I going to do? The cafeteria's closed and I won't be allowed to take food into the room." I could tell that he was still afraid and now was finding any way he could to get out of taking this exam.

"So, Mike, you're worried you'll get hungry."

"Yeah, yeah. You know I can't wait that long to eat. I'll faint."

"All right. I'll ask her about food as well. We'll see whether we can make an arrangement for you to get food if you need to." I knew I needed to just be patient with him while he wound himself down from the fit he had worked himself into. I knew it would take time so I just kept on showing him how I could help him work out the problems he thought he would face.

"Well, yeah, if you would ask her about the food that would be great," he conceded.

"Okay," I said, "so that's our deal. You're going to go up and get ready for bed, finish your homework, make it an early night. Then you'll be fresh in the morning to take this exam. And I will call your assistant principal in the morning to tell her about your concerns."

"Okay. That sounds good. Thanks, Dad."

I said goodbye in the morning, gave him a big hug, put him on the bus, then called his assistant principal from my office. When I reached her, I told her about Mike's concerns. She chuckled at first. Then she said, "Mr. Hofmeyer, Mike doesn't know this but we're going to have a pizza party at one o'clock to relax the kids; there'll be soda and snacks in the room where they are taking the exam; it only takes about ninety minutes to redo; and, at least ninety kids out of the 140 sophomores are retaking it. He'll have plenty of company. I bet he thinks he'll be in there by himself. That couldn't be further from the truth. You can tell him this if you like. Or you can let him be pleasantly surprised." I was smiling by the time she finished telling me this.

I thanked her for her time and hung up. Within minutes the phone rang. It was Mike.

"Dad, did you call her?"

"Yeah, Mike. She said you'll be fine. She said she's never seen anybody take longer than two hours. She's more than happy to check on you every half hour. And if you are really hungry by the time you write, she'll make arrangements for some food to be brought in. If you have any more questions, she'll be more than happy to talk to you."

"You really called, Dad?"

"Yes, Mike, I really called."

"Cool. Bye."

Later that afternoon, Mike waltzes through my office door. He'd taken the train downtown so he could catch a ride home with me. He's all smiles. "Guess what, Dad. It only took me an hour and a half. And they had pizza . . ." What a change. Less than twenty-four hours before he was kicking the kitchen floor in tears. Now here he was walking on air and wanting to hang out with his old man. You know, that experience taught me two things: One, that when I father my son in just the way he needs to be fathered, I feel fulfillment. Two, I learned that patience, seeking first to understand, and making and keeping commitments are the basis of building trust in any relationship.

I believe that if a person loves another in five ways synergy results, love is received, and bonding takes place. The first way is simply to understand, particularly feelings and deeper meanings. The second is to seek to be understood, also particularly feelings and deeper meanings. The third is to explicitly affirm the worth of another in words—to say what you feel about them, and to affirm their potential, that they can "do it." The fourth is to pray with and for them if the individuals believe in this. And the fifth is to sacrifice for them, to do something for them that would be outside what they would normally think you would do. Such sacrifice was the real key of the relationship in this story; the father was willing to sacrifice outside the boy's perception of his father's comfort zone, and that made all the difference.

Marriage: Valuing the Differences

CELEBRATING THE DIFFERENCES

SPORTSCENTER

LOVE IS A VERB

THE GREENHOUSE

MY FREE-SPIRITED HUSBAND

MERGING MISSIONS

MISS SUPERWASHERWOMAN

Celebrating the Differences

This is an absolutely extraordinary story of the synergy that came from diversity inside a family. It teaches how a higher value of family love and respect for differences gradually evolved through heart-wrenching difficulties and problems. Notice what profound happiness and peace was produced inside this intergenerational family.

Marriage is a wonderful yet challenging journey, especially when trying to blend cultures, customs, religions, and ethnicity. Fifteen years ago when I got married, I learned many difficult but valuable lessons. I am of Indian origin born on a little island halfway across the world. I grew up in Washington, D.C., in a fascinating and cosmopolitan community due to my father's position in the diplomatic corps.

Growing up in the States my family adopted many Western ways, but there was also embedded in my upbringing many cultural attitudes and practices which were very traditionally Hindu Indian. When I met my husband-to-be, many things came into question because he was of an entirely different background—white American from the West, and from a deeply religious Christian family. Naturally, some conflicts arose—mainly from our families, which had different expectations.

I will always remember the day when I almost walked away from my relationship simply because I felt so tugged at from all sides. On the one hand, my family had strong reservations about such a marriage because of the differences, especially in light of my wish to adopt my fiancé's religion and our plans to live in a remote and uncosmopolitan town out West. On the other hand, my husband's family had reservations because of their expectations for their son to marry within their own religious community and in a family with a similar religious tradition.

I quickly realized that while I understood where each family was coming from, I also knew that I had to find the courage to forge my own path. I did not shy away from the challenge; in fact, my husband and I decided to take charge of our lives. With love and respect for our families, we decided to forge ahead and build our family relationships with love and kindness.

After finishing my university education, I returned home with many fears because setting my own course, I knew, would be difficult. I grew up in a culture where children were to be seen and not heard. For the first time in my life, I had to make myself heard. My dad is traditionally authoritarian in his role as father, and I played the role of a peacemaker and accepting whatever came my way—good or bad. Now for the first time in my life I was trying to stand up for myself.

My dad's reaction to my plans was exactly what I expected. He was upset and forbade it, telling me that the man I wished to marry was not welcome in our home. With all the courage I could muster, but with great calmness and sureness, I replied, "Then I cannot stay here either."

After this, we both retreated to the cold war of not speaking of it until the next day when something strange happened—I was finally heard! My dad asked me to go with him into town and I accepted—just as I always did whenever he invited me to be with him. He is a very private man, and does not share much conversation, but being in his company meant something.

We had been in silence for quite some time when my dad, out of the blue, asked me to invite my fiancé home. When he said this I kept silent and just listened. For one thing, I am not always sure what to say to him—so I listened. He also asked that we plan a party for friends and associates to formally announce my engagement. Now, I was stunned into silence! Just twenty-four hours ago, he forbade this relationship and now he was giving me his blessings. I was both relieved and grateful, knowing how far my dad had to move himself to get to that point.

My fiancé did come shortly after this for his first visit with my family. It was wonderful having him there, and he was introduced to many foreign things: our culture, our foods and music, and also our Hindu customs. For this party, I wore my mother's sari, a traditional Indian dress. A traditional Hindu prayer was also performed for me and my fiancé, blessing our relationship and future wedding. It was wonderful to see my fiancé so accepting of what must have been very strange customs to him. I think this may also have been a comfort to my family.

Our wedding ceremony was the beginning of a beautiful blending of two beautiful families. I wore my traditional Indian sari of pink and silver brocade and my husband wore a suit. We exchanged flower garlands, which is customary in Hindu weddings, and our pastor performed a simple but memorable ceremony in which both families participated.

In the years to come, my brother and sister were supportive as they always had been; however, my parents' feelings were different—they felt they had lost their daughter. With time, however, feelings slowly began to soften. A memorable turning point came when I had my first child, a beautiful baby girl. She was my parents' first and only grandchild, and having this child to share among us brought us closer together, and a sense of acceptance began to blossom.

I will never forget the day, during a visit home, when my mother kindly offered to raise my baby girl should anything happen to me or my husband. I was so profoundly touched not only because of her love for me and her grandchild but because she offered to raise my child according to my new religion. I could only imagine what it must have taken for my mom to reach such a place in her heart. It was at that moment that I felt her acceptance and peace—this experience is forever etched in my heart.

During those years, my father also showed his love and acceptance in peculiar but meaningful ways. Many times, he used his influence in the diplomatic community to help the efforts of my new religion. Often, my dad went the extra mile to do good for this religious institution, and I always wondered why he did those things, considering his feelings. This was also a humbling and unforgettable experience for me.

I felt complete acceptance three years ago. When my dear brother passed away, my family was split apart halfway across the world. As we gathered together in love and grief, we found a way to connect as never before. My mother asked me to offer a prayer and remarks at my brother's memorial service. I was surprised because my mom knew it would be a Christian prayer, yet that did not matter to her. It was such an honor for me to be asked to do this, and I also knew she was embracing my religious practice and faith. During this glorious interfaith service, my prayers joined many others—Hindu, Muslim, Buddhist, Christian, and Jewish—and I felt the beauty and power of the divine and universal principles which govern all beliefs. I'm sure my brother was well pleased that day, for his life was a remarkable example of celebrating the differences of people everywhere.

Today, I am raising my own three beautiful children who are very proud of their Indian heritage from their mother and their Danish, English, and American heritage from their father. With the encouragement and support of my husband, I do my best to make my Indian culture and Hindu background part of our family—my children know that I still consider myself Hindu along with my newly adopted Christian religion. Through it all, my husband and I are trying to teach our children to appreciate the common threads that bind us all, as well as to celebrate our differences.

Through love, courage, faith, and hope, my family's circle has grown—my family and my husband's family feel proud of us, and we all share one common thing: a powerful love for one another—and love conquers all.

The French national motto surrounds three basic values. The first two, equality and liberty, if pushed to their extreme, are divergent of each other. But when they are subsumed in the third, fraternity, they become convergent and serve each other.

The critical moments that help produce such transcendent values and that enable divergent values to become convergent usually come when great courage and kindness are evidenced. It is relatively easy to be kind when you don't need to be courageous; it's also relatively easy to be courageous without being kind. The essence of true integrity and maturity, as my Harvard professor Rhand Saxenian taught me, is to be courageous and kind simultaneously.

SportsCenter

*Notice in this story the growing awareness of how hard it is to
sincerely listen, and how it reflects the value one places on another.
The quality of relationships is reflected in the quality of
communication.*

During football season a couple of years ago, I was really into
Steve Young and the San Francisco 49ers. One Saturday morning during the playoffs, my wife, Angie, and I had this "issue" we were talking about. She had a lot of energy about it. The two of us were sitting
at the table, face-to-face. Just over Angie's shoulder I could see the TV.
SportsCenter just happened to be on so I started pretend listening,
sneaking a peek every so often. I thought I was doing pretty well and
that she thought we were really "connecting."

Then suddenly, on comes a clip of Steve Young. I guess I got a little too absorbed in the screen. Before I knew it, Angie really got upset
with me, and rightfully so. Now the conversation switches to how
rude it was of me to pretend to listen when I was really watching
SportsCenter.

We don't resolve that one very quickly. We're on the outs with each
other for a few hours. My whole day is shot because I can sense how
upset and unhappy my wife is.

Fast-forward to Saturday night. Angie is no longer upset about the
original issue we were discussing earlier. It's gone. Now, she's ticked
off because I don't have the decency to listen to her. "After all," she
says, "I'm home all day with the kids, I need an adult to talk to, and
my husband, who's supposed to value me more than anybody,
doesn't even have the courtesy to really listen."

Now, it's ten or ten-thirty at night, we're in the upstairs bedroom,
and *SportsCenter* is on again. We're talking about me watching TV
while I'm pretending to listen to her. I'm in the middle of apologizing
to her, saying how rude it was of me, and what do I do? I actually
wander off again and start watching Steve Young! Ouch.

Needless to say, we didn't resolve that one until well into the
next day.

Really seeking first to understand is not easy. Sometimes I *think*
I'm practicing Habit 5, when in reality, I'm just going through the mo-

tions of the technique while my heart is somewhere else. When I do this, Angie senses I'm up to something and it's very hurtful to her. People know when you're insincere. They really do.

Fortunately, Angie knows enough 7 Habits to be dangerous. Sometimes she even says to me, "Don't practice that Covey stuff on *me*." Yet when my heart is right, when I'm really focused on my wife, she never thinks, feels, or says that. Things are just good.

I'm learning.

I have found that Habit 5 is a litmus test of our character. If we are into ourselves, into our own thinking, into our own world, we simply do not listen. Even if we attempt to practice listening, we're only pretending. Practicing the empathic technique of simply reflecting back what the other person has said is essentially manipulative and will probably be counterproductive. Like the proverbial iceberg, the technique is the tip and the motive and attitude of genuinely wanting to understand is the great mass under the water. This is why the private victory of the first three Habits is so foundational and also why the spirit of respect found in Habit 4: Think Win-Win is foundational to Habit 5: Seek First to Understand, Then to Be Understood. When the Private Victory is won, people feel inwardly secure and at peace with themselves. They can afford to venture outside their own world into the world of another.

Love Is a Verb

Notice the amount of patience and persistence it took for this woman to practice specific acts of love until the feeling of love for her husband returned.

"Love is a verb," I kept saying over and over in my mind. I had learned this phrase from the story in *The 7 Habits* of a husband who didn't feel loving toward his wife anymore. The advice he received was to "Love her!"

"But how do you love when you don't feel love anymore?" the husband asks. The story goes on to explain that love, the feeling, is the result of loving actions.

I believed this was true, and I decided I was going to live it. My feelings of love had drained out of our marriage, and left a stale relationship. I hypothesized that if I did thoughtful, loving things, and treated my husband courteously, the feelings would come back.

One day, while walking down the aisle at the grocery store by myself, I was feeling discouraged over some recent conflict between us, and I started repeating under my breath, "Love is a verb, love is a verb . . ." I kept doing this for a while, but after several months, I still didn't feel a whole lot better. I turned to some close friends who would listen to me when I needed to vent my frustrations, and they supported my efforts. I remembered the words that if you don't see the results right away, just persist.

I remembered hearing a quotation by Rainer Maria Rilke, "For one human being to love another: that is perhaps the most difficult task of all . . . the work for which all other work is but preparation." I must admit I didn't always feel love when I listened to my husband's point of view or kissed him when he came home from work. I realized that although it was difficult now, at one time my loving feelings had been real, and our relationship had been sweet and comforting. I wanted those feelings back.

So I started looking for small things he did for me, and expressed my appreciation for his help, like when he vacuumed the family room after a night of popcorn and videos. I picked up his favorite candy bar at the drugstore. I complimented him on how he dressed when we went out, and praised him when he remodeled our basement. I looked for the good to appreciate, and criticized less [Emotional Bank Account].

It has been eight years since I read that story and made the conscious decision to "love" my husband. It took quite a bit longer than I expected. We still have our ups and downs but now when I say "I love you" there is a sweet feeling inside. I am "in love" again, and happy together with my husband. Love is a verb. I proved that, and it was worth all the work!

> Over the years since I began teaching that love is a verb, amazing
> things have happened. People have told me that they have found that
> envy is a verb, that forgiveness is a verb, that anger is a verb, that
> courage is a verb, and so forth. As the space between stimulus and
> response becomes a part of one's conscious awareness and when we act
> within that space on the basis of values rather than feelings or events,
> we gain more and more control of our attitudes and actions. The net
> result is that our life becomes a product of our decisions, not our
> conditions.

The Greenhouse

Two wonderful things happened as this woman sincerely tried to understand her husband. First, she redefined what win and lose were for her. Second, a new sense of meaning and purpose extended her husband's life.

My father had been a superb dentist for thirty years when he was diagnosed with amyloidosis, a rare disease similar to cancer. The doctors gave him six months to live. Because of the effects of the disease, he had to give up his practice. So, here sits this man who had always been extremely active, with nothing to do all day except think about his fatal disease.

He decided he wanted to take his mind off things by putting a greenhouse in the backyard where he could grow his favorite plants. This wasn't a fancy glass greenhouse that you see behind Victorian mansions. This was one of those kit greenhouses complete with corrugated plastic for a roof and black plastic sides. My mother didn't want that monstrosity in her yard. She said she would die if the neighbors saw it. The g-word topic got to the point where they couldn't speak civilly to each other about it. I think the issue became the site of all their redirected anger about the disease.

One day my mom told me she was thinking about really trying to understand my father's point of view. She wanted to resolve this situation so that both could be happy. She knew she didn't want a greenhouse in her backyard. She'd rather have morning glory in all her perennial flower beds than that greenhouse. But she also knew she wanted my father to be happy and productive. She decided to step back and let him do it. Some people might say she went for lose-win. But from her perspective it was a win. She decided that my dad's happiness meant more to her than either the backyard or the neighbors.

As it turns out, that greenhouse kept my dad going long after the doctors had given up on him. He lived for two and a half more years. At night, when he couldn't sleep because of the chemotherapy, he went out to the greenhouse to see how his plants were doing. In the morning, watering those plants gave him a reason to get up. His greenhouse gave him work to do, something else to concentrate on while his body collapsed on him. I remember my mom commenting that supporting my dad's desire to build the greenhouse was one of the wisest things she had ever done.

⊗ *Initially the greenhouse was a "lose" to the wife until she subordinated her judgment to her husband's happiness and welfare. This teaches that when you understand (Habit 5), you redefine what win-win is (Habit 4). Nevertheless, had she not initially felt enough respect (Habit 4) to want to understand what was important to her husband (Habit 5), she wouldn't have made the shift. Interestingly, the energy that resulted was not a third alternative solution, it was a third alternative attitude. The first alternative was to not have the greenhouse. The second alternative was to let him have the greenhouse grudgingly. The third alternative was to truly understand him, to cheerfully and lovingly find her happiness in his satisfaction at having the greenhouse. This is often the way synergy works. An outside observer might say it was a compromise, but if you were to talk to this woman she would surely deny that she was compromising herself. She fulfilled herself in her husband's happiness and well-being. Such attitudinal synergy is a magnificent expression of mature love.*

My Free-Spirited Husband

The power of self-awareness is absolutely amazing; it is so uniquely human. In this little story this woman reflected upon her mission statement and allowed its words to challenge her to live by it—to value the differences in her husband. Study how she came to see her husband differently once she had her own epiphany. Even though her paradigm shift was evolutionary, it resulted in a revolutionary consequence.

I've always struggled with taking personal responsibility [Habit 1: Be Proactive]. I find it far easier and reassuring to blame somebody or something for the way things are. Somebody or something other than myself, that is. So, after writing my mission statement, I put it on the farthest corner of my desk and left it there. For six months. While I was traveling, I read an article in *USA Today* that sparked my interest in giving the Habits another try. As I reviewed the principles, it dawned on me that what I lacked was the experience of Private Victory.

The opportunity was just around the corner. I picked up my mission statement and read it through. Right in the middle there's this sentence about cherishing the good in my husband. A little voice inside of me challenged, "Well, do you?" I shrugged it off and made a commitment to read this mission statement every Monday to remind myself of what I was about. So I heard the voice every Monday morning. Whether I scanned over my mission statement on an airplane, or just visually thought about it, these few lines hit me in the face. I heard, "Well, do you?" And I thought, "Am I actually living by this?" I began to examine myself.

My husband and I are very different people. I'm very structured, organized, and even-tempered. He is just the opposite. He is unorganized and very headstrong. I suppose some people would call him intuitive and emotionally liberated. In my attempt to make myself feel good and cast the blame, I had always thought about his qualities in the negative. That way I could blame him for the problems we encountered together. I had also come to believe that there was nothing we could do to resolve these issues; Larry was the way he was. I couldn't change him.

As I thought more about this man I had been married to for twenty-three years, I started to see him in a different light. I realized that were it not for his free-spirited sense of adventure, all our vacations would have been organized down to the last minute and rest stop. We would never have discovered the penguins on a little beach in Cape Town, or that restaurant overlooking the canal in Amsterdam. When I planned the vacation, we would know exactly where we were going, where we would stay, how we were going to get there, and what time we expected to arrive. I also saw that what I had always viewed as his negative traits were only negative because they were different from mine [Habit 6: Synergize]. I had always been reluctant to embrace things that were different, even from my husband. In some ways, I had kept him at arm's length for twenty years.

I now had a new appreciation for Larry. I could see him in a completely different light. This paradigm shift also gave me one of my very own Private Victories. I had managed to replace false perceptions with accurate data all on my own. I felt empowered by that paradigm shift.

⊛ *The two most powerful ways I know of to connect the conscious to the subconscious mind, where life's deepest scripting and programming has taken place, are first, in visualizing and affirming things that have great meaning to us, and second, in writing, which is a psycho-neuromuscular activity that can literally imprint the brain.*

These two powerful activities are joined together in the preparation of a written mission statement (Habit 2: Begin with the End in Mind). It optimizes the likelihood of overpowering, eclipsing, and perhaps even erasing earlier negative programming.

Merging Missions

There are probably few experiences as bonding as when people share their mission statements with each other. Observe in this story the mutual learning that took place well before this couple shared their missions. Then notice also the impact that this sharing had.

I work as a trainer for a large corporation in Illinois. As part of my training, I certified as a 7 Habits facilitator. I train the employees at our plant and also offer community programs. My wife and I have been married for thirty years. It's been a pretty good marriage: she's a special education teacher, we have three daughters, and we live on one of those wide, tree-lined streets in central Illinois.

In my years of facilitating the community seminars, my wife had never taken one. Oh, we've talked about it a lot and she knew the lingo. Sometimes, when we're out together, I'll act up if I'm not getting the service I think I deserve. She'll elbow me in the ribs and say, "Hey, I'm going to call your boss and have your facilitator license revoked."

Then one week, about two years ago, my wife came through a session with a group of the teachers from her district. Talk about intimidation. Every time I would explain a concept, I could hear them whisper, "Hey, Kris, does he do that? Does Dave really do that at home?" I could hear her laughing. Despite my credibility problems, the session went really well. And our relationship soared to a higher level.

Now that we shared an understanding of the material, we suddenly had a way, a language for talking about what we want out of life. As Kris wrote her mission statement, I realized I had never shared my mission statement with her. Not because it was secret, just because I had never thought to do it. So we shared our mission statements. I think I always knew what would be important to her. But reading what she had written made her goals really clear to me.

Because I read Kris's mission statement, I understand how strongly she feels about education. And I make sure I do all I can to support her in her goals. Kris started a little later in life. We're part of the old generation where women mostly stayed home to raise their children. She took twenty years to get her bachelor's degree. Then she got her master's, and is now working on her doctorate. Her career is far more important to her than mine is to me at this point. I'm sixty, approaching retirement in my life. She's thinking about her career, what she can do in the time she has left. I'm trying to be supportive. So when she doesn't get home until seven-thirty at night (I told you I'm out of the old school), it helps that I know why she is doing what she is doing.

I really feel that with each of us having peered into the heart of the other through our mission statements, our marriage, and especially our communication, has just gotten better and better. And it was good before.

⊗ *From my observation and experience there is only one other activity that is more powerful than merging missions and that is the creation of a new mission between husband and wife or within a family (Habit 2: Begin with the End in Mind). If it truly comes out of the hearts, minds, and deepest parts of those involved, if it is done with great patience and with everyone's involvement over time, and if everyone knows that it will be used as the criteria by which all decisions will be made, nothing is more profoundly uniting and bonding than creating a mission.*

Miss Superwasherwoman

*Notice here the shocking realization of why understanding another
must always be the first deposit in the Emotional Bank Account.*

When I learned about making deposits in the Emotional Bank Account, I decided to try it. I thought I would do something special for
my husband to improve our relationship. I figured that having the
kids in clean clothes when he got home and getting the laundry done
quicker would really make him happier.

After about two weeks of being Miss Superwasherwoman with no
feedback from him—I mean nothing, I don't think he even had a
clue—I started getting a little ticked. "This stuff ain't worth nothin',"
I thought. Then, suddenly, one night when he'd gone thoughtlessly to
sleep between clean sheets, I saw the light bulb click on above my
head.

"Oh my gosh. He doesn't give a hoot about Zac's clean face or his
clean jeans. That's what makes me happy. He'd rather have me
scratch his back or organize a date for Friday night." I could have
kicked myself. Here I was killing myself over laundry and making all
these deposits that didn't mean a thing to him.

I learned a simple truth in a very laborious way: a deposit must
mean something to the other person.

⊛ *The reason that understanding another is always the first deposit in
the Emotional Bank Account is that we do not know what a deposit is
to another person until we understand them and the way they see
things. Take any deposit you want to look at, whether it be kindness,
promise keeping, treating people with fairness and respect,
apologizing, or whatever—it always must be done within the frame of
reference of the other person. Otherwise, what we consider to be a
valuable deposit may very well be a meaningless deposit or even a
withdrawal to them.*

3

Community and Education

"Alone we can do so little; together we can do so much."

—HELEN KELLER

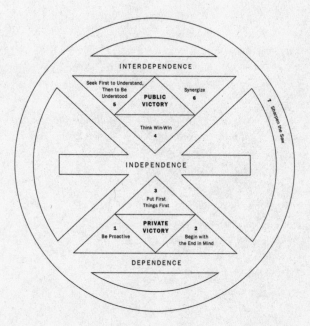

Building Community

BRENDA KRAUSE EHEART,
FOUNDER, HOPE FOR THE CHILDREN FOUNDATION

STONE

THE RABBI

LEAVING A LEGACY OF SERVICE AND HUMILITY

SYNERGY OF A COACH

SAVING A HISTORICAL TREASURE

SOUTH BEND, INDIANA:
REACHING ACROSS GENERATIONS TO BETTER A COMMUNITY

Brenda Krause Eheart,
Founder, Hope for the Children Foundation

One of the things that I love about this story is that this woman had no knowledge of the 7 Habits, yet you can see each one of them beautifully illustrated in her life and efforts. I did not invent these principles, and cannot take credit for them. I simply organized and sequenced them into a framework. This story shows that these Habits are self-evident, universal, and timeless—that you can observe these principles in practice in all enduringly effective people, families, communities, organizations, and societies.

For seven years I worked with a colleague in the clinical psychology department at the University of Illinois in Urbana delving into some of the most heartbreaking aspects of the foster care system. We wanted to know what happened to the "unadoptables," the children, adolescents, and teens that spent their entire youth being bounced from one foster home to another. They were crack babies, children with AIDS, victims of mental, physical, and sexual abuse, or afflicted with cerebral palsy, sickle cell anemia, and other illnesses of the body and mind.

We found that even those lucky few who were adopted often were returned to the foster care system because the adopting parents were simply not equipped to deal with these deeply troubled or chronically ill young people. A frightening number of them went from foster care into prison or mental health centers, and too often, even committed suicide. Our findings were backed up by other studies showing that at eighteen years of age, 46 percent of foster care children had not completed high school, 38 percent had not held a job, 25 percent had been homeless at least one night, and 40 percent ended up on welfare. Sixty percent of the young women in foster care had given birth by the age of eighteen.

At the end of the 1980s and in the early 1990s, we had one thousand kids a month coming into the foster care system in Illinois and at about the same time leaders of the U.S. Congress were talking about building more orphanages. I thought we had to come up with a better idea than that. Then I heard a statistic that really put me over the edge. It said that one third of the kids who enter foster care will never go back to their birth parents nor will they be adopted. I thought, "Enough is enough."

Upon completion of our research project into the foster care system and its most problematic children, I called together a group of colleagues and friends, many of whom were also adoptive parents, and formed the Hope for the Children Foundation [Habit 1: Be Proactive]. Together we created a model that would provide what we believed to be a child's most vital needs: "At least one person who is always caring, a sense of security, and a sense of community."

I envisioned creating the sort of place that I would want for my own children should my husband and I become unable to care for them [Habit 2: Begin with the End in Mind]. I'd had considerable experience working with low-income families and unwanted children. Before that, I was a social service field worker assisting housing project residents in Chicago. I also had worked in Philadelphia and overseas, both as a child welfare advocate and as a volunteer.

My dream was to create a place where the "unadoptable" children would be adopted by caring parents who would themselves be supported by professional therapists and psychologists as well as backup adult guardians to provide relief from the stress of dealing with extremely troubled or ill children.

That dream was still being formed when I attended a speech given by Maggie Kuhn, founder of the Gray Panthers, an advocacy group for senior citizens. She talked about the untapped resource of senior citizens and how they should be allowed to work in public service rather than "scrap-piled." Kuhn's message resonated with me. I'd grown up on my family's dairy farm in upstate New York. My grandfather and father worked alongside each other on the farm. My brother and sister and I felt very secure with our parents and grandparents watching over and supporting us. From Maggie Kuhn's speech and the memories it stirred, I came up with the idea of involving senior citizens as a vital part of the "village" I wanted to create for foster children. I wanted those children to know security and to have the support that I enjoyed as a child.

Once we had developed a basic model for our village and all of its elements, we began searching for both funding and a site [Habit 3: Put First Things First]. It was an eye-opening experience. After more than a year, it appeared that our model community for unwanted children would never become reality. Then in 1992, I learned that the federal government was trying to sell surplus property and housing at an abandoned air force training base in Rantoul just fifteen miles north of Urbana in central Illinois.

When I first toured the grounds of the former Chanute Air Force Base, I could hardly contain my excitement. It was perfect. There were hundreds of well-maintained, spacious homes along winding, tree-lined streets. There were parks, baseball diamonds, swimming pools, even a golf course on the grounds of the 2,400-acre base. Some portions of it had already been sold off for residential and commercial development by private developers. And so I returned to Urbana thinking that it would be no problem to convince the Pentagon to donate or sell us part of it for our planned village for the unwanted children in the foster care system. I was a little naive there.

The military establishment had a process for selling its surplus property to for-profit businesses, but no experience at all in dealing with nonprofit entities. Our bid to buy a portion of the former air base in Rantoul became mired in the bureaucracy for two years. In exasperation, we sent a telegram to the White House, imploring newly elected President Bill Clinton to take up our cause. Our desperation ploy worked. Suddenly, the Pentagon found a way.

In the fall of 1993, we won approval to purchase sixty-three duplex houses on twenty-two acres of the property. Our foundation paid the $215,000 tab with a portion of a $1 million appropriation we wrangled from a financially strapped state legislature through the help of an unlikely political coalition that included Democrats and Republicans, liberals and conservatives—all of whom bought into our dream.

One year later, the first "unwanted" child from the state's foster care system found a permanent home in a comfortable brick house with two welcoming parents at Hope Meadows. Today, our village population includes more than forty former foster children who have been adopted by the fourteen families who reside there free of charge in exchange for agreeing to permanently adopt up to four children [Habit 4: Think Win-Win]. Many also come to Hope Meadows with their own biological children. Each family receives an annual subsidy of $19,500, so that at least one adult can serve as a full-time parent in the home.

The parents are themselves supported by an amazing network of fifty-three senior citizens who are allowed to rent their homes on the grounds for $325 a month in exchange for putting in at least six hours a week as volunteer grandparents. Most put in at least twice that much time because they come here out of their love for children and their desire to make a contribution.

Irene Bohn is a seventy-three-year-old widow and retired school-teacher who was among the first foster grandparents to move into Hope Meadows. She tells me that we have created "the best of all worlds here for these children, and for us. My own two children are grown and my husband was gone and after I retired I got a little apartment and I was doing a lot of mall walking, but I decided there had to be more to my life at this stage."

Irene told me that she and the other seniors at Hope Meadows give a lot to these children, but they get just as much as they give: "One morning a while back, I got up feeling bad. I'd just lost one of my brothers and I was feeling all alone," she told me recently. "Then I walked out into the yard and all of a sudden somebody hollered, 'Mornin', Grandma!' and I got goose bumps all over. That brought me back."

The volunteer grandparents baby-sit, tutor, serve as crossing guards, and monitor playgrounds at Hope Meadows. They also fix bicycles, play catch, work in the library and computer lab, and, in Irene's case, even go on "dates."

One of her favorite foster grandchildren is Tabian, an eight-year-old boy who came to Hope Meadows after his addicted mother finally consented to give up parental rights to him and his ten-year-old sister, Shamon. The children often awoke screaming and cursing. Tabian had never learned his ABCs before Bohn began working with him. He now reads to her nearly every day, and he has appointed himself her personal escort.

"One evening he came to my door with a dollar bill all crumpled in his hand and some sweaty pennies," she recounted.

"Grandma, may I take you to the movies?" he asked.

"It was my first date since I don't know when," she noted.

The adoptive families at Hope Meadows are also supported by a team of resident child therapists and psychologists, who provide professional guidance and greatly reduce the stress that, in the past, has caused many well-meaning adoptive parents to give up.

I'd define Hope Meadows as a community, not by physical dimensions but as a network of caring relationships. And those relationships are just very, very powerful. Everyone works hard to see that these are successful adoptions.

Our model for child care has been itself embraced by the Ronald McDonald House Foundation of the McDonald's Corporation, based in suburban Chicago, 130 miles to the north. In 1998, the hamburger chain's charitable foundation provided a large grant to our foundation so that we could develop a similar village in a rehabilitated neighborhood in Cleveland.

Anyone without foreknowledge of the troubled histories that accompanied the young residents of Hope Meadows would have a difficult time recognizing it from any other small-town neighborhood. Children of all races pedal bicycles, Rollerblade, dribble basketballs, and skip on sidewalks along meandering streets under the watchful eyes of parents and "grandparents" posted on lawn chairs and front porches.

The soothing normalcy of it all is very much the end that we had in mind when we decided that enough was enough. Normal is good. Normal is what we want here. We only have one sign and it is like that designating any subdivision. Our office is unmarked. We want it to look like a regular neighborhood. We don't want these kids to feel different than others. They've already had enough of that.

There are many challenges awaiting us. There are no guarantees that the deeply rooted trauma, either mental or physical, suffered by these children will not lead to serious behavioral problems as they grow into adolescents and teenagers. This is a social experiment that will take years and years to measure.

But all agree that it is a start, a good start, at addressing a critical societal problem. I truly think we are doing just about everything humanly possible to meet the needs of these traumatized kids. In many ways it is a utopia for them, but there are undoubtedly going to be some kids who still don't get enough here. The greatest reward for me is knowing that we are helping people, not only these kids but also the seniors and parents. It really is incredibly gratifying now, and even though my heart will always be here, it will be even more gratifying to see it spread across the country.

Recently I was speaking with Jeanette Laws, a dedicated Hope

Meadows parent who has adopted two children with troubled pasts. She gave me a great gift when she told me that if nothing else, the children in our village have learned one very important lesson already: "My kids now know that no matter what has happened to them in the past, or what may happen to them in the future, there is a better way, a better life."

Imagine what would happen in every community or society that worked within their Circle of Influence and followed the kind of vision, passion, and discipline of a Brenda Krause Eheart. It is a common vision that creates the magnanimity of spirit and largeness of soul that transcends and subordinates self-interest and littleness of soul. When you challenge people to a greater vision, they become consumed by a larger purpose that transcends petty misunderstandings and turf issues. This could happen throughout our nation. This could happen throughout our world.

I believe that if every functional and relatively healthy family would psychologically adopt either an unstable, dysfunctional family or a child that is seriously at risk, and do whatever is necessary to help them become functional, successful, and contributing, we would strike at the very roots of almost all of our social problems throughout the world. This is possible; it's achievable; it's doable. Neighborhood coordinators could be set up to provide training and some kind of accountability.

Unless we as families take this kind of action, our social problems could deepen, expand, and become so exacerbated that they could disrupt our entire society, undermining the economy and feeding upon themselves until we became gang-infested communities of confusion and chaos. Gangs are simply surrogate families. We must all become surrogate parents, caring mentors, to innocent, vulnerable children who otherwise have little hope.

Stone

The following true story is the script of a short film made by
Franklin Covey Co. It has won many awards, and I use it
continuously in my teaching. It is one of the most uplifting,
inspiring, and thrillingly challenging stories people have ever heard.
Notice the amount of proactive muscle and sincere caring, and notice
the kind of leadership that truly develops and empowers others.

My wife and I first came to Uganda five years ago. Our original plan was to take a year off school before we went on to law school. We saw a lot of suffering around us, and a lot of poverty. We found ourselves slowly getting involved in one small thing after another and so we decided to stay.

About three years ago while working together in Kampala, one of the things that really struck us was the number of young men who were unemployed. They were about sixteen years old and didn't have the money to continue on in school. They were without direction. We met a couple of them and questioned them about what they would like to be involved in. They said they would like a soccer team.

So we began a soccer team with those few boys, told them to bring their friends, and told them we would practice every day at such and such a time, at a certain field. That went on for a while. Soon the boys came and said they had found their coach and they wanted us to meet him. This man basically told us he would like to coach this team and we shouldn't worry about paying him, he would just like to do it. From that time on we became friends with Stone and we began working together.

Stone began playing soccer in high school and he was recognized as a really talented soccer player. When he was about eighteen, he was picked up by his first professional team. He played at the professional level for ten years. By that time he had been chosen to be on the national team, which is the goal of all Ugandan soccer players; then you have the opportunity to play in Europe. You're seen by scouts from the European clubs.

Shortly before he began his international career, he was on a breakaway for the goal. Before he shot, a guy cut him down from behind and tore the ligaments in his knee. It wasn't an accident; he did it intentionally. This put an end to Stone's professional career.

In a country where revenge is really commonplace, where sixteen years of war and corruption have been centered around revenge, Stone just said to this man, "Don't worry about it. You did what you had to do [Habit 1: Be Proactive]." Stone's ability to forgive this man, after pursuing a career for so long, was really remarkable. We knew that the sort of integrity he had within him was exactly what these boys were going to need in order to get direction in their lives. Stone explained it this way:

"Some of these boys were druggies. Some were pickpockets. There were some wild boys who just walk on the streets aimlessly without direction at all. We look at these boys to give them a sense of direction. And in this, we also try to give them some skills, then some resources, then a frame of mind, you know, which can really help them in the future [Habit 2: Begin with the End in Mind]. We just don't look at them as footballers for their future. We want them to be good citizens. We want them to be self-reliant, to draw upon those skills to help them in the future."

The boys Stone started with were basically rejected by their families and their community as being troublemakers and problem children. Stone really loved the boys and showed a lot of trust in them. He said that love was the key to the team's success:

"We keep these boys just by the love that we give them. We don't give them money, we don't give them things. But they just come because they feel they are at home on the team. It is love that makes everything. You can never be happy unless you have love. So we really work on that. That's the basis of the team. Love and forgiveness."

When Stone teaches about love and forgiveness, the boys can take this back to their own families. They can learn how to love the people immediately around them, and learn how to forgive them.

A lot of the teaching of this principle is shown by Stone's life. He lives in the same area as the boys. They know his wife, his children, the way he interacts with his family. They see that he's actually living everything he's teaching. That's the most powerful part of what he does, even more important than what he says. His example challenges the boys to be like him.

Leadership isn't about being famous. So even though Stone may be affecting only a couple of hundred people in his community, those couple hundred people will be affecting villages and those villages will be affecting other villages. Stone emphasized the importance of his work like this:

"We are trying to teach them how to lead themselves, how they can have responsibility. Not that I will be there all the time. Because most of these kids are boys and they will be fathers. Now what type of families will they lead if they are left as they are? We try to tell these boys that there is nothing which you cannot do. It is through hard work that all things are possible. Your life is entirely on you. What you have in your mind is what will shape your future, is what will shape you."

Stone is an amazing person, totally dedicated to the young men of his country. He has undoubtedly blessed, directly and indirectly, thousands of them. How easy it would have been for Stone to have gotten bogged down in the quicksand of self-pity, victimism, and revenge. He chose a different path—a path of contribution infinitely greater than only becoming a star soccer player. Stone is poor, but he is truly rich. He is like a Mother Teresa, whose motto was "The fruit of silence is prayer; the fruit of prayer is faith; the fruit of faith is love; the fruit of love is service; the fruit of service is peace."

The pathway to the kind of moral authority of a Stone is always sacrifice. Sacrifice has to be defined as giving up something good for something better. Stone did this. He is still doing it. What a noble and inspiring soul!

The Rabbi

Notice in this story how the people involved moved back and forth between independence and interdependence, between scarcity and abundance, and between win-lose and win-win. Notice also how growing self-awareness created sufficient freedom to act with wisdom during the struggles so that the tremendous benefits of interdependence could be realized. Notice finally how if just one person's mind and heart are filled with the spirit of Think Win-Win (Habit 4), others are drawn into that spirit of abundance, and synergy (Habit 6) usually results.

Between congregations, there is at times a sense of competition. Unfortunately, the competition usually boils down to membership, because membership boils down to much-needed funds. As a result of this need to draw members, synagogues often duplicate programs and services unnecessarily.

We have had a successful youth group in our synagogue called the Israel Youth Group. It has had up years and down years, but has been doing well recently. In fact, last year we were able to employ a part-time advisor who has been able to involve not only our own congregants, but teenagers from other congregations as well.

Another congregation here in town, which has had very limited success in being able to establish a youth group, decided that they wanted to establish a youth group affiliated with the same organization as well. In other words, duplicate our service completely. They approached the regional director and said, "We are going to open our own Israel Youth Group, and in our city there will be two Israel Youth Groups."

I thought to myself, "Why are they doing this?" A sixth-grader from my congregation will be in the same class as his friend from the other congregation, and up until now they have been going to youth group activities together. All of a sudden there will be issues of loyalty and competition between them. And can you imagine having awards at the end of the year? Kids would be competing for their awards, one chapter against the next. If our community represented a major metropolitan area I could understand having more than one chapter of the youth group, but our community was not big enough for this.

"This is insane," I thought. I knew that we could figure out a way to make this situation a win-win, so I contacted their rabbi. "I understand you've petitioned the regional office to establish your own youth group in your synagogue," I said. "Let's talk about a collaborative effort. Let's talk about a joint chapter." He listened and heard what I said. At least I thought he heard what I said.

The next month on the front page of his newsletter, he announced that his synagogue had applied for and expected to receive a charter to establish its own Israel Youth Group. "There will be two Israel Youth Groups," it said. "One at so-and-so's congregation, and one at ours."

I was just livid. I could not believe this. I asked the regional director to come into town and have a meeting. He set up a meeting with leaders from both congregations. I came to the meeting with my youth advisor. The other rabbi brought a whole army of representatives. We sat and started discussing what a youth group sponsored by both of our congregations would mean.

First, it would mean sharing a name. Second, it would mean that the chapter advisor we had hired already would work on behalf of both groups, and we would split the cost. Third, it would mean that some of the activities would take place at our synagogue and some of them would take place at their synagogue. Fourth, it would mean that if there were regional events, we would also alternate synagogues. Fifth, it would mean that we would both comply with the same standards set by the regional organization.

In the process of working everything out, including some technical concerns, everyone involved seemed satisfied. Then, one of their representatives turned to me and said, "I don't understand. What do you have to gain? It seems to me that as we are describing this, we have everything to gain. You have everything to lose."

"What do you mean?" I asked. "Well," he replied, "you have a viable youth group and we don't. So by sharing this, your group will not be as unique as it is right now."

I went on to explain to him, "Look, you need to understand that this is not a win-lose situation. It's a win-win. Look at how much I gain by doing this. The group will have much larger numbers. Because the numbers will be larger, the kids will be more excited about going and being involved. And if they are more excited about being involved, then ultimately, they will travel to the conventions and become more inspired. If they are more inspired, they will come back to the synagogue, and we will share in that inspiration. So, the question is what do we have to lose?"

These words were like an epiphany for him because he had never thought about it that way. His whole mind, his whole training as a lay person and lay leader was that he had to be the best. If we are the best we have to be better than the other group to attract more members than they attract. Otherwise, they will take our members. But the reality is that if we work together it reflects positively on both organizations.

That was the first step. Subsequent to that, I decided to take a bold step on another issue. We have been trying for about four or five years to create a Sunday School program for children in our congregation, but we can never get the critical mass of children we need.

The other synagogue has a substantial number of kids, but they need more as well. And they are having some financial problems. They had started trying to create different incentives to bring in non-affiliated students, but they still needed help.

I called the rabbi and said, "Look, we did it with the youth group. So why don't we create a collaborative effort with this school program? It could be another win-win for both of us." The rabbi said, "What a great idea."

The next thing you know, we called another meeting. But this meeting was different. In contrast to the first meeting, the only people who came were the rabbi and his president, me and my president, the principal of the school, and one of my teachers. Six of us. A very nice little meeting. We talked, we worked things out, and the meeting went very smoothly. So much so, in fact, that they magnanimously said to us, "We'll offer all of your kids the member rate, even though they are not member kids. If they are members by you, we will give them the member rate."

And as we were leaving, they added, "We won't charge you any fees for being involved." Sometimes when synagogues work together, the hosting synagogue charges the other one an annual fee, but in this meeting, they said, "We'll waive that. And as far as we're concerned, you just come."

I guess the lesson is that win-win begets win-win. Once people think that way, they realize they can continue down that path and there will be much more for them. In a collaborative effort, you are not asking either side to abdicate its own personal standards. That's not what a win-win is. People think that. They think compromise. They think, I have to give. But that's not what a win-win is. Win-win is based on what we already are and that there is always room for mutual efforts.

I think we all learned that. We did not ask them to be something they were not and they did not ask us to be something we were not. As we work together in the future, neither of us will give up our identities, but we will mutually benefit one another and provide for our youth the best inspirational and social experience possible.

Independence is much easier than interdependence. My guess is that it takes about one tenth the effort and the emotional energy. People often resist working on an interdependent basis, so the price must simply be paid. This story is a beautiful illustration of win-win begetting more win-win. An upward spiral of the Abundance Mentality creates a kind of immune system so that small difficulties are transcended, new challenges are met, and higher and higher purposes are served.

Leaving a Legacy of Service and Humility

The following story beautifully illustrates the intergenerational impact of anonymous service.

My great-grandmother was a French girl taken in an Indian raid who stayed with the Choctaw tribe. Her son, my grandfather, grew up in Oklahoma speaking only Choctaw and a few words of English. At the turn of the century, he received his call to be a minister. Even though he didn't speak English, and was hardly any more fluent the day he died in 1974, he answered the call.

He worked where he felt he was needed. He never owned a home but lived in whatever parsonage the church provided for him. As I grew to know him in the 1950s, I got used to his odd hours and appearances. He pastored at one church in the morning and another in the evening, sixty miles from the first. I thought of him as a simple, uneducated man who worked hard to help the people around him. After all, he could hardly string a sentence of English together.

There were a few strange things that happened from time to time. Sometimes, he would disappear. Grandma would say, "Oh, he's off to Washington." I thought she meant on the West Coast. At other times, checks would arrive in the mail. And he'd give it all away to whoever he thought needed the help.

It was only after he died, when we were going through his papers and correspondence, that I realized what a phenomenal man my simple, unassuming grandfather actually was. The Washington my grandmother referred to was actually Washington, D.C. In his papers, we found letters from governors, senators, U.S. representatives. Some congratulated him on his fiftieth wedding anniversary; others thanked him for his help with legislation issues and for his community service. I sat there thinking, "Did they know the same man I did?" He had no eloquence, no wealth, not even his own home. Yet here were famous, powerful people corresponding with him. I realized that his life had been lived not to acquire things for himself, but to help other people. He had lived a life of integrity, honesty, and dedication to family and community all the while toiling in relative obscurity and humility.

I reflect often on my grandfather's life and his choices to live it the way that he did. Once, before he died, he told me that there are two reward systems: people who will be rewarded here and people who will be rewarded later. "These are not the same people," he said. He continued, "For all that you don't see in a reward system now, you will see some other time."

One incident from his life epitomizes his philosophy of thinking first about the impact on others, of not seeking only our reward but working to bring about good in the lives of others:

As we searched through his papers after his death, we discovered a title to land dating back to a land grant given to all Native Americans in Oklahoma. Each family received 160 acres of land, some parcels close to the recipients, some not. My grandfather's property was 180 miles from the town he lived in. By chance, my grandfather's piece of land was rich in oil. The oil companies negotiated with him to drill on his land. In return, he received bonus checks, sometimes thousands of dollars a month, from the oil companies. Those were the checks I remember him disbursing to his parishioners. He hardly kept anything for himself. I suppose he thought his reward would come later.

As we researched the land, we discovered something that would give us the choice to act as my grandfather would have or as we would have liked to. When he died, only 20 of the 160 acres remained. The other 140 acres had been taken for back taxes. When we tracked down who now owned the property, we discovered that the tax assessor, the very same man who had put a lien on the property in the first place, had bought the property to pay the back taxes.

Apparently what had happened was that, even though a law established that taxes did not have to be paid on the land grant properties for forty years, the tax assessor started proceedings long before the forty years was up. When the nonrequired taxes were supposedly not paid, he placed a notice at the local courthouse notifying the owner. Of course, my grandfather lived 180 miles away in his hometown that he hardly ever left. He would never see the notice in time to pay the taxes. So the tax assessor bought the property when my grandfather failed to pay taxes that weren't supposed to be paid in the first place. When we visited the property, Sinclair Oil had built a huge oil refinery on the 140 acres taken from my grandfather. Next door, the old tax assessor lived in an opulent home, all on the land my grandfather had been given by the government.

We debated long and hard what to do about the situation. Should we sue him to take back the land? Should we let it alone? Shouldn't he have to pay for his wrongdoings? Then we thought about what my grandfather would have done. He felt so strongly about honesty and integrity, about taking no credit for his accomplishments. He would never tell people, in many instances, who had given them money, he would only send money or deposit money on their behalf and tell someone to notify them that it was there under the stipulation that no one would know where it came from. In the end, we knew. We knew what he would do. He would let it alone and allow the taxpayer to reap whatever rewards his behavior would cause him to reap, whether here or later.

My grandfather might not have been able to leave us 160 acres of oil-rich land in Oklahoma but he left us something far more important. His insistence on humility, on compassion, on spending his life trying to help those around him with no thought of reward or praise is now our family legacy. He has changed generations of people with the help he gave. Can you put a dollar-and-cents value on that? I say absolutely not. We now have a value I try to instill in my own family to continue the legacy started by the Choctaw preacher who never owned his own home.

⊗ *There are a few sources of gaining an intrinsic sense of worth and value. One of those sources is in giving anonymous service. It reminds me of my own father. He was a humble, modest back-bencher who worked for years on projects of surpassing significance that no one knew about. In fact, the day after my father passed away was the first time that any of us ever went into his private rooms in the basement. There we discovered the nature of his life's work, the interest he had pursued, the depth and extent of his scholarship, the books and designs he had authored, and the source of the contributions he had made. Growing up, I explicitly remember my father telling me to not talk about things that might in any way make others feel lessened—to not be a person who drops names and places or who talks of one's possessions.*

I have become increasingly convinced that as we seek "to live, to love, to learn, and to leave a legacy," not only will we have a sense of fulfillment and peace of mind, but our life will be truly synergistic—producing new energies, new insights, new opportunities, and larger responsibilities and resources than we would ever imagine.

Synergy of a Coach

Notice in this story how simply redefining the goal or mental
expectations became the foundation to a synergistic "championship"
season for these little kids.

I am a businessman who traveled a lot while my kids grew up. I
decided when my youngest son was in the fifth grade that no matter
how busy I got, I would volunteer to coach the community basketball
team for his age group. Being a former college basketball player, a
high school coach for years, and a coach for a European Olympic
team, I felt pretty confident that I would be able to get these kids in
shape and produce a super team. I play to win and have taught my
three boys to do the same. They are all outstanding athletes.

My son Jason was a real talent, and with my coaching help he
would finally have the chance to shine. He had played on another
fairly successful team, but we transferred him to my new team full of
hope and excitement. I went to the first practice and came home dev-
astated. The kids stunk! There were probably only three players that
had any potential and the rest were completely spastic and awkward.
They could hardly catch the ball. Every practice was a nightmare, and
I felt rotten about having transferred my son to this much inferior
team. His entire season was going to be a waste.

After the first couple of games it became obvious that I would
have to keep the three good players on the court the entire game, or
we would be slaughtered. Even with them in all the time we lost
games, and I never felt good about them or me. In my ears I kept
hearing comments I had made about other coaches my son had had
in the past: "He is just coaching to enhance his own son's chances." I
had seen it and felt it time after time, and worried that maybe deep
down, this was also my reason for sacrificing my time and energy. I
am still not sure it was, but I worried so much about it that I felt I had
to do something.

I decided to forget all ideas of winning and make the season about
something completely different. I called the parents and players together and told them I had decided to let all players have equal time
on the court regardless of their talent. I asked everyone about their
expectations, what they hoped to get out of the season. I asked the

parents how I could help each of their sons progress and feel good about himself. Then I let them know what I expected from them as their sons' coach. They were so surprised at my initiative about their kids that they wanted to help me in every way they could. They became part of that season in a way I have never experienced before in coaching.

The kids still stunk—but they didn't know it. They played their hearts out. We stopped keeping score—we didn't care—we had fun and they felt great about themselves. The three good players struggled in the beginning with this approach, but quickly learned to just go with the flow. At the end of the season my ten-year-old son said, "Well, Dad, it wasn't a very good team, but the kids sure like you and they all say it's the first time they ever got to play as much as the good players. So I guess that was fair. They are all asking if you will coach again next year."

🌀 *Isn't it interesting how we want our Little League youngsters to behave like adults, while parents on the sidelines often behave like children! What a marvelous capacity this coach had to reinvent the name of the game from win-lose competition to learning and fun. He did it by using his self-awareness, involving the kids, and getting emotional buy-in from the parents. Almost everything depends on how you define "win." If winning means to beat, all behavior and attitude tend to flow from that. If winning means having equal participation, having a lot of fun, and learning, then all behavior will flow from that. It is terribly important to get a clear and common sense of what "win" means at the very outset.*

Saving a Historical Treasure

As you read this story, try to feel the excitement and proactive muscle of a mother who engaged her entire family in a significant community service project. Just imagine the profound life lessons being taught here.

My husband I had plans for him to finish his schooling before we planted ourselves in our dream house. Until then, our three children and we were settled in a small apartment in the center of town. Just a few blocks from our window I often looked out to an old historic building called Academy Square. It was falling to ruin, but I could still feel its splendor of days gone by. I learned that this beautiful building had been a marvelous center of learning at the turn of the century, and it was now one of the most valuable historical sites in the western United States.

I soon grew to love this historical treasure. Every time I drove by, I wondered about the stories contained within its walls and about its fate. My children often looked out for the Academy landmark during trips around town, making their own comments about the old building.

One day during a trip to the city library with the kids we discovered a plan to renovate the old Academy into a new city library. I was overjoyed, but I also learned that if the proposal failed, the building would be torn down. There was growing opposition to the plan because of budget concerns, but I was convinced that a new library at Academy Square was the right thing to do. My family also has a love for libraries—we often visit old libraries when on vacation, so this was a perfect match.

I quickly gathered my husband and children when I realized a bond election for this project was being voted on. I decided to get involved and so with only one week before the vote, I made handouts, flyers, and signs for our friends and neighbors. The evening before the vote, I gathered my children with our homemade signs to rally at the old building. Soon, some students joined us in the rally and before we knew it others also joined in.

Despite the cold of the evening, my children (ages seven, four, and two) and I stood waving our signs at passing cars. My kids jumped with excitement as they chanted, "We're gonna save the 'Cademy so they don't wreck it." That evening we appeared on the local TV news, and the children were so excited we decided to continue the rally the following day—the day of the vote. That day, we had many, many more people join us in the rally to save our history.

It was such a thrill when the bond election succeeded, yet the job wasn't over. A citizens organization promised to raise an additional $6 million with only four months to do it. This was a do-or-die situation—if the money was not raised in time the building could still be demolished. My family's heart was already deep into this, so I joined the citizens group to raise funds.

I felt very lost thinking of raising $6 million! What money connections did I have? I was simply a homemaker with three children. My family was struggling to make ends meet. No one I knew had more than a few dollars to donate, but I felt that it was *very* important for people like me to be involved in saving this important landmark.

I gave a great deal of thought to ways I could help. I felt very strongly that families, the common people of my community, should be a part of this valuable effort. The more I thought about it, the more ideas came to me. This led to my leading the Nickel and Dime Community Action Campaign. My ideas wouldn't raise millions of dollars, but they would raise the awareness of the community and make the efforts of families pay off.

During the four months of vigorous fund-raising, my family was immersed in the effort. Anyone calling our home heard our children's gleeful message on the answering machine: "Sorry we're not home, we're out saving the Academy." It was one of the busiest times of our lives, but also one of the most enjoyable and gratifying.

I was convinced that my family had a lot to offer, and I used all of our talents as best I could. I received tremendous hope and encouragement knowing that my children would walk the hallways of the new library, just as their grandmother did when she attended classes there forty years ago. This was, undoubtedly, a part of my children's heritage and a part of their future. I wanted them, and the other children of our community, to be able to say, "I helped save the Academy."

My children and many other children participated in an art and literature contest I helped organize. We had over a hundred entries from schoolchildren, and the senior citizens at senior care centers were delighted to judge the entries.

I watched my children save up their pennies for donations. Several times a month we visited the library to drop off the kids' pennies in a fish tank. Karen kept her pennies in a little teapot, Joey kept his in a little cardboard box, and our little Kate dropped as many pennies in the tank as she could hold in her little hand. This became a familiar ritual for other children as well, and they were all so proud so see the tank fill to the top.

I also helped organize a 5K run and we had hundreds of people—young, old, and also disabled—join the race to save their heritage. Seeing the faces of so many was touching to me—I felt a real sense of pride in the community that day.

The activity that touched my heart the most came during our Clean Up Academy Square Day. I watched my children happily pull weeds, sweep up muck, rake leaves, and pick up trash. I especially felt such pride seeing my two-year-old working without any complaining or groaning. There were many others by our side, neighbors, family, friends, other citizens—all volunteers doing a labor of love.

To do the job right, my father brought all kinds of yard tools and a gas-powered generator to run the electric tools. My mother helped the children plant flowers in the old abandoned fountain in front of the building. She came back faithfully twice a week for months with my children, lugging pots of water to water the flowers. The children watched those flowers thrive with tender loving care until the following autumn, when they died as all flowers do.

Finally, the day I had anticipated came. The dreadful deadline for saving the Academy building I had given my heart to was upon us. A dramatic eleventh-hour effort brought the full $6 million in—dollar by dollar, penny by penny! The entire community could celebrate this victory—individuals, families, organizations, and especially the children. It was an unforgettable time.

Because of the tireless efforts of so many, the precious legacy of my town will live. The Academy will greet a new century with children once again running through its halls, looking for books to read. I would like to think that my family made a difference in this noble effort, but more importantly, it made a remarkable difference to my family, especially my children. My children now know that what they do, what they believe in, and what they work hard for can pay off. Their efforts are important, and if they believe—they can achieve.

⊛ *Something marvelous and magical takes place when people have a goal that is larger than self, a goal that is larger than me or mine. This story beautifully illustrates that point. When we live outside ourselves in love and service we not only find ourselves, we model magnanimity of soul.*

Can you begin to imagine the impact that this mother has had on the lives of her children by involving them in such a worthy cause? Can you imagine the impact of such a vivid experience with the power of shared vision (Habit 2: Begin with the End in Mind)? Her ladder is truly leaning against the right wall. No amount of social recognition or wealth could compare to her intrinsic and transcendent achievement, the lesson that true happiness and joy come only from service and contribution.

"I don't know what your destiny will be, but one thing I know: The only ones among you who will really be happy are those who have sought and found how to serve."—Albert Schweitzer

South Bend, Indiana:
Reaching Across Generations to Better
a Community

Many have wondered how the principles of the 7 Habits could be taken to an entire community. The following account is longer than most of the stories and will require a little more effort and study, but I encourage you to put in the effort. I believe that this story will arouse a vision of what is possible in communities around the world. Notice how the key lay within the fire-lit individuals who worked within their Circle of Influence (Habit 1: Be Proactive). They worked on things they could do something about, however small or large. It illustrates the Inside-Out Approach. You will notice that it is not a story of miracles or quick fixes, but rather a slowly evolving pattern of understanding, caring, and respect between people. I am the narrator.

Fifty years ago, South Bend, Indiana, was a thriving blue-dollar industrial town. It was the home of the Studebaker line of automobiles. Most of its tax base was rooted in the automotive industry and its many tiers of suppliers. Today, South Bend is generally known as the home of Notre Dame University and aside from the Roman Catholic priests who lead that prestigious institution, the bulk of the town's workforce today is employed in white-collar service or in high-tech plastics and electronics manufacturing.

South Bend remains a diverse community, however, and not at all immune to the problems plaguing society as a whole. Single-parent households, latchkey children, and the disintegration of the extended family are at the root of many of South Bend's problems. Like many cities across America, those challenges range from juvenile crime to gang violence, teenage drug abuse, and a workforce that is ill-prepared at a time when the aging of the baby boomer generation and lower birth rates have caused increased demand for qualified workers.

In 1993, David Jarrett, a certified public accountant in South Bend, completed 7 Habits training and emerged with a mission as well as a mission statement. His mission, he decided, was "to spread the 7 Habits throughout the community."

"I was on the board of the Youth Services Bureau in South Bend and we dealt a lot with abused kids, runaways, unwed teen mothers, and troubled young people," Jarrett recounted. "I'd been on the board eight years and already I was seeing the cycle repeat itself in families. We'd been successful in helping some individuals, but breaking the cycle in which the abused become the abusers is more of a long-term challenge. We were constantly asking ourselves what we were going to do for the next generation. It seemed to me that low self-esteem played a big part in most of the problems we were seeing. I thought if we could find a way to provide young people with something that would make them feel better about themselves and their lives, it might have a greater impact on their lives and on the community."

Jarrett decided that a positive first step would be to make the 7 Habits training available to a wide range of South Bend's residents by applying for a license as a Principle-Centered Community. This process involves bringing together organizations from throughout the community and creating a vision and a plan for teaching and applying the principles of the 7 Habits at the grassroots level.

In South Bend, that meant marshaling the collective resources of the Chamber of Commerce, Notre Dame University, hospitals, nursing homes, schools, libraries, the YMCA, and a variety of local businesses and service agencies and clubs. The South Bend Chamber of Commerce became the licensee for the material, and over several years thousands of people were trained in courses offered by their employers or organizations. Jarrett became a facilitator and his public accounting firm, Crowe Chizek, has trained nearly four hundred of its employees.

Bringing Two Generations Together for a Community-Wide Win-Win

Jarrett's simple goal was to introduce the material throughout the community and plant the seeds that would take root and blossom. He understood that it was a long-term process and that the fruits would not be visible for many years, but already some very encouraging offshoots have appeared.

After one woman, Kathy Newman, went through the training in

South Bend, she saw an opportunity to apply the material in addressing two areas of concern to her. Newman is a full-time volunteer in the middle school system of South Bend. She is also the wife of Edward Newman, who is the CEO of Holy Cross Care Services, which operates three long-term elderly care facilities in this Midwestern city of 110,000 residents.

In her volunteer work in South Bend's middle schools, Kathy Newman had observed that a large number of schoolchildren appeared to be low in self-esteem, lacking direction, and highly vulnerable to negative influences. The short-term impact of this was disciplinary problems in the schools and increasing juvenile crime. The long-term impact was societal corrosion and, among other things, a generation unprepared to make a positive contribution either in the workforce or in the community.

Through her husband's career, Newman had learned that societal isolation and disengagement existed also at the other end of the generational spectrum. Many of the elderly residents in the community's nursing homes were also vulnerable for reasons related to the fragmentation of families and isolation from the community in general.

Newman was not alone in making these observations, but she was in a unique position to do something to address these problems when the opportunity arose. Shortly after South Bend was licensed as a Principle-Centered Community, she joined forces with school administrators and the Principle-Centered Community Resource program in seeking a grant from her husband's parent company, Holy Cross Health Systems, and its Mission Outreach Fund. The goal was to address problems in both generations by bringing the young and the elderly together for their mutual benefit.

Their campaign took the form of an "intergenerational enrichment initiative" that has enhanced the lives of a wide range of South Bend residents and brought national attention to this community. Launched in 1997, it is called the B.E.S.T. (Businesses Encouraging Students and Teachers) program. It features a three-pronged approach that incorporates the principles of the 7 Habits.

In the first step, specially designed 7 Habits training courses are offered to seventh- and eighth-grade students at three of the five middle schools in an effort to help them deal more effectively with relationships and their personal development. The middle school teachers at these three schools were offered the training so that they could better incorporate and reinforce the language and principles in the classroom.

Rather than teach the 7 Habits in a step-by-step course, the material was integrated into the curriculum when individual teachers found the opportunity to illustrate a principle or reinforce a particular Habit. If, for example, a student made a disparaging remark about another person, a teacher might take a moment to talk about the Emotional Bank Account and the concept of honoring those who are absent.

Eighth-grade science teacher Pat Shagdai taught the 7 Habits as life science for about forty-five minutes each week to her students at Jackson Middle School.

"In a way it was easy because the message is so much about family matters," she said. "I started with an overview and then went into each of the Habits and got the kids talking about their family lives and problems they have dealing with siblings and parents. It got to be more of a group discussion. It was like someone opening a gateway to a beautiful mountain. They were eager to talk about their lives.

"If you approach the material correctly, it seems to peel away so many of the defensive layers that people have already formed. You have to approach it as a way of talking about their lives, not as a system of rules that they have to live by."

While her students were eager to share their feelings of rejection and isolation, they were less inclined to accept responsibility for their own happiness and their own lives, Shagdai noted.

"I can teach proactivity until I am blue in the face," she said, "but we are a blame society. It is everywhere and it is deep. If you can begin chipping away at that, it makes my job in the classroom a lot easier. The 7 Habits training teaches that you have to change yourself first before you can change others, and I tell my students if they follow this philosophy their lives will change for the better."

Seeking Understanding Between Generations and Building a Sense of Self-Worth Within Them

The second component of the B.E.S.T. initiative was designed to address alienation among both young and old in South Bend by creating a program to encourage interaction between middle school students and the elderly residents of three Holy Cross health care facilities. The goal was to provide affirmation and positive reinforcement for students by giving them the opportunity to practice relationship skills, to seek understanding of another generation, and to appreciate diversity more deeply.

"Talk about beginning with the end in mind, when you are a teenager working with the elderly, it can be a wonderful way to start thinking about how you want your own life to play out," said Shagdai. "It is also a great method for practicing seeking to understand, which we did with some preliminary sensitivity training."

The program was designed also to enhance the lives and experiences of the residents of the long-term care facilities by allowing them to interact with the middle school students, and giving them the chance to establish relationships with younger members of the community and their families. This intergenerational relationship building was initiated by pairing the students in one of each of the three middle schools with the residents in one of each of the three care centers.

The third element of South Bend's B.E.S.T. program addressed concerns about the future of the workforce in the community. The B.E.S.T. program coordinators presented a health career program to make the young people aware of the town's many opportunities in a wide range of health care professions. Most of the students also participated in job shadowing in which they followed and observed health care workers over the course of their workday.

A nationwide study conducted by the Bureau of the Census in 1997 found that companies with close school involvement have a turnover rate among young employees that is as low as half that of other companies. "By actively engaging their local education systems, establishments may be helping to generate a future labor force that is more stable, more work-ready, and presumably better matched to the workplace of the future," the researchers said in a *New York Times* report.

The Power of an Expanded Vision

On paper, this all may sound rather cut-and-dried, but when several hundred South Bend middle school students took these principles on the road to an equal number of senior citizens, the results were heartwarming, inspiring, and rewarding for all concerned.

Imagine scores of animated teenagers planting flowers around nursing homes as the elderly residents offer assistance and direction. Imagine high-energy young dancers trading lessons in the Macarena step for step with seniors who then demonstrated their own generation's dance crazes—the Lindy Hop and the Jitterbug.

Imagine also the enlightenment experienced by a group of young soccer players as they discover that the frail white-haired man trading sports statistics with them is the legendary local coach for whom their soccer park was named.

Imagine the deeper understanding attained when a lesson on the Great Depression is delivered to schoolchildren not in textbooks but in the emotional reflections of men and women who were adolescents and teenagers themselves when their fathers lost their jobs, and sometimes their homes and self-respect as well.

Imagine the joy added to the final days of an elderly man's life when a group of young people find him so interesting that they beg him to return for their next meeting.

It all happened in South Bend.

"There have been so many wonderful little things that occurred that it is hard to describe. It is a look in the eye. It's a touch. It's having fourteen-year-old kids, who at first were reluctant to go into a nursing home, tell you that they don't want to leave, that they wish they had more time to listen and learn and share with the elderly residents," said Libby Bramlett-Jackson, an eighth-grade science teacher at Clay Middle School.

"I think 'seeking to understand' is the number one principle at work here," she added. "It is a key part of this entire program."

Many of the students expressed hesitancy and even fear about going into the care facilities. They didn't think they would have anything to talk about with the residents. They feared being rejected by them, or annoying them. But in the end, they learned that the elderly were often more accepting of them than they were of themselves.

"I can think of four of my guys in particular who were a little freaked out at first but I watched them go through such growth in a short period, it was amazing," said Shagdai. "We went on a bird-watching trip and to see these four guys standing outside the bus and one by one, with their heads lowered respectfully, escorting these frail people as they stepped down, I almost broke down crying. They had been so scared but they built rapport so quickly. When I told my students how proud I was, they got tears in their eyes. It was like their hearts had been touched and they weren't afraid to show it and some of them were rough-and-tumble kids."

Students in the birdwatching group, who partnered with the nursing home residents to participate in a national birding program, were particularly taken with an elderly gentleman who showed up for their first meeting wearing a coat and tie and carrying a package. The man, who had rarely left his room or socialized, stood at first to show the students his collection of old Audubon prints and then he began talking to the students about observing birds from his office window during his years as a professor at Notre Dame. Warming to his audience, he went on to inform them that he had also been a local sportscaster and the author of a book on Notre Dame, which he also displayed.

"He opened up to them and something about him really grabbed the kids," Shagdai said. "When he asked if anyone wanted an autographed copy of his book, a bunch of hands went up. I'm sure some were just being polite, but when one of the boys showed disappointment that there weren't enough copies, the man went back to his room and returned with an autographed baseball card. The kids really flipped out when they realized that it was him on the card. He had been a major league ballplayer. No one in the nursing home had known."

The elderly man seemed to feed on the energy of the young people and when they asked him to come back to subsequent meetings, he was obviously delighted. He came to two more, but before the third meeting, the home's administrators notified the school that the man had died unexpectedly.

"It really got to the kids, they were very emotional, and I was surprised, but I think there was a lesson in that, too," the teacher said.

Although some teachers had expressed concern that the barriers between young and old might prove too great, the young people seemed eager to be with adults who were not judgmental, and who leaned on them for support.

"There's a give-and-take between these two generations that is missing when middle-aged people are inserted into the equation. We take things so seriously and those two groups don't," said Kathy Newman. "When a student shows up with purple hair and a Grateful Dead T-shirt, our inclination is to send him home, but the residents get a kick out of it."

The students became especially involved with their elderly partners during an exercise in which they were asked to compile the life stories of residents at their nursing homes and then they enthusiastically expressed those life stories in a wide range of creative means.

"There was a lot of artwork. A few did dramatic presentations or songs. We had one student who was so fascinated with her resident's life story and developed so much respect for her that she quietly made a quilt with twenty or thirty story squares depicting the woman's life. She didn't tell anyone she was doing it. She simply did it out of caring and compassion and a desire to please the lady. When her teacher saw it, she was absolutely flabbergasted," said Kathy Newman. "And the resident's family said that they noticed a huge change in her social ability. Before the program with the middle schoolers, this woman, a former teacher who'd had a leg amputated, had rarely left her room, but when the young people started coming around she suddenly was up and dressed without assistance every morning. The students would find her waiting at the door in her wheelchair. She even asked her son to bring some mementos from home so she could share them with the young people. Her whole persona and attitude changed. It was wonderful to see the interaction between them."

Walking in Another's Place Can Lead to Self-Discovery

Libby Bramlett-Jackson's students were paired with the residents of Holy Cross Care and Rehabilitation Center. Like the 350 other middle schoolers who have participated in the first two years of the B.E.S.T. program, her students were first taught to understand their elderly partners, many of whom were wheelchair-bound or suffering from Alzheimer's, Parkinson's, or other debilitating illnesses of aging.

"Before they came to our facilities, the students spent a whole day in a community park involved in activities that taught them about the effects of aging while also dispelling many of the myths about the elderly," said Edward Newman. "They had wheelchair races in gravel. They wore special greased goggles to learn what it was like to view the world with cataracts. They were seeing some of the problems faced every day by the people they were going to be meeting so that they might better understand them."

Bramlett-Jackson noted that many of her students gained self-confidence and insight into their own lives as they bonded with their elderly partners in the program. Her class was named Class of the Year by the South Bend Agency on Aging for their participation in the B.E.S.T. program, which itself was selected by *Woman's Day* magazine as one of the most innovative educational programs in the country. The outside recognition was appreciated, but the internal rewards were undoubtedly far greater.

"One of our boys was very introverted, to the point that he had difficulty speaking in front of others and had not made many friends, but by the end of the year he had become much more willing to speak up and he'd even found a girlfriend," the teacher said.

Teachers were particularly struck by the transformation of another male student, Josh, a rebellious and trouble-prone eighth-grader with a gruff manner, when he bonded with the elderly residents, in particular with a woman named Violet. They were left speechless one day when they observed the boy tenderly and carefully painting Violet's fingernails for her. "Josh's attendance and grades began to improve. Finally, Josh felt effective at something—and it was carrying over into the classroom," reported one of his teachers.

For their part, Bramlett-Jackson's students said that getting to know the residents of the care facilities helped them better understand that they need not fear growing old.

"It gave me a whole 'nother outlook," said one student, fourteen. "Listening to their stories makes you think more long term about how things you do now will affect you later in life."

"A lot of kids were afraid of old people and dying and stuff but when we got to know more about them we realized it isn't so bad to grow old," noted another student, thirteen.

Increased understanding is not the only reward shared by participants in the program. Many of the residents at St. Joseph, a senior health care facility, suffer from Alzheimer's disease and other forms of dementia that have served to isolate the elderly from the rest of the world. The presence of young people willing to reach out to them has sparked new life in many of the elderly patients and it has increased the sense of community for everyone involved.

"I've seen magical things occur when the two interact and bond," Greg Perkins of St. Joseph's staff said. "Last year we had a middle school girl who came here on Valentine's Day. She hadn't been asked to the school dance and her heart was broken. Her teacher said she had been crying and was very upset. She came to visit one of our Alzheimer's patients who is nonverbal and unresponsive, but when the girl sat down with the resident, they both blossomed. The patient reached out and touched her hand as if she could tell she was distressed. It was heartwarming to see two people, young and old, respond to each other's needs.

"Now we have young people and their families coming to visit their favorite residents over Christmas and on holidays," he added. "They have bonded over and above their involvement in the school program.

"Those memories will be saved as a living history of the community and a new way of understanding life here," he said. "Everyone wins with a program like this. It is like throwing a pebble in a pond. The waves just keep expanding outward. We have created a whole new generation of concerned kids. I believe if you can create one memory of community service, it will grow and grow for many years."

🕸 *One of the important concepts I've learned in my professional work is that when people live outside themselves in love, and focus on some goal or vision which is greater than themselves, it taps into their deeper energies and motivations and unleashes the higher faculties and talents of their nature. When we get two or three or more people involved in such a common enterprise, true synergy results. The whole becomes greater than the sum of the parts—not in small ways, but in large ways. You can see the wisdom of sociologist Émile Durkheim, who said, "When mores are sufficient, laws are unnecessary; when mores are insufficient, laws are unenforceable." These kinds of norms or mores inside a group, community, or larger society represent the meta-habits of a culture. I also believe it is necessary to eventually build these mores and norms into the laws so that they become institutionalized. Then the laws represent the standard and official expectation, so that nonconforming elements in society are held accountable, while with the vast majority, these laws become essentially unnecessary.*

Lord Moulton, an early-twentieth-century British parliamentarian, talked a great deal about the third domain being the enabler of effective community life. The first domain is positive law or government, which represents force. The second domain represents individual free choice. The third domain represents the overlapping area where individuals freely choose to live by manners, civility, and values that lift and integrate a community, which keeps it unified, at peace, and in a state of constant improvement. Moulton called this middle or third domain "obedience to the unenforceable." In a sense, it is not the outside-in approach of government, but the Inside-Out Approach of individuals, volunteering to live by principle-centered values, which become the heart and soul of the critical mass that enables a healthy civil society to come about.

Back to School

SHARLEE DOXEY-STOCKDALE, SIXTH-GRADE TEACHER,
MONTE VISTA ELEMENTARY SCHOOL

FACING TRAGEDY

JUST CUT THROUGH THE BULL

STUDENTS: THE CUSTOMER?

JUST TRY DISMISSING A TENURED TEACHER

THIS CLASSROOM BELONGS TO . . . ME!

Sharlee Doxey-Stockdale, Sixth-Grade Teacher, Monte Vista Elementary School

As you study the objectives and methods of this outstanding teacher, notice how she encouraged her students not only to understand the 7 Habits, but to constantly refer to them in identifying different behaviors. A common social language is basic in culture building.

A couple of years ago, during an awards ceremony at Copper Hills High School in South Jordan, Utah, twelve students were presented with Sterling Scholar Awards for academic achievement and leadership. There was nothing unusual about the ceremony, except that one of the parents present noted that half of those students being honored had passed through the same sixth-grade teacher's classroom. They had all been my students. I hadn't been aware of that until the parent came to me and asked what my secret was for consistently turning out such high-achieving students. I told her it was no secret. It was simply the 7 Habits.

I recently put together a collection of letters handwritten by children from my classes, and while they are all very dear to me, there is one that will always strike a particular chord. It begins: *"I came to Ms. Doxey's class one of the worst panikers* [sic] *ever. I have been proactive in learning to control my panic attacks."*

This letter is from Heidi, who entered my fourth-grade class as a shy, withdrawn child whose intelligence nonetheless shone through her reticence. Still, the child was all but crippled by her fear of failure. Anytime she failed to respond correctly in class, she became distraught, crying and tormenting herself to the point that she often could not function for the rest of the school day. I have seen the situation many times in my more than thirty years in the classroom. I recognized Heidi's nervousness and emotional volatility as perfectionism. This little girl lived in great fear of failing.

Her paradigm was "I can't solve problems without help because I might make a mistake." She didn't trust herself, which is common with the gifted child. Perfectionism and fear of failure can seriously handicap bright children if they are not taught early that failure is part of the learning process. To help Heidi overcome her fears, I both modeled and taught proactivity. To help solve the problem of perfectionism, I have a poster on the wall showing the 7 Habits. This I present as "The Rules of the Room" and from the first day of class each year, I model the Habits and define what I am doing so that the students begin to understand. I go through the vocabulary and tell the students that these are the rules that govern our class. I also send a paper home to each of their parents explaining the Habits. The second week of school I ask the children to bring back examples from home for each Habit. In class, I consistently incorporate the Habits into my teaching by modeling them and by using examples in the curriculum. For example, when I identify a problem and begin to work on a solution, I tell them, "I am being proactive now" or "I am beginning this with the end in mind." I also have the children verbalize when they are being proactive or ask them questions such as, "If you were going to be proactive, how would you respond?" Students find proactive behaviors in stories, in history lessons—even in math! Every subject can model the Habits.

Heidi had to overcome her learned behavior, which was primarily reactive, so for the first few weeks of school she was often frustrated by these exercises based on the 7 Habits. When she discovered she'd left a book at home the second week of school, she panicked. When she burst into tears, I said to her, "Let's look at the problem together." I listened to her talk about it and then I asked, "Now, what Habit am I practicing?"

She said, "You are seeking to understand what the problem is."

Then I asked, "What Habits are going to help you solve this problem?" She couldn't identify how to proceed, so we talked about being proactive, and what the possibilities were for her in this instance.

In the following weeks, I walked Heidi and the other students in the class through similar scenarios dozens of times with the goal of making them second nature. This was very difficult at first because panic was so ingrained as her response, but little by little she began to transform from a problem spotter to a problem solver.

To help the students understand the 7 Habits more clearly, I set up an Emotional Bank Account system. I give out little printed points certificates to reward appropriate behaviors such as problem solving, prioritizing, or proactive behavior. I also award them when the children make deposits into each other's Emotional Bank Accounts by being kind or thoughtful. I use these points as a physical reinforcement for using the Habits. Students can use the points for privileges or as makeup for a late assignment or a low score.

I encourage students to analyze their behavior in terms of the 7 Habits and I emphasize that students are expected to live the principles in my classroom. In social studies or math we find examples of the Habits being used. I integrate them into every lesson. The students quickly learn.

If a student says that his homework isn't done because his mother made him go to bed early, I call that "mommy dumping" and tell him it is an unacceptable solution. They pick up on that and become quick to identify the mommy dumpers and the proactive problem solvers.

To build self-awareness, I conduct role-playing sessions in which the children act out scenarios—playing the role of historical figures, novel characters, parents, and children—and identify behaviors that are not in alignment with the 7 Habits. It doesn't take them long to figure out that the problem wasn't that Mom made them go to bed, it was that they didn't put first things first and do the homework instead of playing.

I also have a problem board that students can sign. It entitles them to a private conference with me to resolve problems. If they left their homework at home, we work out a win-win solution but I require them to have evidence, such as a note from a parent saying that they did the work but forgot to put it in their book bag. If they come up with the evidence and a solution then there is no late penalty because they have been proactive. But if they don't have the assignment, and they don't have evidence, a zero is earned. They learn to be proactive, and also learn that there are negative consequences as well as positive ones for decisions.

Through this daily exposure to proactive behavior and the 7 Habits, Heidi slowly began to understand that she had a choice to rise above circumstances and to apply her intelligence in far more beneficial and satisfying ways.

One day six or seven weeks into the school year, she came to me with a solution instead of a problem. When she dared to take that risk, to come to me with her solution, I knew she had experienced a breakthrough. I witnessed many such moments since with her and hundreds of other children. I had the pleasure of working with Heidi again in sixth grade. She still uses the Habits!

Usually about halfway through a school year, the students will look at their own behavior and say, "I didn't put first things first when I played instead of doing my homework." They reach a level of awareness where they can identify the behavior that caused the problem; to me, that is an incredible step. I've even had parents tell me that students go home and scold their brothers and sisters for not synergizing enough or for not seeking to understand each other! They have internalized the Habits.

The letters my students have written offer the greatest testimony to the effectiveness of modeling and teaching the Habits. Here are a few more samples from those letters from my fourth-grade class:

I sought to understand then to be understood when we were doing comprehension cards and my partner was being slow. I asked her why she was being slow doing the cards. She said that she just read slow. Then I understood.

I begin with the end in mind when before I play I clean and do homework.

I have been proactive at doing my homework. I was one of the kids who never did it. I have gotten real good scores now.

Think win-win. When I play I always think I'll play a good game, I don't care if I lose.

Seek to understand then to be understood. I have started to see what other people want to do, it's not just what I want to do.

When I put first things first . . . I go to the store and I get the most important things first and always get candy last.

There was a teacher standing at the front of the room. I could not see the white board. So instead of asking the teacher to move it, I did. That was an example of proactivity. One time we had a pioneer trek and our handcart fell over and we synergized and cleaned it up.

My sister wanted something of mine and I wanted something of hers. So I made a deal with her and we both won!

Think win-win. My friend and I were playing basketball and we kept passing to each other and we won the game!

I've had a great deal of career satisfaction since I began using the 7 Habits in the classroom. I'm not always successful with every child, but my goal each year is to teach myself out of a job, to teach the youngsters to become independent so that they don't need a teacher, so that they are ready for life. It turns kids like Heidi, who was paralyzed by her fear of failure, into problem solvers and into functioning people who will take risks because they understand that failure is not a dead end. It gives the children the power to govern themselves, and if we teach them to govern themselves and expect them to do it, they will do it.

Incorporating the Habits in the classroom has produced classes that are delightful to work with all year long. No longer am I a stressed-out teacher trying to control thirty children. They are controlling themselves and synergizing with each other and with me. Together we are soaring! My work has become much more enjoyable because we synergize.

Instead of being the sage on the stage, I'm the guide on the side, and that is energizing. I don't have to know all the answers: my job is to help the students discover the answers for themselves and that gives us both a great deal more satisfaction. They are becoming problem-solving citizens of the world.

✳ *In his brilliant book* A Guide for the Perplexed, *E. F. Schumacher identifies four levels of being and their unique characteristics: the first level, rock, which is mineral; the second level, plant, which is mineral plus life; the third level, animal, which is mineral plus life plus consciousness; the fourth level, human, which is mineral plus life plus consciousness plus self-awareness, which is the ability to think about your thinking. Self-awareness is the least cultivated of the four unique human gifts (self-awareness, imagination, conscience, and independent will). Yet the more it is cultivated, the larger the space* between stimulus and response becomes. People are no longer a product of their genes, their parents, or their present relationships and circumstances. They are a product of their choices in response to these things. The more people train themselves in the language of self-awareness, the more it is cultivated. Words are symbols of meaning; they are tools for ideas. People cannot think outside of their vocabulary. Just try it and you will see how your thinking is confined to your language.

When this marvelous teacher trained her students in the language of proactivity, Emotional Bank Account, and other positive behaviors, both their awareness and their behavioral repertoire increased. Also, when people move from being unconsciously effective to being consciously effective they can teach the principles to others by both precept and example. Such conscious effectiveness increasingly cultivates independence, rather than continued dependence upon a teacher. It also deepens understanding of why a principle works and why a particular practice that is not based upon a principle does not work. It's no wonder that so many of Sharlee Doxey-Stockdale's students were recognized for their outstanding performance!

Facing Tragedy

*Notice how this school superintendent exercised self-awareness the
very second he heard of the tragic accident. Because he was able to
observe his own involvement through the whole experience, his
catalytic leadership enabled him to flow with reality and adapt to
whatever needs arose with great caring and empathy.*

I am a school superintendent. One afternoon, just an hour before
school let out, a six-year-old child ran off the playground into the
street where she was struck and killed by a semi. As a superintendent, there is no textbook or manual to tell you how to handle this.
The first thought in my mind as I was walking out to the accident
was, "Be Proactive [Habit 1]."

When I arrived at the scene, I found a young newspaper reporter
there. He was taking pictures of the incident, and asking the kinds of
questions that just stir up everybody's emotions. I didn't want that.
So I asked him to leave. I know that some might say everybody had a
right to see those pictures splashed across the evening newspaper.
But we had lost a child here. I didn't want to turn the tragedy of this
child's death into a tabloid report to the public. Our school and
kindergarten class had lost a friend. We needed ample time for the
community to come to grips with this loss. Subsequently, I shared my
comments and the statements of the witnesses with a local newspaper that was more sensitive to the emotional nature of this situation.

During this tragic afternoon, I felt the power of Seek First to Understand, Then to Be Understood. For me to be of any help to the parents of the child, to the faculty, the other students and their parents, I
needed to know what their needs were. I was in almost hypersensi-
tive listen-and-plan mode.

That afternoon, I had to view the body of the child on the road (I
had nightmares for several weeks afterward). Then I had to go with
the Highway Patrol to tell the child's parents. I realized people
needed to be able to talk about the experience in a sympathetic group.
As hard as it was, I met with the staff personally to talk about the
tragedy. We immediately formulated a letter to send home to the parents of all 550 students that same afternoon. We told them that we
had experienced a terrible accident, so would they "Please, under-

stand if your child comes home upset." Later that afternoon, I brought the supervisors on duty who witnessed the accident to my office. We took their statements there. They were already under a lot of stress, and taking care of it quickly meant that the next day they didn't have to recall it all over again.

That night we assembled a team of eighteen counselors and ministers to provide mass counseling for the students and teachers. The next morning, all of these professionals were in the library and we held a formalized session. We scheduled three debriefing sessions with the staff. We were being proactive to provide every classroom an on-site counselor to deal with the grief and pain of this dreadful accident.

One member of the school board mentioned to me that legal action might be taken against the district and me personally. I told him I was ready to accept that responsibility, should it happen. It did not. He told me later that he was so amazed at the way I handled this event that he went out and bought the 7 Habits book to see where I learned how to behave in such a situation. Instead of reacting to this tragedy, we acted in the face of it. Everything I did in those two days was done because I wanted to gain control over what was a devastating death, and what could have been a devastating trauma to the community. I think because we acted so quickly and calmly many fears were allayed and hearts started to heal a whole lot quicker than they otherwise might have.

⊗ *There is a time to involve others and a time to simply take control. This superintendent first got complete control over himself and then took control of the situation. When you act fast and are full of wisdom and compassion in a crisis situation, people identify with you. They want direction, leadership, comfort, and help. They have been humbled by the force of the circumstances and by the depth of their grief. Your assessment of a situation may tell you to stop listening and to simply act. Sometimes being proactive means you choose not to act. Sometimes it means subordinating your feelings to your values and doing that which is right. In every case, whether taking action or not, each response requires initiative and strength of character.*

Just Cut Through the Bull

This is the story of a difficult, complicated, even disastrous family-school situation. Notice the difference between the failure of the outside-in approach and the success of the Inside-Out Approach.

An incredible thing happened to our family when my daughter, Kelsey, entered fourth grade. Within the first few months, she became a different child. A typical conversation went something like this:

I asked, "How was your day?" She answered in one-word sentences, "Fine." I persisted, "Well, what did you do?" or "What did you learn?" She said, "Nothing." If she did decide to talk about school, it would always be in negatives, "So-and-so made fun of me today."

When we asked to see her work, she wasn't eager to hold up her pictures. She didn't want to share the stories she had written. All her homework papers came home wadded up in her backpack or remained crumpled in her desk at school.

Things progressed to the point where my wife, Terry, and I had to actually walk Kelsey to school. She started waking up "sick" every morning. After school, if we could get her to go, she just sat and watched TV or went to her room and shut the door. Previously she was a happy child so this behavioral change was unsettling.

Eventually, we figured out it was probably something to do with school. We asked the school to test her in reading and math. To our amazement Kelsey tested two grade levels behind. We couldn't believe it. The school had just promoted her to fourth grade. Didn't they pick up that she was behind? We were so angry that at the first couple of meetings we just vented our frustration. I know it didn't help our cause at all. When you call the third-grade teacher and the principal inept and uninterested, you don't build a strong foundation to work from. Ironically, while we were expending all this energy to make things right, things just got worse for Kelsey. She'd say to us, "I'm stupid. I don't belong in fourth grade."

Even my relationship with my wife began to suffer. When I got home from work, she and I took long walks to talk privately about what was happening, what our course of action should be. Sometimes we walked three or four miles. We'd end up arguing about what to do and have to walk home in silence. We wrote letters, made phone calls, sat through meetings, talked with other parents. Nothing seemed to work. We couldn't create a positive learning experience for our child by ourselves.

One day I suggested to my wife that we try to think win-win [Habit 4]. We asked ourselves, "What steps can we take to have a more positive influence over this situation?" We looked again at the situation, trying to see it with new eyes, trying to understand all those involved [Habit 5: Seek First to Understand, Then to Be Understood]. We realized teachers were under tremendous pressure to solve a myriad of problems. We wanted to make sure we weren't pointing the finger unfairly. We questioned ourselves. Maybe the problem was with us. Maybe we weren't giving our daughter enough support at home. Perhaps the problem was with Kelsey herself.

I suggested we write a Win-Win Agreement among us, Kelsey, and the school. Terry wanted to cut through all the "bull," as she called it. "Let's just fix the problem, Dan." So I shared with her some successful experiences, and the philosophy behind Win-Win Agreements. I showed her the win-win form with the five main points and room to write. She said she would try it.

We agreed on the desired results, getting a better learning experience for our daughter, but we were both on different paths trying to get there. I could feel the tension rising again. So I backed off. "I'll put my thoughts down. You put yours down. We'll come back later and talk, okay?"

Over the next few days, Terry wrote and rewrote several drafts. I went through the same process. Then we came together to work out the win-win. We tried to understand the situation from the school's perspective. We reviewed the school mission and vision statements. We discussed the guidelines and resources available. We identified how we were going to hold ourselves and the school accountable and what the consequences were, good and bad.

We sincerely wanted to make this a team effort. So we made another appointment with the principal and teachers (I'm sure they were just thrilled to see us walk through the door). We were a different set of parents though. This time we wanted a solution that would benefit all involved. Our emotions were under control so we could focus on the facts.

As we came to the table with this new attitude, the school administrators were willing to reexamine themselves. They realized that in some things they weren't following their mission statement. They saw the inconsistencies and the need for changing some policies. They admitted that sometimes, while trying to meet the requirements for state and federal funding, they lost their vision.

One such change was letting students retake tests so they could grow and expand their knowledge in areas they were weak. Teachers were encouraged to reflect the student's mastery level with a number, or a percentage, rather than ranking the students with a letter grade on their daily work. They altered their curriculum.

On our end, we offered to put Kelsey in private tutoring classes and agreed to sign homework assignments to demonstrate we had reviewed them. We monitored whether she needed to retake a particular test for improvement. Kelsey committed to work as hard as she could to catch up.

We didn't get everything we hoped for. The school maintained its policy not to move students out of a classroom if the student didn't get along with the teacher, unless it was the last resort. They wanted time and opportunity to work things out between the student and teacher. But, overall, the results were wonderful. Kelsey was very determined and worked through the summer until she surpassed her grade level in reading and math. Her love of learning returned and school became a fun place of instruction again, not a battlefield in a war zone.

If this couple had persisted in their outside-in approach with their child, with the school, and with their own relationship, everything would have likely continued to deteriorate. Until one understands the complexity of such family dynamics, one might simply conclude that pushing harder or adopting a positive attitude might be the solution, when in fact the real need is to go into the heart of the complexity to realize how truly simple the solution is. By simply taking an Inside-Out Approach—thinking win-win and seeking first to understand—synergy can eventually evolve.

Students: The Customer?

Sense how a student-customer focus inspired and guided the principal and faculty in this story to take one step at a time in transforming the entire educational experience.

As the principal of an alternative school, I was always looking for a curriculum that we could use to help us work together better. When I looked at the business philosophies, they all had helpful little pieces, but they didn't seem complete. Some gave us new language to use, but that wouldn't help us with our ability to work together. When I found the 7 Habits, I realized this was a more complete map: we could move from Private to Public Victories. We could learn to take responsibility for our own actions, then we could move toward our responsibility for the actions of our students [Habit 1: Be Proactive]. We could form a mission statement together as a faculty that would govern our behaviors toward others [Habit 2: Begin with the End in Mind]. I really thought these habits would help us gel together to accomplish our common goal.

In the past, our behavior as faculty had been reactive to say the least. During faculty meetings, we spent an awful lot of time looking externally, pointing fingers at each other, confessing the district's sins and parents' sins. We moaned about parents not sending kids that are ready to learn. We complained that parents don't value education, that the community wasn't willing to support us in our very taxing jobs. We griped about how permissive society had become, how kids were so disrespectful and uncivil they couldn't even learn to read. I guess you could say not much constructive was done in those faculty meetings.

When we began working with these principles, we recognized that there were things we could do besides talking about what was out in our Circle of Concern. We could be more focused on things we could do something about [Habit 1: Be Proactive]. We could deal with the kids that did show up by listening to them and adapting to what they needed, instead of complaining about the kids that weren't there [Habit 5: Seek First to Understand, Then to Be Understood]. We could be clearer about what we wanted the kids to learn [Habit 2: Begin with the End in Mind]. We could agree as a school on classroom discipline. We could be more hopeful. We could admit that maybe we didn't see the complete picture inside the school walls. Instead of thinking we were the experts, we could be humble enough to go to the families and ask them what they needed us to do.

To help us in our new approach, we developed a mission statement. We took our time because we wanted this mission statement to reflect the needs and hopes of the students, the teachers, the parents, and the community at large. We worked on it every Friday afternoon for a year. Parents, students, and businesspeople were invited to our meetings. We asked them, "What should we continue doing here?" "What should we start doing?" "What should we stop doing?"

The feedback we received was specific, insightful, and helped us improve our approach as teachers. Parents told us they would like us to hold their kids responsible, to be clear what the objectives were, but not to hassle them over trivial things. They wanted us to be more careful that when we were having a bad day we didn't take it out on the kids. They wanted more contact with the teachers, especially parents of kids that were struggling. So we took the intercom system out of the school and put a business telephone system in. Every teacher has a telephone on his or her desk so they can call parents whenever they want.

To help us better work together to meet the students' needs, the faculty agreed to have all of their preparation periods during the same period of the day so they could meet together if they needed to. That violated the union agreement, but the teachers wanted to do it. So we did. A history teacher and science teacher can now call the parents of a student and meet together with them during the same free period. Little changes like that helped us feel as if we were all working together toward this goal of a better-prepared student and citizen.

We noticed some students were being kept home during school hours. So we asked the parents why their children were not in school. They said they had to keep their older kids home on occasion to tend younger brothers and sisters while they worked. How can you fault a parent for trying to put bread on the table? Instead of criticizing them, we asked how we could make this a win-win. In business terms, we were open to new insights that allowed us to change our delivery system in the market.

We developed remarkable new levels of customer service. Because we understood the parents' situation, we tried to think of new ways to deliver education to these families. We sent teachers into the students' homes. Kids could do computer lessons over the phone lines. We developed a complete home study curriculum for periods of time when a student needed to tend kids at home while a parent was on a graveyard shift. When the students returned to class they brought in completed lessons that the classroom teacher was willing to accept. They could pick up where they left off.

We began to understand our students' concerns about education. So we made changes that were beneficial to them and allowed them to learn at their own rate. Not all kids could learn the Civil War in the same ten weeks. Instead of saying you didn't do it in this ten weeks so you get an F, we considered them not yet finished. As soon as they could demonstrate mastery, then they were finished. The win for our kids was they were feeling good, that they could show they had learned the material successfully. We allowed kids to pass their high school credits with what some call authentic assessment. The kids said they wanted ways to demonstrate to us that they knew the material other than sitting an hour in a seat taking a written test. They wanted to come up with real-world ways to show competency. Because we tested our kids in a different way, we gave ourselves permission to say, "The national standardized testing does not ask our kids to demonstrate competency the way we have. It is reasonable that the test scores have not gone up very much." However, the scores did not go down.

Among the faculty, we decided we needed fewer policies and procedures implemented to maintain control. All meetings became voluntary. If you weren't at the meeting we tried to develop a culture where people didn't say, "Where's so-and-so?" We wanted to communicate the feeling that if they weren't at the meeting, there must be a good reason. They are professionals. Not everybody wanted to participate, but we stopped focusing on the few who didn't and started focusing on the majority of faculty that were there faithfully. The others either came along and improved, or they stayed the way they were, but things didn't get worse. The culture got better because of the energy and excitement of working together and because of the mission statement, which centered us.

We communicated our larger vision by opening the school building to all the teachers. Everybody had a passkey that could open any of the doors. That built a much higher level of trust. We unlocked the copy machine. Now anybody could make copies anytime they wanted. It wasn't unusual to see students in the copy room working for their teachers. Amazing respect was built among faculty members. One exchange I remember would have been unheard of a couple years ago. One department said to the other, "Well, you've really wanted new textbooks longer than we have. Why don't you get them with this year's budget, and we'll use the budget next year for our books." Instead of fighting over scarce resources we began to grow a co-mission culture. We really believed we were all here for the same reason.

As a result of our using the 7 Habits and trying to implement the principles, we had increased graduation, increased attendance, and an increased number of families wanting their kids to come to our school. I think we started to think like a business: These are our customers, we deliver a service. What is the best way we can go about doing that? That was a fun transformation to be a part of.

🕸 *In a very real sense there are only two roles in any organization, customer and supplier, and interestingly, we are all simultaneously customers and suppliers. As the reader of this book, you are my customer, and I am your supplier of stories and ideas around those stories. You are a supplier to the customers you serve. Owners are suppliers, bankers are suppliers, employees are suppliers, suppliers are suppliers. Everybody is a supplier, but each is simultaneously a customer as well. The essence of all organizational life is the quality of the relationship between customers and suppliers. Everything else is minutiae, or the fruits of that relationship.*

The essence of leadership is to build a culture with shared vision and a principle-centered value system. Once such vision and values are embedded into the hearts and minds of the people and into the norms of the culture, then the management problem is essentially solved. People will manage themselves because they have within them the criteria for decision making. The establishment of those criteria is leadership.

Just Try Dismissing a Tenured Teacher

Evaluating someone is very difficult and usually causes more problems than it solves. That is why many people don't do it. They simply won't participate in performance appraisal processes. If they do, it's done in either a superficial, mechanical way so that the threat isn't present, or in a very officious and formal way so that no authentic human interaction takes place. This dilemma usually creates a division between the formal and informal organization so that the norms don't support the formal rule. Unionism and other forms of collective resistance usually follow. This story represents a powerful third alternative.

In our high school, every faculty member, staff employee, and administrator has been through the 7 Habits training together. This has taken us three years but the results have been worth it. We function in what I like to call an empowering culture. Even then, some faculty members find it hard to live up to the agreements they have had a part in making, which is particularly hard to deal with.

One situation comes to mind:

Each year in place of teacher evaluations, our administration initiates Win-Win Agreements [Habit 4: Think Win-Win]. As part of the process, a teacher is asked to perform a particular service for the school in compliance with state regulations, e.g., teach three sections of classical civilization and one section of Latin. In return, we ask each teacher: "If we could do something better this year, what would you want it to be? What could we do that would add value to your experience teaching at this school?" They'd respond something like, "I would like to be able to develop a space module in my free period. I need some financial support for that." Together, the teacher and the administration would work out an agreement that allowed both sides to benefit. At the end of each year, or whenever assessment was required, we used the accountability section of the Win-Win Agreement to determine whether the promises had been met.

Because of this new approach and the new levels of involvement, the faculty and staff essentially became self-reporters. They would constantly be monitoring their own progress. I hardly ever had to go in, observe, and do a formal assessment unless they asked me to observe them for the purpose of giving feedback. These Win-Win Agreements changed our attitude toward improving performance. Before, the mandate to improve had always descended from on high. Now, the teachers were the impetus for their own changes. They got to determine how they were going to improve.

One year we had a faculty member who could not account for her stewardship under the Win-Win Agreement. She was our special education teacher and so was responsible for keeping accurate records of treatments, programs, and time. We were legally bound to keep these records for the state and federal government. She just couldn't do it. She could not get the files into compliance with state and federal regulations. I think she really wanted to do it. She just couldn't. Her inability to keep these records had severe repercussions: parents wouldn't know what treatment their kids were receiving; kids could conceivably receive inappropriate, even harmful, programs; government money could be suspended because of noncompliance.

So I met with her to try to help her get organized. I met with her three times. That means we crafted three Win-Win Agreements. She actually said three different times, "Okay. This will work. I feel happy with this. I can do this." Then she'd not follow through on her agreement. After the third time, I decided to recommend that we not renew her contract the following year. The children could not be harmed because of her inability to follow through on her agreements. Even if she did have tenure.

So we moved into a mentoring remediation process. In this process, the main goal is to improve the skills of the teacher through training and support. Once the union saw the three Win-Win Agreements, they realized that we had in good faith worked with this particular teacher to improve her skills. Normally, when a school tries to remove a tenured teacher, the discussion gets heated. But the union was supportive of our position. They could see this woman would not, or could not, account for her failure to live up to her personally crafted contract.

After six more months of trying to work with her, she still was not in compliance. So when I said, "I don't think we'll renew her contract this next year," the union was supportive of our position. They allowed us to find her a different position within the district. In fact, if we hadn't been able to find her that position, they would have allowed us to fire her. That's how strongly documented our case was. To this teacher's credit, she found work in a mental health unit for teenagers, where her skills were a natural fit.

I learned something really valuable about Win-Win Agreements through this experience. When they are crafted well, they are powerful. They help people choose their very own best way. They hold them accountable for results, not just methods. They also increase an individual's responsibility for his or her performance. Sometimes a person gets paid for undergoing the process no matter what the results are. These Win-Win Agreements helped us be more results-oriented. They helped us see whether the process really elicited the results. And if it didn't, these agreements were a vehicle for faculty and administration to figure out a way to get the results both needed.

⊗ *Win-Win Agreements take a lot of courage and a lot of kindness—in short, a lot of integrity. Integrity is the foundation that enables you to be both courageous and kind at the same time. This kind of integrity enables you to carry on a win-win discussion—you don't give in and go for lose-win, you don't throw your weight around and go for win-lose, and you don't give up and go for no deal. All good relationships are based upon the five elements of a Win-Win Agreement: desired results, guidelines, resources, accountability, and consequences. They can be formally written up or informally carried in the hearts of those involved. I've found that they can deal with almost any conceivable contingency, personality, or relationship. The key is to make them clear, tailored to the people involved, and flexible. It's an open psychological-social contract, not a closed formal legal one.*

This Classroom Belongs to . . . Me!

Every teacher in deeply troubled schools and neighborhoods should carefully study the following story. In fact, any leader, parent, or teacher dealing with a difficult, challenging situation should study this story. Notice four things as you do. First, notice how this teacher gained trust by being an example before attempting to build relationships. Second, notice his depth of sincerity and integrity in building relationships. Third, notice how he constantly developed third alternatives. The students were used to either strong authoritarian rule or "everything goes" permissiveness, but this teacher made trust a verb by involving them and giving them responsibility inside their Circle of Influence. Fourth, notice how he constantly affirmed their potential, taught them principles, and helped them experience the power of vision.

After I graduated from college with a degree in secondary education my first teaching job was in a junior high school that served an extremely poor, gang-infested, crime-ridden neighborhood.

I believe that only poverty of the spirit can diminish a young person's ability to learn. There are scores of incredible schools and great teachers in poor inner-city and rural areas around the country. Unfortunately, I found that at this school, many teachers had surrendered any hope of making a difference in the lives of their students.

I was fresh out of college and I still believed that change begins from within, often with one small gesture after another. And so I did not worry about what existed all around me at the junior high. I focused instead on the positives and also on those things that were within my power to change in spite of existing conditions [Habit 1: Be Proactive]. But, in truth, I felt I didn't have a lot of choices.

On my first day, the principal showed me my classroom. It was painted a depressing pink and green, but it was a big room on the third floor with a lot of space, so I decided to take it. I asked the principal if I could get some of the broken and missing ceiling tiles replaced and if I could get the room painted. He just kind of laughed and said they couldn't do that now. I then asked if I could undertake the remodeling project myself. "Okay, just don't tell anybody," he said.

I purchased all of the paint, brushes, rollers, and new ceiling tiles with my own money and set to work. A lot of the classrooms were terribly run-down, so the building custodian and principal were amazed at how good the room looked with a fresh coat of paint. I cleaned the room and repaired a dozen desks so the writing surface and seats would stay on. To liven up the room, I added bulletin boards, posters, and pictures of everything under the sun including two Einstein posters, van Gogh's *Starry Night*, and posters of basketball heroes like Dr. J, Michael Jordan, Kareem Abdul-Jabbar, and Magic Johnson. I was teaching U.S. history at the time so I had pictures of the presidents above the chalkboard in a time line. I wanted to help them start dreaming about who they could become [Habit 2: Begin with the End in Mind].

One of the most significant additions I made to the classroom was a sign that, in effect, notified my students and fellow teachers that this room was within a Circle of Influence that we controlled. At the beginning of the year, the sign said, "This classroom belongs to Mr. Roberts," but as the students progressed by doing well on tests or making good grades, I added their names to the ownership sign. I wanted them to feel that this classroom belonged to them, too, so that they could take pride in it and in their accomplishments.

My approach attracted both those who shared my philosophy and supported it, and those who were leery of it. My first ally was the school's maintenance engineer, who saw the value in creating a positive environment for students. Anything I needed, he would help me out. He knew I tried to take care of the classroom and not tear it up.

From the first day of classes, I worked to win the students' trust and the most effective way I found to do that was to show them that I was sincerely interested in their welfare. Shortly after school started a heat wave hit. It was 98 degrees with incredible humidity. Our floor, the third, is the hottest part of the building. At one point, I went to the hallway to get a drink and discovered that the water in the fountain was warm. I was dying of thirst but I couldn't very well have something cold to drink without sharing it with the students, who were also suffering in the heat. So I went down to the cafeteria and out of my own pocket bought a bunch of Sunny Delight fruit drink. The cafeteria managers wondered what I was up to and when I walked into the classroom carrying a tray of Sunny D, the kids were shocked, too. It was as if they couldn't understand why somebody would do something for them.

Another gesture that helped improve the classroom environment was our quote of the day. I would take a positive or uplifting quote and write it on the chalkboard, and that was our thought for the day. We'd discuss it for the first five or ten minutes of class. It got things off to a positive start. It made them feel good and think in a positive light. In fact, they liked it so much they started bringing quotes to me.

These were small gestures, but they helped further the difficult process of building trust in a culture permeated by despair. I was able to really build some good relationships right from the beginning but it was not easy at all. There were kids who didn't care about anything and often it seemed like the system had given up on them, too. The principal told us not to fail kids, just to keep passing them on through the grades.

The school's administration also gave in when it came to discipline within its classrooms and hallways. The principal didn't do anything unless there was a serious fight or a weapon was involved. I had students who were being loud and obnoxious or wouldn't cooperate and I'd take them down to the principal but he'd refuse to do anything. He'd tell me to call their parents myself, putting the problem right back in my lap. It was a struggle to maintain order under those circumstances, which is why one of the first things I did was let my kids know that their behavior would determine how the class worked. I told them we could do a lot of fun things but if they got out of control, then we wouldn't be doing them. I gave them the responsibility, which is the essence of learning to become proactive.

I think that approach surprised them. You could look in the eyes of most of the students and see a light come on. Some thought it was the neatest thing they'd ever heard of. Others were "Oh yeah, whatever." And some just didn't care what happened. In an attempt to get more students to view education as a way to elevate their lives, I had them write Personal Mission Statements, of a sort [Habit 2: Begin with the End in Mind].

I told them to take out a pencil because we were going to have a quiz. They were all upset at first, saying I was crazy, but they got interested with the first question: "What year will you graduate from high school?" Some of them needed a little time to even figure that out. Then I asked them where they would be going to college, what jobs they would have, where they would want to live, whether they would marry and have kids, and finally, how each of them would like to be remembered after they die.

Some of the kids made fun of it, claiming exorbitant things they never could accomplish. Some took it seriously, though, and after they had answered all the questions, we talked about it. To show the mind-set of the kids that I was dealing with, only about five saw themselves living outside of this city. They'd never seen anything else. They thought any chance of going to college was nonexistent. That was one thing I set about to change. From that point, every time I had an opportunity I would refer to their finishing high school and going on to college. I tried to say that at least once a day to them, just drill that into their heads like that expectation was drilled into mine as I was growing up.

The mission statement exercise disguised as a quiz proved to be a first step toward drawing the class together. It created a possibility, an expectation, and the first seeds of a new sense of self-worth and vision for their future. It was a small step, and its impact was not the same on each student, but I could see that at least some of the students were slowly starting to view the world differently.

Of course, there were some hard-core cases that were far more difficult to reach. I had some rude awakenings with some of my students. One day, I gave out a short exam of twenty-five questions. This one student with a juvenile record didn't even look at it. He wrote his name on it and then added his own grade, "zero F plus," before handing it back to me. Then he put his head down on the desk and went to sleep.

I looked at the exam and at him and wondered, "How do I get through to him? What can I do to help him?" Looking around the room, there were many students with that attitude and because of them, I really didn't do much testing because they were conditioned to accept failure. Instead I'd have them do reviews of the material in the form of game shows in which the winners were rewarded for knowing the answers. But I knew something was getting through to these students. Some would be out dealing drugs in the morning, would come to my class in the middle of the day, and then would go back out.

There were other students who were eager for the opportunity to rise above their circumstances. There were six kids that I took a special, almost adoptive, interest in. One doesn't know who his dad is and his mother died during childbirth. He could well have become the worst kid in America because he bounces back and forth between two aunts' homes, but he is an honor roll student. I saw that he was acting out because of boredom. He'd complete his assignments quickly and then create problems. It came easier for him so I tried to offer him more. I'd also take him out for a hamburger now and then to offer him some of the things he wasn't getting socially.

I came to understand that often my students were forced to focus on survival rather than self-improvement through learning. Most joined gangs. Some were required to sell drugs on the streets. It was not unusual for our students to be involved in a shooting. My students would tell me they wanted to stay out of trouble, but in their situation, they were in trouble a lot. I had to learn to deal with the different neighborhood factions. I learned to spot trouble brewing and, when I could, I tried to stop it. They'd tell me the whole story over pizza and I'd tell them that if it got violent someone would get arrested or the violence would escalate.

Often if there was something going on outside the school that was disturbing to the students, I would invite the students to work through their feelings. I would tell the kids, If you have a problem with another student, don't fight about it, talk to me about it, talk to somebody about it. I'd tell them that if they knew somebody has a weapon they could shoot you or they could shoot your best friend. There were three times in my two years here that students came to me and said someone had a gun. I'd always try to resolve the tensions by sitting down and just listening and talking with them [Habit 5: Seek First to Understand, Then to Be Understood].

Some of the other teachers came to resent my approach. Because I was observant of the gang activity in the school, some students even suspected I was with the police. The administrator who probably disliked me the most was in charge of the Title I money the school got each year from the federal government. It was about a half-million dollars but if I'd ask to go on field trips with the students, he'd say no. I asked for maps in the classroom, he'd say no. So I went out and spent about a thousand dollars on maps myself. I took the students on a hundred-mile trip to Shiloh, the Civil War battlefield, and had a disciplinary note placed in my permanent file because I violated procedure. I footed the bill for all but six of the kids. I wanted to take another trip to a black history museum but was turned down. Another teacher was told to take her class instead. It was tough.

I didn't always win, but when I did see a student break through it was a great feeling. Seeing one of them have just one little ray of light in their life, seeing them progress in class, I loved that. I enjoyed being someone they could turn to to listen and trust and be honest with. I also had a great experience with some of them when we went to a Chicago Bulls and Portland Trail Blazers exhibition game in their city. I took five kids who got to sit courtside, meet all of the players, and get autographs, thanks to a helpful and generous general manager. My kids interacted with the other kids well. They were friendly and happy. It's significant because one day they will be in the workplace and they have to learn how to interact with all kinds of people.

Because I took the time to really get to know my students, I reaped the rewards. They came to feel I understood them and that I was willing to be influenced by them, so they were willing to be influenced by me. Once that trust was established, it became easier to teach them to practice synergy by working together—a skill that could be vital to their survival in the world of work. We would do a lot of things in a group setting, teaching them to work with two or three people and share responsibility. We'd do exercises in which they had to work as a team and struggle and use each other's individual talents for the benefit of the group [Habit 6: Synergize].

I left this junior high position after two years to teach at a less troubled school in the same city, but I will never forget that school and my experiences there. Already I remember those small victories far more than the failures or the difficult times. I was just thinking about an eighth-grade girl in my fourth-period history class of my first year. She had failed one grade before. She had also been in trouble for fighting and cutting classes. She came from a troubled family. She was quiet and didn't turn in a lot of her work but out of my 150 students that year, I'll always remember her.

In the first six weeks of school she did poorly, probably less than 50 percent, but as a new teacher, I didn't want to start off by giving anyone a failing grade. I told her I wanted to give her a chance to improve. She was very thankful. She promised to work harder. She did not miss an assignment the rest of the year. She went right to the top of the class. Not only did she improve in my class, but she started excelling in the rest of her classes. In the second semester, she made honor roll for the first time in her life. She became a leader in the classroom. She volunteered for everything. She even began helping other students who were struggling.

By the end of the school year, her name was on the classroom plaque that said "This classroom belongs to . . ." because she had taken ownership of a much brighter future. Even after she was no longer taking my class, she would come and show me her report card. She really turned her life around and went from being someone who was in trouble a lot, to being one of the better students and very popular. In fact she began feeling so good about herself that she looked into modeling classes. She is now in high school and doing well. She is working at McDonald's, too. I know because I gave her a recommendation and took her to her training classes because her mother doesn't have a car. Best of all, she is setting a good example for her younger brothers and sisters.

I gave her a journal at the end of the school year and told her to write down her daily thoughts all summer. She filled it up and now every six months I go to Barnes & Noble and get her another one. She feels good enough about herself that now she can write things and share them. She's a fantastic success story. She's come out of the shadows because she really caught a vision.

Trying to get these kids to see themselves in a good light was a challenge. Many were convinced that all they were ever going to do was be on welfare. They didn't care about graduating from high school or getting a job or going to college or anything like that. My goal was to get all of my students feeling good about themselves, even if it was for just an hour in the classroom. Then perhaps they could build upon that. I wanted them to realize that they have value, that no matter what kind of background they came from, they had value.

⊗ *Two very powerful movies were made on the same pattern evidenced in this amazing story*—Stand and Deliver, *starring Edward James Olmos, and* To Sir with Love, *starring Sidney Poitier. Both movies dealt with very challenging and troubled kids and with teachers who learned and modeled the same principles. The teacher in this story had hope and infused it into the souls of his students. His classroom was an island of excellence in a sea of mediocrity. He created value by investing himself, sacrificing, and being willing to listen. He valued these troubled teenagers until they came to see value in themselves. The greatest gift we give others is helping them discover who they really are.*

4

Workplace

All true and lasting change occurs from the inside out.

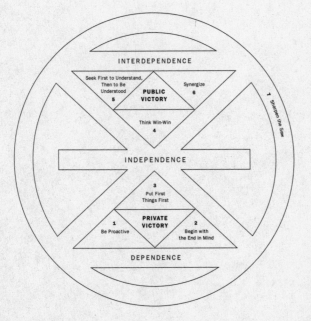

Increasing Your Influence

NINETY DAYS

IF LOOKS COULD KILL

I'VE TRIED FOR MONTHS TO OFFEND YOU

DO YOU JUST NOT LIKE WORKING HERE?

GOSSIP ADDICTION

Ninety Days

Notice the metamorphosis this person goes through from fear to exercising some courage. See if it doesn't give you courage to take hold of your situation and improve it in some way.

When I came on board as director of human resources, I heard horror stories about what my boss was like. I was actually in his office when he lost his temper with an employee. If words had edges, the employee would have been standing in a pool of his own blood. I vowed then and there never to get on my boss's bad side. Nothing, not even the greatest frustration or biggest legal action, was worth running into him on a bad day. I made good on that promise. I spoke nicely to him in the hallways. I had all my reports in on time to his secretary. I made sure I wasn't one of the last people out of the office for lunch so he wouldn't single me out. I didn't even want to play golf with him in case I beat him.

A short time later, I started seeing myself in all my cowardly glory. I was consumed with things on the job that I had no control over. I'd spend precious creative energy devising solutions to problems that hadn't even happened yet. Because I was scared, I wasn't giving the company my best effort. I wasn't an agent of change. In fact, the only change I felt comfortable instituting was me changing to another company. I even had an interview scheduled.

Ashamed of myself, I canceled that interview and committed to focusing on my Circle of Influence for just ninety days [Habit 1: Be Proactive]. I began by deciding I wanted above all to create a sound relationship with my boss [Habit 2: Begin with the End in Mind]. We didn't have to be best buddies, but we did have to interact like colleagues. So with that goal in mind, I returned to the office thinking, "Just ninety days. I'll give it my all for just ninety days."

One day my boss came into my office. After some discussion and after swallowing and practicing the words in my head a few times, I said: "By the way, what can I be doing to help you be more effective here [Habit 5: Seek First to Understand, Then to Be Understood]?"

He was perplexed. "What do you mean?"

I forged bravely on. "What can I do to alleviate some of the pressure that you have in your job? It's my job to make sure your job gets easier." I gave him a big, sort of nervous, please-don't-think-I'm-weird smile. I'll never forget the look on his face. That was really the beginning point of our relationship.

At first, I was asked to do just little things, things I couldn't really screw up, like "Type this memo up for me" or "Do you mind making this call for me?" After six weeks of doing that, he came to me and said, "I understand with your background you know workers comp pretty well. Do you mind working on this aspect of insurance? Our rates are high, see what you can do." It was the first time he had asked me to do anything that had a significant impact on the organization. I took a $250,000-a-year premium and got it reduced to $198,000. Plus I got them to waive the fee for terminating midstream on our contract by negotiating over some mishandled claims. This was an additional savings of $13,000.

Once when we had a disagreement I proved to him that it stayed behind closed doors. He didn't hear about it later on from the marketing department. I soon discovered that my ninety-day test was paying off. My relationship and influence did grow by focusing on what I could do to change the environment in which I worked. Today, the trust between my boss and me is very high, and I feel I am making a contribution here.

✢ *Increasing your influence usually takes a lot of patience and persistence. As confidence in your competence and character increases, inevitably a larger trust is given. Ninety days is usually a good period of time to test something. Sometimes it can even be done in thirty.*

If Looks Could Kill

The subordinate in this story gave strong but needed negative feedback to her boss and was able to do so because of great security within. As you study this story, try to empathize with the situation. With your mind's eye try to see the confrontational environment and the belittling that was taking place. Try to sense the amount of courage it took to give this piece of feedback and the peace of mind that resulted.

I was working with a high-powered executive team at a retreat for a week. Each morning of the retreat, one of the executives would be asked to talk about a personal experience with one of the 7 Habits. To be honest, some of them were pretty hard-nosed. Most pooh-poohed the whole idea. But we were starting to make breakthroughs with the personal experiences. As they articulated these success stories in front of their peers, the realization that perhaps these might work was spreading.

One morning, we were working on seeking first to understand. Jacques, one of the presidents and natural leaders of the group, shared a personal experience. Then we moved on to other areas of training. In the afternoon, this rather obnoxious exec started to say something about a business approach he was struggling with. The group pounced on him: "Well, have you tried this? Or this? What about this?" To be honest, I would have liked to pound him myself. But I knew it wasn't my place. Then, I heard Jacques laughing out loud, right in this guy's face. He was actually making fun of him in front of the whole group. Of course, the group jumped on the bandwagon.

I was stunned. Only a few hours ago, Jacques had shared this moving experience about the value of waiting your turn, trying to understand a person's actions. Now, he was doing the very opposite. I couldn't very well reprimand him in front of the whole group. So, I just glared at him. Jacques read me loud and clear: "That was ugly. If you don't do something to rectify this right now, I will kill you." Really. I was so angry, I was ready to walk out on the whole group. They had just reverted to their old, combative behavior and poisonous group dynamics.

He stared back at me. I pulled myself up taller in my seat and glared, "Back at ya, pal!" He shrunk back in his seat. I kept on looking right at him. This went on for about five minutes, during which his team members were still crucifying the poor guy. Then all of a sudden, Jacques stopped the meeting. He said, "Stop, I did something wrong. Darren, I want to ask your forgiveness."

"For what?" Darren was a bit baffled. Things were normal as far as he knew.

"That was inappropriate of me. I shouldn't have laughed. We didn't listen at all. We just jumped right on you. Will you forgive me?"

I thought that Darren, this senior VP, would say something like, "No problem. Don't worry about it." But his response was amazing: "Jacques, I forgive you. Thank you." Do you realize how much more courage it takes to actively forgive rather than trying to forget something happened?

I sat there. I was overwhelmed with emotion by Jacques's behavior. He didn't have to apologize. He didn't have to seek forgiveness in front of the whole group. He's the head of an eighty-thousand-person division. He doesn't have to do anything he doesn't want to. After the meeting, I went up to him, with emotion still in my voice, and said, "Thank you for doing that." He replied, "It was the right thing to do. Thank you for glaring at me." We didn't speak about that incident again. But we both knew that we had risen to our best that day.

✳ *Giving negative feedback is one of the most difficult communications there is. It is also one of the most needed. So many people have serious blind spots they never come to grips with because no one knows how to give them feedback. People are too fearful of rupturing a relationship or of having their personal future compromised by "taking on" their boss.*

The hypocrisy in this belittling situation became so evident to the offender that it wasn't an issue of having a blind spot, but one of ego. The courage and integrity of the person who gave the feedback was more powerful than status and position. That's why it worked. Sometimes it isn't more powerful and it won't work, which may necessitate going to the person privately and making reconciliation. The best way to give feedback in that private circumstance is to

describe yourself, not the person. Describe your feelings, your
concerns, or your perceptions of what was happening rather than
accusing, judging, and labeling the person. This approach often
causes the other person to become open to information about their
blind spot without being so personally threatened.

I've Tried for Months to Offend You

The following story is very straightforward and self-evident. Just do one thing as you read it. Try to put yourself into the mind of the writer. Try to sense what your natural tendencies would be while being so maligned and unjustly bad-mouthed, both openly and behind your back.

I joined the company I work for straight out of Harvard Business School. At the same time, a division head position came open. Because the company didn't know who to appoint, they grouped together four of us in an informal team to study how this division should be run. For about three months, the four of us worked together to figure out how to run this portion of the business. Suddenly, Rob Kimball, the design guy, really wanted the job. We could all sense it. But, as fate or luck would have it, they gave it to the new guy, me. Rob got assigned to something else that was just as important. But you could tell he thought my job should have been his. He set out to get revenge.

In every meeting we were in, he would say things to cut me down: "Oh, just 'cause you're a Harvard grad doesn't mean you know squat about design." He'd bad-mouth me behind my back, he'd be offensive to my face in front of twenty or so group members. I held my tongue. Sometimes I even bit it. He kept on hassling me. Other people sensed what was happening. Sometimes you could almost cut the air with a knife. When I returned from a vacation, a few people said to me, "Do you have any idea what Rob has been saying about you while you've been gone? If you only knew what he was doing to you behind your back." I'd just smile and say, "Well, some of us say things we don't mean. He doesn't really mean it."

You see, I had determined not to react to Rob. I was going to act the way that I wanted to [Habit 1: Be Proactive]. What I wanted to do was hold my tongue, be loyal, give him the benefit of the doubt, and just be nice. Sure, I wanted to beat his face in sometimes. I wanted to jab back at him, talk about him at the water cooler. But I wasn't going to let him determine how I would act.

Finally, months later, he came around. I remember one meeting in particular. He said something really rude, then he stopped and chuckled. "Geez," he said, "I've tried for months to offend you. You haven't taken offense once." Everyone laughed—that laughter of release. He said those very words, "I've tried to offend you but you won't get offended." We've actually become good friends.

From that experience, I learned the fruits of not being offended, choosing not to take offense, and just being consistent and loyal. There were a few things though that helped me not to react to Rob:

First, I had seen other people not react when they were put down. I admired their integrity, their sense of self-worth. I wanted to be like them. I wanted people to know that I could be trusted, that I was loyal, that I would not speak behind their backs.

Second, I knew that Rob had influence with a lot of people. He had clout in the company. It wouldn't have done me any good to take him on. (That's just practical business strategy there.)

Finally, I believe very strongly that all of us have good in us, that if we love people and are patient, the good in them will respond to the goodness we show them. It's only a matter of time. And a chunk of swallowed pride.

⊗ *It's ironic, but when your security comes from within and your effectiveness comes from without, you care more about other people's opinions because they're not vital to your sense of personal worth. It is also ironic that when both your security and effectiveness come from without, you don't care about other people's opinions because you can't afford to; you are at too much personal risk. That is why the first three habits are so foundational in building security.*

People usually get back what they send out. This is the law of restoration. You will notice that people who don't judge others are usually not judged. People who don't cut others are usually not cut. He who lives by the sword of criticism, dies by the sword of criticism. Those who are competent, even to the point of threatening other people, but who are also accepting, usually lubricate the human interaction processes and eliminate almost all threat.

Do You Just Not Like Working Here?

Feedback brought this person up short and caused him to reflect on working from within his own Circle of Influence.

When I joined my current organization, I was a stressed-out, reactive person. I brought with me eleven years in an intense industry, only to lose my job, as our local facility was closed. It took time to get over the past difficult years. It was easy for me to look at problems within my new company and want to fix them.

Though I enjoyed my new job, it wasn't hard to find things to complain about. Systems were obviously broken and I felt I had the answers to these problems. My boss had to listen to me every week during our update meeting as I suggested how to fix other people's problems. I even had a special section on my written weekly report I had titled Circle of Concern Issues! Somehow I thought that if I constantly raised these issues, they would be solved. In some strange way, I think I actually thought I was being helpful. One day during one of my complaining sessions my boss turned to me and said, "Ross, do you just not like working here?"

Well, *that* wasn't the problem! I did like working here. I just couldn't stand to see the inefficiencies and errors happening when the solutions were so *obvious*—to me. But the question did cause me to reflect on my behavior. In light of my boss's comment, I finally realized that all I had done was complain about things that weren't my concern. In my desire to share my great ideas, I had focused hypercritically on others and what I thought was their inability to perform their jobs correctly. To make a change, I committed to look at the problems around me from within my Circle of Influence. I would notice and act only on those issues I really had the power to change. No matter what, I wouldn't cross the boundaries of my influence [Habit 1: Be Proactive].

I soon had an opportunity to test my resolve:

One day, out of the blue, a new travel policy appeared in my mailbox. I thought the policy was poorly thought out and premature. I had two choices: I could complain yet again to my boss, or I could look at the problem from within my Circle of Influence.

I chose the second option. I drafted a document listing my concerns about the policy from the viewpoint of a traveler. Some of my concerns were with the policy itself, but most of them expressed my feelings about being left out of the communication process. The policy had appeared like a decree from Mount Olympus and I was expected to adhere to it. After I had written what I felt was appropriate, I contacted the person who had written the policy and asked if we could meet for a few minutes to go over my concerns. She wasn't thrilled. She'd caught nothing but flak over the new policy for the past two weeks. She said she'd see me anyway.

We met, and after understanding each other, not only did I have most of my questions answered, I was able to give her some thoughts on dealing with discontent about the policy. So really, we both won. And because I stayed within my Circle of Influence, I was actually able to expand it. I was also able to be a positive influence on others while avoiding the stress of trying to fix the things I couldn't.

Even though you may have a small Circle of Influence, if it touches on someone who has a larger Circle of Influence, communicate your complaint to that person; you are still working within your Circle of Influence. Over the years many people who have decided to focus on their Circle of Influence have come to the faulty conclusion that they can't complain or give negative feedback. This is not at all the case; it all depends on the quality of your relationship with the person who has the larger Circle of Influence. If it isn't that strong, then perhaps you have to figure out other ways to work inside your own Circle of Influence. At least you could test the waters and begin the communication. Sometimes we must care enough to confront. That's what the boss did when he asked the question, "Do you just not like working here?"

Gossip Addiction

As you read the following story, think about this statement: "The greatest battles of life are fought out every day in the silent chambers of one's own soul."

When I hired on at my present company, one of the first things I noticed was the destructive work environment. Our department thrived on gossip. People gained influence by getting the latest gossip and sharing it around the department. It didn't seem to hurt to backbite as much as you could, as long as you got away with it. As soon as somebody left the room, they became the topic of conversation. When person one returned, and person two left, the conversation switched targets.

I thought I had only two choices: I could either pick one side, or I could pick both sides and gossip indiscriminately. I realize now how weak that sounds. But I was new to the company and felt the need to curry favor with the power brokers. I thought it was their way or the highway.

Then I started thinking more deeply about the principle of taking personal responsibility. I took some hard looks in the mirror. My behavior was pretty ugly. I realized I needed to choose to interact with others in a different way. But how? How could I break the cycle I was a part of and that dominated our office culture? I knew I was not comfortable with gossiping, but what to do about it I just didn't know.

To help me figure out what to do, to give me a starting point if you will, I asked myself the question: "What is my role in this situation?" I knew my role was to stop doing something that was not helping others. That wasn't hard to figure out. To implement that role change was a little bit more difficult.

I saw that others didn't feel a need to change their behavior. They might go right on with the gossip. I couldn't change them. But I could be responsible for my own behavior [Habit 1: Be Proactive]. I recognized that perhaps the office culture was temporarily outside my area of influence. My own behavior wasn't. That I could influence.

I knew I couldn't change overnight, so I told myself I had to be patient. I also told my wife my plan to improve. She encouraged me every day. I failed every day most of the day in the beginning. I had to keep confronting myself and saying, "Here is stimulus, here's response, and here's the chance to act in the middle. As of right now I'm not doing this." Then I'd grit my teeth and bite my tongue, and think, "I have plenty of opinions about that person, but I'm not going to say them."

Gossip is so alluring it can suck you in before you even know it. I knew I had to just walk away. Even though it sounds so simple, I found it difficult to consistently exercise my integrity [Habit 3: Put First Things First].

Eventually I gained the reputation of not contributing to the gossip. People began to trust me; they knew that gossip did not have currency with me. I'm not completely over the pleasure of hearing about other people's lives. I still have to fight my tendency to want to listen. But at least I've made progress. At least I'm getting better.

As I've taught the idea of the Emotional Bank Account over the years the one deposit that seems to get more attention and response than any of the others is the idea of being loyal to the absent, not bad-mouthing people behind their back. I think it hits people the hardest because it is a behavior that so many people relish and from which they get their psychological jollies. Inwardly they know they shouldn't. But I have come to believe that not bad-mouthing is only one element of being loyal to the absent. Other elements include speaking up in favor of the absent, planning a time to communicate and give feedback to the absent, and representing the point of view of the absent.

Managing: Think Win-Win

FIFTY YEARS OF LOYALTY

BE PATIENT . . . THEY'RE LEARNING

THE MILLION-DOLLAR QUESTION

SHAPE UP OR SHIP OUT

CLOSING DOWN THE PLANT

THE TROUBLED EMPLOYEE

BILL PHIFER, GENERAL MANAGER,
COSMO'S FINE FOODS

THE DEAL IS OFF

FINDING THE THIRD ALTERNATIVE

Fifty Years of Loyalty

Look for two things as you study this story of win-win synergy: first,
in spite of the tendency of the procurement manager to see the world
through his nightmare work problem, notice how he transcended it
and became both analytical and empathic; and second, the power of
genuine human interaction.

I work for a multinational corporation in Malaysia. I am the procurement guy—that means I am responsible for the purchasing of materials, equipment, and services for all corporate operations in Malaysia. When I first started, I had about five thousand suppliers to keep track of and negotiate with. Imagine five thousand suppliers—each with individual products, contracts, purchase orders, and invoices! The paperwork alone was a nightmare.

As I looked closely at these suppliers, I knew we had to reduce the number as much as possible. My greatest problem was the haulers—six hundred truck drivers who carry the parts to and from the work sites. There were a few companies with large fleets, but most of the haulers were very small, often one-man, single-truck operations. I thought, "If I can reduce their numbers to about one-fifth the size, my job would be four-fifths easier." I made up my mind to consolidate by concentrating on expanding my relationships with the larger companies while eliminating many, if not all, of the onesies and twosies.

I called a meeting to announce the contract terminations. There were about forty people in the room. Just before I was about to stand up, an older gentleman sitting next to me turned and said, "I just want you to know how grateful I am for this company . . ." I'm thinking, "Oh no, man, not now, not here please. I'm gonna fire you in two minutes." He went on, "Because of this company, my father was able to raise a family. About fifty years ago, he saved his money to buy his truck and began shipping supplies for the company. From those contracts, he raised our whole family. I am the second generation of my family to drive trucks for the company. I have my father's business, which has supported our families for fifty years. Thank you for letting us provide for our families in this way."

What could I say? My stomach churned. I just smiled at him and then got up. When I stood there looking out into that room, I realized each one of these men had a similar story. I wasn't about to reduce my paperwork: I was about to destroy many fifty-year-old family businesses. So, I just went for total honesty with the group: "Look, I've got a problem here. I have this list of suppliers thirty-nine pages long. I can't keep track of so many people, plus I have to negotiate contracts every other week. The company is losing money. And we're running inefficiently. The most logical approach would be to let you all go. But I don't want to do that. So, how can we come up with a solution that's good for all of us [Habit 4: Think Win-Win]?"

After a bit of discussion, one trucker said, "Would it help if a couple of us got together, then we would be bigger and could handle more loads with fewer contracts? Would you consider keeping us if we did that to save our jobs [Habit 6: Synergize]?"

"Sure. If you're willing to do that, that's a win for me," I replied.

Then a few other men started another ball rolling: "Well, what if five or even ten of us got together. We could buy our tires at a group rate, and get our petrol cheaper. And if one of us gets stuck on a job, we could have a backup to help out." Suddenly, these guys were excited. Here they were forming this company with a whole fleet of trucks and group discounts to boot. Not to mention, my job was getting easier by the minute.

I must have gotten caught up in the excitement of the new concept. All of a sudden, I saw the big picture: I had five hundred of these suppliers. With five hundred, I could buy tires and parts at an unbelievable rate. So I suggested that I would buy their tires for them, act as a middleman, and sell the tires to them at a rate even less than they could have gotten by themselves in their group. Then our company would make money as well as save them money. I tell you, that room was buzzing with the excitement that synergy brings. I was grinning down the home stretch—it felt so good to be there.

I learned a very important lesson from that first conversation. Decisions and ramifications are never purely economic. I sat in a room that changed, in my mind, from being one filled with suppliers who were causing me problems to one filled with families, fathers, husbands who had been loyal to our company for fifty years and who deserved my best effort to retain them. I realized, luckily not too late, that when we see each other as human beings, we work differently together, we act differently toward each other.

The basic principle that this story teaches is simply this: involve people in the problem and work out the solution together. Most people hesitate to get others sincerely involved because they don't believe that it would help. They also believe that it would be a torturous process with no way of predicting the outcome. When people do involve others in the problem, they often hesitate to get fully honest and authentic, involving them in only part of the problem. They usually don't openly share their own personal feelings, dilemmas, and struggles. Because they don't, the other person tends to react out of their own feelings, dilemmas, and struggles. Consequently, true intimacy (in-to-me-see) in communication doesn't happen and mutual understanding is not achieved. The more authentic people are with each other, and the more communication is accurate, honest, and real, the more likely it is that creative juices will be released. When mutual understanding and respect is present, the spirit of synergy inevitably starts to develop.

The key reason breakthrough synergy occurred in this story is that one supplier got very authentic in expressing deep gratitude. Such open sharing profoundly affected the spirit of the procurement manager, which in turn led him to be equally open and honest regarding a tough issue.

Synergy is always exciting and tenuous because you are never quite sure where it's going to lead you. All you know is that it's going to be better than before, better than what either party had proposed.

Be Patient . . . They're Learning

Notice three most interesting points in this story. First, the amount of self-awareness and self-control it took for the manager to make the conscience choice to move from a traditional authoritarian style to a principle-centered participatory style. Second, how he kept his commitment by listening to a person whom he never would have considered listening to before his determination to change his style. And third, how he not only listened, but was influenced to be more patient.

In the past, I used to lead the people I was responsible for in a very traditional manner. I made unilateral decisions. I liked to ride in on a white horse to rescue people from their problems. I talked a lot and hardly listened at all. But I'm learning to have patience. I'm learning that I need to include people more in decisions that affect them. I'm learning that there is a wealth of talent and knowledge in the organization that I couldn't tap into because I was always talking and never listening. I'm also learning that sometimes I made the wrong decisions because I included the wrong people in the decision-making process. The people with the most expertise were often on the factory floor. Traditional thinking held that they shouldn't be involved in decision making at all. Leading according to principle means making the best decisions by including the best people with the most expertise and knowledge.

I made a decision to lead in this new way. Soon after, we had to make a very difficult decision to close a plant in North Carolina and consolidate in New York State. It was difficult, but nonetheless the right decision for the company. As a result, we had to hire new people at my facility in New York and train them to be upholsterers. Upholstering is a difficult job. It requires a lot of manual dexterity, hand-eye coordination, physical stamina, and an eye for symmetry and detail.

After a few months, management consensus in the upholstery department was that these new guys were not going to make it. A year ago, I would have fired them on the spot. But I decided to manage a better way. I went to listen to the person who really knew the situation, one of our young upholsterers and trainers. I had known him for a long time. Though he was a new trainer, we chose him to train new hires because of his enthusiastic personality. He is always ready to help out. He told me something that put the situation into a much clearer, kinder perspective.

He said, "You know, I'm not the best upholsterer here. I wasn't the fastest learner either. I think these guys are coming along just fine. Okay, maybe they're not where we want them to be. But we're not where somebody else higher up wants *us* to be either. I think we're just being a little impatient. Some people catch on in three months, others take longer. I think these guys will be great upholsterers."

We're at the twelve-month point now with these new hires. They are doing a great job. If I had made the decision the traditional way, we would have fired those guys ten months ago. I would have listened to the first person I spoke to and made a decision without all the relevant information. But I didn't. Because I was thinking about the habit of seeking first to understand [Habit 5: Seek First to Understand, Then to Be Understood], I chose to make the decision a better way. I listened first, and I listened to a person who would not normally have been involved in the decision-making process. By including someone that many would view as "just" an upholsterer/trainer, I know I made a better decision all the way around.

⊗ *The tendency of bottom-line-oriented people is to look at training and education as an expense instead of an investment. Without any question, an investment in people has the greatest leverage of any investment there is. It's like moving the fulcrum over. As someone put it, "If you think that training and education cost a lot, try ignorance."*

The Million-Dollar Question

Notice how this attorney transcended his adversarial legal training and put his faith in the synergy that comes from building a relationship of respect and understanding.

As the outside legal counsel for a large business, I became involved in negotiations to purchase another company owned by the widow of the founder. There were teams of lawyers on both sides, but the negotiations reached an impasse. Or perhaps I should say that the negotiations reached an impasse *because* there were teams of lawyers on both sides.

I am an attorney, but I am not blind to the fact that sometimes our win-lose form of advocacy causes more problems than it solves. In this case, the stumbling block was rather straightforward. The widow, who was the sole shareholder, wanted $1 million more than my client was willing to pay. We thought her departed husband's business was worth $2 million. She wanted $3 million.

At least that's what her lawyers said she wanted. Too often in these matters, you never get to hear directly from the parties involved. That has troubled me in the past, and so when my client's attempts to buy the widow's company reached an impasse, I made a final plea to her attorneys. I asked if I could speak directly to the widow.

I explained that as far as my client was concerned, there was no way we were going to pay another $1 million for the business. So the deal was dead unless we could come up with a third alternative. It was in their interest to let me speak with her. There were no other potential buyers and, in fact, the nature of the business was such that my client was one of the few companies that would ever be interested in purchasing it.

It was a strategic fit for my client's business but my client was prepared to walk away at her $3 million price. Her advisors had a bit of a stake in the company being sold, so they were willing to let me try a one-on-one telephone interview with the widow.

When she called, I took my lawyer's hat off and listened to understand her point of view to better appreciate her position [Habit 5: Seek First to Understand, Then to Be Understood]. I asked her about the business and how her husband had founded it, how much involvement she had had, and what her goals were for her children, all of whom were grown except for one teenage daughter.

I was curious as to why the final $1 million was so important to her. "This business is our destiny. I've got commitments," she responded.

The widow explained that her late husband had committed to "take care" of a friend who had helped him start the company. She noted also that she wanted to build up enough funds so that her children and grandchildren would always be well provided for, even after she died.

Two million dollars would not cover all of her commitments and responsibilities, she maintained. "I've got to have another million."

As soon as I understood her situation, the answer to the dilemma became absolutely clear. I fully understood her purpose in holding out for that extra million. So I suggested, "Let's do this. Our company will buy an insurance policy on your life for a million dollars. We will pay the premiums until you die or we'll pay one single premium, whatever way will be the least costly for us. In any event, we will make certain you've got a $1 million life insurance policy so that when you pass away, your children and grandchildren will have the $1 million legacy your husband wanted them to have" [Habit 4: Think Win-Win; Habit 6: Synergize].

That's all it took to close the deal. Given the widow's age, the premiums would likely end up costing us $50,000, but that is a lot cheaper than the $1 million in cash she was demanding.

There are so many deals that reach an impasse when people just can't break through and can't resolve huge differences, whether it's money, deliverables, performance, or concessions. Whatever the impasse, if you really work to understand the reasons behind the impasse, it seems there is almost always a third alternative that neither party envisioned.

I have long believed that all attorneys should be trained in the use of synergy in the prevention and settlement of disputes. I know many attorneys and judges who have used this approach of synergy based upon mutual respect and understanding as an alternative to costly, drawn-out litigation. They find that when they do, the whole game changes and people become influenced in such a way that creative juices are released and a third alternative usually results.

Shape Up or Ship Out

*When most people hear others complaining about someone they tend
to join them in their judgments and then take arbitrary action.
Notice how this supervisor exercised self-knowledge and self-control,
and followed the principle of involving others in the problem so that
all could become part of a synergistic solution.*

I supervise a staff of about twenty-six housekeepers for the local
hospital. We hire a lot of local college kids because we can offer a flexible schedule that fits their school schedule.

A couple of full-time employees came to me complaining about a
college student on their team. They said he was always late, that the
quality of his work had dropped off, and that he'd take hour-long
lunch breaks instead of the allotted thirty minutes. By the time they
finished their report, they were pretty worked up.

I knew this student quite well. He was a good worker but he had
transferred to a college sixty miles out of town. His commuting took
a heavy toll on him. As I thought about his situation, I remembered
the principles of being loyal to the absent [Emotional Bank Account],
to avoid blaming [Habit 1: Be Proactive] and instead, to focus on the
solution. I decided to do that.

In the past, I would have been pretty direct and autocratic. However, I wanted the two complaining employees to feel part of the
problem-solving process. So we started talking about their relationship with him while still remaining loyal. I asked them when the
problems started [Habit 5: Seek First to Understand, Then to Be Un-
derstood]. Then I told them about his transfer to the state university.
With this information, they could sense why things were changing. I
could tell that just identifying the root cause of the problem empowered them. Now they felt part of the solution.

I told them what they could expect. I would meet with the employee, work out a solution, and if things didn't improve, we would
get back together. Before understanding these habits of effectiveness,
I would have called this young college student into my office and
come out blasting, "These are the facts, if you don't straighten up and
start getting to work on time and doing a good job, I am going to cut

your hours." Instead, when I called him into my office, I knew it was important to guard his self-esteem.

"Ivan," I said, "we need to talk about what is going on with you." Then he explained his situation. In response, I asked him, "How can we help you be successful? School is very important to you, and we also have a set standard of performance at the hospital. How can we work this out [Habit 4: Think Win-Win]?"

He suggested, "How about I cut my hours back to two days a week? On those two days I can do my very best work. I can also devote all my energy on the other three days to school [Habit 6: Synergize]."

The solution was quite simple. His co-workers are happy to work with Ivan. He felt part of the solution and was able to maintain his self-esteem. My job became easier all the way around because I followed sound principles of management.

🔯 *Isn't it interesting how the space between stimulus and response can become larger by simply pausing and thinking about the principles that are involved? This is a remarkable illustration of the power of self-awareness and determination to act on principle. You can see how unilateral arbitrariness is really the spirit of independence, not interdependence.*

Closing Down the Plant

How to downsize or close a plant and keep morale high is a
commonly discussed question today. Try to get a sense of the kind of
empathy, feeling, and commitment this manager had toward his
people and their future.

Within a span of eighteen months, we had involved our entire division in learning and applying the 7 Habits. We grew together in a common way of thinking and were grounded in our common mission statement. My vision was that over three years we would change the culture of our whole company. Suddenly, in the middle of those plans for the future, headquarters announced we were closing our division. I was asked to be in charge of the closure.

This wasn't a job I would have volunteered for. But I am doing things differently now. Normally, we would have waited to announce the closing at the very last legally allowable minute. Of course, we would offer a severance package of our own design with the announcement. People would be so devastated they would take it, whether it fit their needs or not. Eighteen months before the projected closure, however, I went to the senior management. Since we had irrevocably decided to shut the doors, I said, "Okay, now is the time to tell the folks."

We didn't have any jobs for anyone to go to, we didn't have any training in place. They said, "Are you nuts?"

I said, "No! I need all of these people to start working on moving forward. I need some people to work on shutting down the business. There is equipment to dispose of, negotiations with vendors to wind up. I need other people to help me work on looking for other opportunities. Word is going to leak out anyway. If we tell everyone, then we give them the trust and empowerment they deserve to get a grip on their lives, and to get their affairs in order [Habit 4: Think Win-Win]."

"Go ahead. But if it falls apart, it's your head!"

We called everyone together. I made the announcement to a roomful of people who went into shock. It almost broke my heart. We had worked so hard to create our team; now it was being torn apart. We didn't let them grieve alone though. Group follow-up meetings were held every two weeks: I gave an update; they asked questions [Habit 5: Seek First to Understand, Then to Be Understood]. We tried to come up with solutions to the problems. Someone suggested that the employees buy the division from the company. When we looked through the numbers, we could see it wasn't feasible. We learned about another division in the company that needed to significantly increase their facilities, equipment, and personnel. We pitched a proposal to them that would move their business to our facility, showing them how it would both save them money and staff their expansion [Habit 6: Synergize].

My view in the beginning was that forty-four people were going to hit the streets looking for work. Today, our productivity is up, we are actually ahead of our schedule to close, and, except for those retiring, we haven't lost any personnel. When we close the doors in a few months, not one person will be without a job. One great benefit is that our closure has become a model for other divisions in the company. Even very hardened, bottom-line-focused senior management is taking notice of our different way of doing things.

People are amazingly resilient and capable of coping with difficult and challenging new realities. The key is that they need complete, current, and accurate information so they can adapt. It is scary business to make full disclosure, and that is why most in management do not. They don't know what is going to happen and often feel that their own motives or earlier decisions will be questioned. It simply opens up a Pandora's box when you involve people. But if you don't, it opens up in other ways—in an atmosphere of low trust, in spawning more cynicism, and in accusations and hostility.

Trust flows out of trustworthiness. So when people are truthful, open, honest, and confront others with the full reality and then attempt to understand the full reality of other people's concerns and lives, the processes of synergy are unleashed.

I know of another organization that not only closed down a plant, but closed it down in a very small city. People were not only losing their jobs, they were having to relocate their homes and families. The media heard that there was going to be some kind of a farewell meeting. Thinking it would turn mean and stir up controversy and public interest, and thinking that it had national byline potential, they showed up at the meeting only to find out that it was a farewell Kentucky Fried Chicken party where everyone was saying goodbye to each other. They were both sad and happy, but the spirit was great. The trust level was high and everyone knew that the synergistic solution was appropriate. Correct principles were followed from the beginning. Alternatives were examined, including an employee purchase, but it was finally concluded that the whole plant was obsolete and could not recover. Great efforts and pains were taken to help people deal with their concerns about employment, moving families, and changing schools. Counseling was given, placement services were provided, and in spite of the profound dislocation and difficulty, the spirit of trust prevailed.

The Troubled Employee

Consider the value system of this general legal counsel. He puts operating on principle, on the value of an employee, on the importance of understanding the dynamics of the situation, and on the desire to do what is right above taking the efficient approach of automatically going along with the recommendations of supervisors and others about a troubled employee. As you read this story you can feel the integrity of this man and the amount of respect he had for this very troubled person.

I am the general legal counsel for a large company. I received an urgent request one day to meet with the director of human resources and one of our division directors about an employee they intended to terminate. They came to my office and made a strong, well-documented case.

This woman had frequently used foul language in the workplace. She'd lost her temper repeatedly with her co-workers. She was uncooperative, irrational, and just plain ornery. On top of that, she was known for coming to work late and for taking extended lunch hours with no explanation.

I asked the normal questions. "Have you talked with her? Have you given her a chance to correct her behavior?" Their responses were satisfactory. It appeared that they had tried to work with her over a period of time but her behavior had not improved. They indicated that she was aware that this was the last straw and that she would be losing her job. It sounded like they had followed proper procedures and done their homework. It appeared that the termination, though never a pleasant thing to do, was unfortunately justified.

Yet I had never met this woman employee, and that bothered me. I like to get my own read on situations, even when I trust all of the parties involved. I wanted to talk with her just to see, perhaps out of an abundance of caution, what her viewpoint was. Truthfully, I also wanted to see if she seemed inclined to sue us over the termination. I really wanted to understand why her behavior was so out of line with expectations [Habit 5: Seek First to Understand, Then to Be Understood]. She had a good job with the company and I wondered if there was something about the job or the culture that needed to be addressed.

I fully expected her to be defensive and to deny the allegations, and perhaps to blame the work environment for her behavior. So I was taken aback when she came to my office, at my request, and said, "I know why you have called me in here. You are going to fire me."

Her directness caught me off guard. I explained that I wanted to understand why she had performed so poorly. I told her what I had heard regarding her behavior: the foul language, cantankerous temperament, and poor punctuality. She didn't deny anything. She said that it was "unfortunately true."

I have to confess; she was winning me over by being so candid. I was heartened that she didn't flinch and that she told me just exactly what was on her mind. She didn't try to make any excuses. She also told me that she liked her job.

"Then why would you act in a way that would cause supervisors and others to conclude that you need to go, that they would need to terminate your employment? Why this behavior?"

She responded by asking if I was really interested in her personal life. I said I was if it would help cast a light on her poor performance in a job she claimed to enjoy.

Then she told me her story. She had grown up in a close and loving family in which all generations took care of each other. And so she had felt responsible when her husband's father, a widower, had become senile as a probable result of Alzheimer's disease. She had fought her husband's plan to put his father in a nursing home. Instead, she had demanded that her father-in-law live with them so she could give him loving care. Her husband told her that if she wanted that, it would be her responsibility and her burden to do so.

It turned out to be a far more demanding task than she had dreamed possible.

"I brought him into our home and it was worse than I thought it would be," she told me. "He is incontinent. I have to change diapers. He often doesn't recognize who we are or where he is. He wanders away, sometimes in the middle of the night. We can't afford to put any kind of security system in our house so I don't sleep well some nights. I dress him in the morning to get him ready for a nurse who comes in and watches him part of the day. I make his lunch so he eats well because people with Alzheimer's often lose their appetite or forget to eat, causing them to lose weight and get sick. Sometimes I have to leave during the middle of the day to go take care of him, to find him if he has wandered off, or to calm him."

She told me how caring for her father-in-law had caused stress in her marriage. "I feel really bad about it. I keep telling myself that I won't do it anymore, but I guess I'm just at my wit's end. I'm just burned out and tired. I don't blame you for firing me," she said.

After hearing that, I didn't feel like firing her. I wanted to pin a medal on her instead. I was more inclined to take disciplinary action against those who had judged her without really trying to understand what was behind her behavior—myself included.

Instead of handing her termination papers, I talked with her further to fully understand her dilemma. She told me that in spite of all the difficulty, she planned on caring for her father-in-law until he died. She said she could not bear to see him go off to a nursing home, particularly since she and her husband could not afford to send him to a high-quality place.

I came to feel that we had let her down, not the opposite. I told her that we had not been very good employers. "You are doing some heroic things and we haven't been sensitive enough to find out what was going on at home," I said.

I asked her what we could do to make it easier for her to continue to work for us while she cared for her father-in-law [Habit 4: Think Win-Win]. We talked about setting her up in a home office with a computer and fax machine, and we discussed giving her a more flexible work schedule. I enjoyed our conversation, and I think she did, too. We both felt good about her future with the company.

She agreed that she would forgive the people who had been harsh with her, who had talked behind her back, and who had accused her of being a poor employee. She said she would be more up-front with people about her dilemmas at home so that they could understand what she was going through. We agreed that she would no longer use foul language, nor would she direct her frustration and anger at her co-workers.

In exchange for those concessions from her, I made a commitment to provide her with whatever she needed to get her work done, as long as she kept up with her duties. I had a bit of explaining to do when I told her supervisor and the director of human resources what I had done. They were angry with me at first, but they reluctantly agreed to give her another chance. They didn't think that she would pull it off. I said, "Trust me. This thing will work. I have confidence in this woman."

We worked it out so she could spend more time at home when she needed to be there for her father-in-law, and she kept her word. She became an outstanding employee, in part, I believe, because she had come to believe that we were on her side and that we were willing to help her get through a difficult time.

She and I forged a strong friendship. She shared her dreams with me, and she moved up in the company. Her father-in-law died just six months after our first talk, and her performance improved even more. She became so highly regarded that, six years later, she was hired away by another company to run an entire division.

Getting to know and to understand her and seeing both the company and this valuable employee benefit was a great learning experience. Initially, I did it because seeking to understand seemed like the right way to approach this difficult situation. It was the logical thing to do, to diffuse a potential conflict by trying to understand the other side.

If we had not met together, if we had simply terminated her, she might have concluded that we didn't care about her or that we had fired her for reasons other than poor performance. She might have sued, or talked badly about us in the community. Instead, something quite beautiful came out of this. A man was allowed to spend the final months of his life in dignity and among people he loved. A troubled marriage was repaired. A career was saved.

⊗ *I've come to feel that being efficient with people in difficult situations is usually ineffective. It is so easy to be efficient, to make quick judgments or to act on other people's judgments without any involvement or effort to understand, and to judge everything in terms of its impact upon the bottom line. Listening is like peeling an onion. There are many, many layers and a soft inner core. Once you get to the soft inner core your whole picture of the situation often profoundly changes, as do your actions. This new correct picture affects your attitude and usually creates in you a feeling of reverence for other people. You cease judging and third-alternative solutions are more naturally produced. When two people are congruent and authentic, when they both say what they feel and what they feel is in harmony with what they are experiencing, creative energies are released and deep bonding almost always takes place. But when there are incongruencies, when people are not expressing what they are feeling, or they are not feeling what they are really experiencing, a seedbed of confusion, frustration, and low trust is sown.*

Bill Phifer, General Manager, Cosmo's Fine Foods

Consider in the following story the power of trust, human
affirmation, and open communication in turning an absolute
business disaster into a success in a little over one year.

"What have I gotten myself into?" was the question I asked myself
after I had accepted the general manager position at Cosmo's, a spe-
cialty food store in Lexington, Kentucky. I had taken on a major challenge with a store that was in financial distress and had no
leadership, no accountability, no clearly defined responsibilities, little
if any customer service, employees disillusioned by previous management, and a definite lack of direction. Despite all those negatives,
I had two powerful positives that could and would change the store's
future.

The first positive was a shared vision with the store's new owners,
Larry and Bunny Holman [Habit 2: Begin with the End in Mind].
They are also owners of a company that provides leadership programs taught by Stephen R. Covey, Tom Peters, Ken Blanchard, and
others. They wanted Cosmo's to be a living prototype of the values
and principles taught in their leadership programs. They wanted to
turn the theory into practice. I wanted to help them do that.

The first principle the Holmans put into practice was the principle
of empowerment. They placed a great deal of trust in the fact that
Anne Hopkins, our financial manager, and I had the same vision and
values for Cosmo's. They empowered us and gave us the freedom to
lead and implement the necessary changes. Now, with trust and empowerment from the owners, where did Anne and I start?

The answer lay in the second positive, the employees. Cosmo's
had employees with tremendous talent and potential, but this group
of employees felt like foster children who kept getting shuffled from
home to home. In order to help them realize their potential and tap
into their talents, I knew we had to provide some stability. For this to
happen, we had to build a trusting relationship that valued people.
That takes time—and I was impatient. I knew that the most important change would be to create a new culture from the inside out,
starting with me [Habit 1: Be Proactive].

We began by letting our people know they are valued; we tried to look beyond the job to the person. We wanted to see our employees as individuals and to understand that they have personal lives, too [Habit 5: Seek First to Understand, Then to Be Understood]. For example, we gave one employee whose good work was slipping because of personal problems a week off to iron things out. As a result, that person is now much more dedicated. I believe that if you make people feel valued they'll become more involved and committed. Sometimes it's a fine line between empathy and being taken advantage of—but the bottom line is that it is well worth the risk. It promotes goodwill for both parties [Habit 4: Think Win-Win].

Another principle we wanted to put into practice was to have a proactive rather than a reactive approach to the business. We took a careful look at each person and the position that person held and realized that many of them were doing things that were unrewarding to them. We had drivers who wanted to be mechanics and mechanics who wanted to be drivers. Through one-on-one meetings we realized that there were many people with talents that had not been acknowledged. An employee well respected for her knowledge of prepared foods is now a highly valued pastry baker for Cosmo's.

We tell our people, "Enjoy what you do; have a passion for it." We promote creativity. I tell them, "Even though your idea might sound crazy, come out with it. Let's talk about it. We don't believe in routine [Habit 6: Synergize]."

We have also created an environment of trust through open-book management. We wanted the employees to know where the store was and where it was going. This proved to be a challenging process. With very limited data to refer to, we relied on the staff to help us put together a profile of where the store actually was. When we reviewed the profiled information with the staff, their reactions showed that they hadn't realized just how serious the situation was. This was a reality check for all of us. With this new information, we began to evaluate as a team where we needed to go and how we were going to get there. I used the example of a staircase. At the top of the stairs was our destination, and the only way to arrive at the destination was to take one step at a time together.

As teamwork and trust have improved, energies are now being directed toward positive pursuits such as rebuilding and establishing distributor relationships that had been damaged and in some cases severed by prior management. We are also concentrating on customer service and innovation and the results have been astounding.

From January 1 to December 31, 1998, Cosmo's enjoyed a 32.2 percent gain in sales, a 22.1 percent gain in gross margin, and a 46 percent gain in customer count. In that same period, inventory was reduced by 15 percent and salaries grew by 14.5 percent. Staff hours actually decreased by 9 percent, while the ratio of labor dollars to sales decreased by 17.6 percent. In just a little less than a year we have pulled out of a $45,000-per-month deficit and are now doing business in the black.

The statistics are great but are only a product of what I feel is Cosmo's greatest accomplishment, the fact that we now have a team of people working in an environment where trust and morale are high and employees have a passion for their jobs and a desire to serve the customer. We take pride in the accomplishments we have achieved and will continue to achieve as a team—what a transformation, what a fun and innovative place to work!

As rewarding as seeing the Cosmo's vision become a reality has been, I want to stress that Cosmo's continues to be a work in progress; but with our commitment as a team that includes owners, management, and staff, the results are promising as we climb those stairs together.

⊗ *Selection is even more important than training. The whole key to this story was the selection and empowerment of the right leader, someone with the Abundance Mentality—someone who didn't define winning as beating. Instead he exercised proactive muscle in involving the heart and mind of every member of his team to release their potential toward the common goal of winning for the customer.*

The Deal Is Off

Sense the presence of mind of this CEO through the whole process of negotiation and deal making. Sense also the deep respect he manifested toward all participants and the effect this had on his ability to empathize and synergize.

I was the CEO of a small venture start-up company in Japan, when a large publicly held company expressed an interest in acquiring our firm. My company's owners and I were ecstatic: here was a huge opportunity to finally recoup our hard work and investment and to ensure a bright and profitable future.

As we began to negotiate, I tried hard to practice Habit 5: Seek First to Understand, Then to Be Understood. Working with the vice president of the potential buyer, I tried to assess the desired results and needs of his company. This company had recently made several acquisitions and there were questions about how much cash would be available for our deal. Additionally, there were issues about getting board support, since previous acquisitions were not bringing results as expected.

Working with this information, I met with all of the shareholders of my own organization and tried to get a better understanding of their needs. How much money was enough? Were there things other than money that were motivational factors in wanting to go through with the deal? What was a win for them?

Once I felt I understood the needs of both sides, I began to think about alternatives that might make the deal more attractive to each party. I was very anxious to put a deal together, so I really tried to think creatively.

One can imagine my despair and discouragement when the president of our prospective buyer told me that his company was not going to pursue the acquisition. I was told that the pressure from the board and the shareholders was just too great to do another deal at this time.

I was discouraged but not dissuaded. I have come to believe in the effectiveness of the 7 Habits in producing results in my business. I decided to continue practicing Habit 5 and see where it would lead us. I started by trying to state the president's position better than he had stated it himself. "Let me see if I understand your situation." I described the acquisitions his company had made, and the delays they were experiencing in showing bottom-line results. I laid out the pressures he was getting from the board and his shareholders and why those concerns were valid. Further, I discussed the limited cash resources that were available to do a deal. Then I said, "Is that a fair summary?" He replied, "Yes, that is exactly our situation."

My reply was: "That's really unfortunate. We had hoped that we could put together a deal that would be win-win for both of us. Based on our understanding of your situation, we had put together some options that we felt would still make the deal a tremendous win for you. But, since you are saying that this will not be possible, we will accept your judgment and look for other ways that our organizations can continue to cooperate in the future."

The president of this company was stunned. If we truly understood his situation—as my summary demonstrated—how could we still think a deal was possible? He replied, "Let's hear about those options of yours." We then talked for six hours, and at the end of six hours he basically said, "We want to buy your company. Let me go back to my board to get the money."

I believe this deal was successful because I was willing to truly understand with the use of Habit 5—both in advance and during our crucial negotiations. I also let go of the need to force-fit a deal; it was either going to be a win-win or no deal.

As a result, all of my shareholders became independently wealthy. Equally important, we also created a stronger organizational presence in our market and produced many new jobs for people in our economy.

⊗ *The effect of being deeply respected and understood is truly astounding. People become open, their defenses are lowered, and they tend toward a creative orientation. The bonding that results from it comes from the overlapping vulnerabilities of the people involved. It all starts with one person being willing to be vulnerable and influenced through understanding the other. This humility almost always softens the stance of others, and when it does, it usually leads to others first becoming open to influence and then to synergy.*

Finding the Third Alternative

This is an absolutely beautiful story of human nature, the lows and the highs. I suggest that as you read it, focus on how this business executive acted with integrity and courage inside the space between stimulus and response, and how it was the root of almost everything else that happened.

I am a senior executive for a midsize manufacturing company, an attorney by training. Several years ago, before I entered the picture, my company signed a contract to purchase a massive, high-precision piece of manufacturing equipment that cost nearly $5 million. It was a bad contract for us, a wonderful deal for the seller.

Basically, as the contract was written, if this high-precision machinery broke down or otherwise failed to work properly, we were in deep trouble.

The manufacturer had no liability for defects. Keep in mind that if this machine malfunctioned, it would result in calamity for our company—missed delivery deadlines, lost production time, thousands and thousands of dollars in ruined raw materials, and many hours of costly labor to perform repairs.

That is exactly what happened, of course.

The machinery that was supposed to run with Swiss-watch precision couldn't tell the time of day. It was a multimillion-dollar lemon and souring our entire operation. It broke down constantly, causing missed deadlines and lost business. Worst of all, the company had made all but one payment on it to the manufacturer, who didn't seem very interested in taking responsibility for its product's failures.

Naturally, my company called out the dogs. I was the leader of the pack.

It looked like this was going to get ugly fast. The manufacturer had a lot of clout and a small army of lawyers. They ignored our demands to either make the machine work properly or remove it and give us our money back.

We called in a big-time trial lawyer who hired experts and conducted an investigation. He threatened to sue the manufacturer for fraud based on a theory that it had misrepresented the capabilities and soundness of the machine. We believed they had known from the start that it was defectively designed.

They pretty much ignored our threats.

Meanwhile, back at the plant, orders were piling up, employees were idle, and profits were plummeting. We knew that if we filed a lawsuit, the manufacturer would stop making even routine repairs on the machinery. It would cost us a fortune to tear it out ourselves, and it would take at least six months to get a replacement up and running.

We asked for one last meeting with the manufacturer, hoping for a resolution. It was a typical lawyer-versus-lawyer confrontation. It went nowhere. I came home angry. I could not believe that a manufacturer would not accept responsibility for its defective machinery.

Of course, I'd spent a good part of my life dealing with situations like this. I'd been trained to go for win-lose when it got to this point. Take no prisoners. Give no quarter.

The problem was that most of the time, nobody wins in those situations. We just chew each other to pieces and go home with the scraps.

When I got over being mad, I decided to ignore my legal instincts and thirst for revenge. Instead, I tried to think of another way to solve our problem. I believe this is called "the pause between stimulus and response."

I brought in a couple of people, including my secretary and others who knew what was going on. I wanted to hear their opinions. I really wanted to understand, to see things through their eyes [Habit 5: Seek First to Understand, Then to Be Understood]. I wanted to make sure that we were all thinking clearly. Then I began to think about the proper response to the real issues that confronted us. We took a time-out to decide what response would be in the best interests of the company.

Putting egos and emotions aside, we came up with a list of our company's needs:

- Production output had to be maintained and ultimately improved.

- We did not want to spend millions of dollars on legal fees and trial costs.

- We needed to have a healthy relationship with an equipment manufacturer so that future growth, as well as immediate production, would be enhanced.

- We wanted to be compensated for losses suffered as a result of the defective manufacturing equipment.

We looked at that list and concluded that only one of these objectives might be achieved by a costly and lengthy lawsuit, while the other, more important objectives would actually be jeopardized by litigation. We also admitted that we'd let our desire for vindication blind us to what was best for our company. It became clear that it was far less important to get even than it was to get production back on track.

With this new end in mind, we began thinking about how to achieve it. The first thing we decided to do was let go of the anger and negative emotions [Habit 1: Be Proactive]. We wanted to build a new relationship with the manufacturer so we could work together instead of being adversaries [Habit 4: Think Win-Win].

After going over all of the conversations and letters and materials gathered in preparation for the lawsuit, I began to understand that while the manufacturer had appeared to be acting unreasonably from our point of view, its actions had probably been entirely reasonable based on its own internal and external pressures. I learned as much as I could about this manufacturer and once I put a few pieces together, I came up with a theory as to why they had been stonewalling us.

To confirm my theory, I telephoned the president of the manufacturing company and asked for an informal, off-the-record meeting. I was not sure he would accept. This guy is tough, intelligent, and experienced. He had dominated all of our previous meetings.

On the telephone, I said that I thought we'd gotten off on the wrong path. I told him I wanted to understand his position more clearly. At first, he held to the same defensive position his company had maintained all along, but as I made it clear that I was only interested in fully understanding his position, he warily agreed to meet with me over dinner.

At the end of our telephone conversation, as the president of the manufacturing company relaxed a little, I sensed that he was beginning to trust me. He shared some information that helped me understand his company's initial defensiveness. This information proved invaluable in helping me construct a third alternative in resolving the dispute between us.

Going into the meeting, I hoped that the manufacturer's candor was a good sign. I went to meet him on his own turf. As we sat down at the restaurant, he initially talked as though I had agreed to drop all demands and give in. I was sorely tempted to react strongly to what seemed to be his exploitation of my kindness and generosity once again; but I restrained myself. Instead, and while it was difficult to do so, I began asking him questions about his company's goals and his personal aspirations. And I offered to share my own personal view of my company's dilemma.

I carefully laid out for him, without assigning any fault or blame, the serious problems and financial burdens that my company had suffered because the equipment he'd sold us had not worked. I tried not to confront him, but I was candid. I explained that we were being dogged by concerned stockholders and complaining customers. I acknowledged that these pressures had helped trigger my company's adversarial and confrontational position.

I asked him to accept my apology on behalf of the company for the way this dispute had been handled so far. He reciprocated with his own apology. I sensed we were finally making some progress.

I told him that I honestly believed his company had done its best to come up with solutions to the equipment's poor performance and that, after taking a step back to listen better and observe more, we believed they were honorable people who wanted to do the right thing. I sincerely meant what I said. As I offered these thoughts, the tension between us dissipated and a new, more collaborative mood settled in. We began to trust each other.

I then laid the groundwork for a third alternative solution to our conflict—what I considered to be a win-win solution. I shared my company's plans and hopes for the future. I did my best to help him understand the human side of our business, what our people were like, what we dreamed about accomplishing.

I guess you could say I shared with him our end in mind, which included a strong synergistic relationship with a manufacturing equipment partner. I explained that based on our growth projections, we would need to purchase millions of dollars of equipment over the next thirty-six months.

Needless to say, that got his attention.

As I shared more of our vision, I explained how his company might play an active role in it. Slowly, he opened up to me, volunteering that his company had also made mistakes. He insisted that they had a solid product line notwithstanding the deficiencies of the equipment we had purchased, and that he was extremely interested in our growth potential.

He definitely wanted to be part of our future. So I told him what he would have to do to be a partner.

With his eyes riveted on me, I said, in substance, "Imagine that eighteen months from now my company will have spent more than $5 million on additional manufacturing equipment provided by your company. Picture my company a few months from now as a loyal client looking confidently to you for additional upgrades and improvements. We could be looking to you for expertise in the design and implementation of a growing manufacturing line. Can you envision other clients coming to us for endorsements of your products and services?"

Then I got personal. "I can even picture you inviting me to play golf sometime."

Suddenly, we felt and acted more like two old friends and business associates than adversaries. We talked about specific equipment we needed. We talked about the services they would provide. We made a lot of notes on our napkins.

But I was not done yet. Now that I had his confidence, I had one more proposal.

"This is what I need from you to build our long-term relationship: I need you to send your best people to keep our equipment running at an acceptable performance level to get us through our busy season. You need to help us minimize the downtime, and you need to provide these services at no cost to us. I need you to agree that we won't make any more payments on the equipment we have. However, we will pay full price on the new equipment we will order from you—minus the documented loss of raw materials ruined by the current equipment. Finally, we will commit to spending a total of more than $5 million on equipment manufactured by your company during the next eighteen months."

When the meal was done, so was the deal. And before we left the restaurant, we also had a golf date.

My company approved the agreement, and with good reason. It ensured that we would recover our losses, return to normal production, and dispose of the defective equipment at no further cost. It also took care of our future needs and avoided a costly lawsuit. It was a sweet deal for the manufacturer.

Later, I called the trial lawyer we had hired and told him about our agreement; he was astounded. He wrote me a letter saying that the deal we put together was better than a 100 percent victory in a jury trial. We had likely gotten more than a jury would have given us.

The win-win played out perfectly, and the subsequent golf outing wasn't bad either.

For us, the new equipment we purchased from the manufacturer has performed perfectly. The old equipment functioned adequately under the constant care of our new manufacturing partner until it was replaced.

For their part, the manufacturer secured a long-term and cordial relationship with a multimillion-dollar customer.

As a negotiator, you are taught that you never disclose your vulnerabilities. You play it like a poker game. You use all the tricks. You bluff. You feign. You stomp off. All of these tactics come from a position of mutual distrust. The "win," if any, is generally a small piece of a ravaged pie. Successful dispute resolution, on the other hand, is built on a foundation of trust, each side sincerely seeking to understand the other. It's a bit tricky. It takes courage and patience.

The key to this type of problem solving—and the beauty of it—is that each individual is given the opportunity to be truly trustworthy. You can't simply posture or manipulate. You have to be strongly principled and, most importantly, you have to be yourself, honest and sincere.

It also demands that you refuse to be cynical. I believe that almost every human being, regardless of his or her past experience or training, if given the chance to be trustworthy, honest, and fair, will embrace that opportunity and act with high integrity.

Given the description of the extent and depth of the problems in this story, how many people would envision a synergistic solution? What kind of a human being is it that refuses to be cynical and who says, "I believe that almost every human being, regardless of his or her past experience or training, if given the chance to be trustworthy, honest, and fair, will embrace that opportunity and act with high integrity"? This comes out of the mind, heart, and soul of a person who is deeply principle-centered and thus inwardly secure. The new dynamic that really made the difference was spending the time, effort, and energy necessary to build an authentic human relationship. Everything flowed out of that relationship. The willingness to apologize, the willingness to sincerely listen, the willingness to courageously express, the willingness to creatively explore new options—these capacities lie within almost all of us, only to be awakened by the example of one who inspires us, who ignites these proven principles from within.

Leading Organizations

COLIN HALL, EXECUTIVE CHAIRMAN,
WOOLTRU LIMITED, SOUTH AFRICA

DOUG CONANT, PRESIDENT, NABISCO U.S. FOODS GROUP

PETE BEAUDRAULT, COO, HARD ROCK CAFE

CHRIS TURNER, LEARNING PERSON, XEROX BUSINESS SERVICES

JACK LITTLE, PRESIDENT AND CEO, SHELL OIL COMPANY

MICHAEL BASSIS, PRESIDENT, OLIVET COLLEGE

WOOD DICKINSON, CEO, DICKINSON THEATRES

JOHN NOEL, CEO, NOEL GROUP

Colin Hall, Executive Chairman, Wooltru Limited, South Africa

This story, told personally by Colin at our Franklin Covey International Symposium, was one of the most electrifying, inspiring speeches any of us had ever heard. It was so profoundly moving that people were almost numbed with a sense of humility, reverence, and gratitude for several hours afterward, some for days and even weeks. You will notice as you get into this story that the key elements were all personal—the inward struggle of a self-reflecting, deeply honest soul that resolved to do that which was right and principled.

I was born just at the beginning of the Second World War into a reasonably affluent, white, South African family. It was liberal. It was sensible. It was a good place to be. It was also unconditional, meaning my mother and father loved me despite the fact that I wasn't the same as them. I didn't do all the things that you are "supposed" to do. There were many times when they didn't like me, but they never stopped loving me. They gave me space to become different.

I went to thirteen state schools, and state education for whites was better than the state education for blacks. It was deliberately so. We got the best. But with the best, we also got heavy doses of the superiority game, of competition, of apartheid. I soon discovered that life was mine for the grasping and that if I didn't grasp it, somebody else would. So I started grasping. I started to climb the ladder of corporate success. I qualified as a lawyer, and in qualifying as a lawyer you learn about win-lose. From there I went into business. I joined a brewing company, South African Breweries, which by South African standards is a big and powerful company. I continued the relentless climbing of the ladder on the basis of win-lose. And it's not surprising because the world that I lived in was a win-lose world. South Africa was a win-lose place. Commerce was a win-lose place. And the company was a win-lose place.

In the twenty years I stayed with them, I rose from a night-shift brewer to the chief executive of the group in charge of all its liquor interests and hotels. It was a fairy-tale story for its time. I was a director by the time I was thirty, which was an achievement in itself. I felt good about that, partly because I chose not to feel bad about what it had cost other people. If I could describe the experience in another way, I was really qualifying for a Ph.D. in power—in raw, naked, ruthless power. It was power not only in the market and over competitors, but power over the guy in the office suite along the hall, and power over my subordinates. And it was a heady experience, as power is.

But all that changed when I came home from work one night and played Monopoly against my nine-year-old son. I thrashed him in the game. I really crushed him. With tears in his eyes he looked up at me and said, "Dad, isn't it a game?" I felt sick about it, absolutely sick.

Though I had been uncomfortable at times about my drive to win at all costs, even against my son, in our games and conversations, I tried to deny my feelings and justify myself: "This is the way the Game is played. This is the way the great guys in the world survive. This is the way you build great businesses. The world is a competitive place and my son had better learn. I'd better knock some spots off him so that he becomes as competitive as I am, so he can find his way through this mess and maze of beating other people." But it wasn't comfortable. And this experience sickened and cut me to the core. I realized that I had been using the same power game at home that I had been playing for years at the office. I could see that you can't play two games in your life. The game you play at work goes home with you. I realized that I had also been playing power games with my wife, Di.

At this crucial point in my life, a mentor of mine gave me a picture of a sleeping tiger with just one eye open. He said to me, "Never forget that in every human lies the power of a tiger, but it is about 99 percent asleep. The great tasks of life are about giving that little tail a twist to see what vigor, what vibrancy, what energy, what excitement, and what real magic comes out of a tiger." I had it on my wall for a long time. I started looking at it and thought to myself, "What am I doing? Am I just killing off tigers here—emasculating tigers, knocking their feet out from underneath them and making them feel bad about themselves?" Instead of getting joy out of watching people grow, I was getting joy and satisfaction out of watching people fail, while I succeeded.

The Monopoly game with my son helped me to the conclusion that I couldn't live with a point of view that I had to prove I was better than somebody at work every day, so I left South African Breweries. My natural inclination was to jump from one power situation to another. Again I got great advice. Somebody suggested that perhaps it was a time in my life sent to me to really reflect and reconsider— that I shouldn't hastily jump back into a familiar situation only to get out my fangs, weapons, and tools of the trade. He suggested that it might be a great time to change pace. "Swap power for influence," he said. "If you are as good as you think you are, see if you can do it without power." So I put up my slate as a consultant.

It was a humbling experience, as you can imagine, because I didn't even have somebody to shout at to bring me a cup of tea. I made my own tea. I couldn't go into a client's office and say, "Do this, and do that; smash the opposition, and do yet another fiendish thing." I had to say, "Have you thought about this possibility? Or have you considered that option? Or perhaps this idea would work a little better than the one we are using at the moment? Or how about this for an alternative?" I found that very frustrating in the short term because I was used to being able to lay structure and to be the boss. I think I was a nice sort of autocrat. But when you are a consultant, you can't be an autocrat. You run out of money.

I began to read voraciously. I redoubled my effort to understand humanity. And the question that absolutely eluded me and began to fascinate and tantalize me once again was, "Why had we not understood what makes the difference between highly effective people and the run-of-the-mill, the ordinary man? We've been together for centuries, and yet we still seem to misunderstand the concept of the sleeping tiger." Why are so many people living what Thoreau described as "lives of quiet desperation"?

After consulting for several years, I joined Wooltru as the chief executive. Wooltru is a large retail group and it started like I did, as a family business with good family values. It was founded by a father and son who could work together despite their differences. But it, too, got caught up in this pernicious determination to be better than, to become a public company. It began to measure everything in terms of bottom line and return on equity. It became increasingly paternalistic, patronizing, autocratic, white-male, racist, chauvinist, top-down, and all the other characteristics of whites in South Africa at that time. It was a master-servant business. And it worked. But by the time I came to Wooltru, our price-earnings multiple on the stock exchange was exactly half that of the sector average. That's poor performance! That was a crisis! Yet, I joined Wooltru because I wanted to see if we could change together. To the group and me it was obvious that with the country in crisis, it wouldn't be long before there would be change—a transformation to a new society, one in which blacks would govern whites.

Deep in the crucible of my life, deep in the crucible of Wooltru's life, and deep in the birth pains of South Africa's life is the same thread of a family, of joy in being different, of unconditional acceptance of one another despite our differences. And it is extraordinary how it got lost. Mine got lost at SA Breweries. Wooltru's got lost as a public company fighting out there in the shark tank of commerce. And South Africa's got lost in apartheid. My trauma, my Monopoly game, was 1980. Wooltru's Monopoly game, if you like, was 1988. South Africa's was 1990. The theme running through all of what's happened since to all three is about difference.

The crises were the same—crises of coercive power getting out of hand, and a system saying, "Enough!" Sometimes when the majority finds out about the dishonesty of the elite system—when the collective power at the bottom of an organization sorts it out for itself, there grows a deep yearning within for something different. That yearning led me to leave Breweries, led Wooltru to seek me, and led President de Klerk to voluntarily hand over power to the enemy—an awesome arsenal of power ranging from psychological power over the mind to G6 missiles. At that time, the enemy was Nelson Mandela and the terrorists in the ANC. What an extraordinary enemy he has turned out to be. His personal mission, against the backdrop of our awful past, is to liberate both the oppressed and the oppressors, because we were all victims of an excessive power phenomenon. That sense of reconciliation, that sense of forgiveness, is far more interesting and exciting than the handing over of power. We have a president who has put on hold the inevitable reactions of whites to blacks and right-wing to left-wing just long enough for us to reconsider what sort of world we want South Africa to be. And he's authentic. In South Africa, we have leadership at this moment in time which is putting together a mission about difference, forgiveness, and interdependence.

In this mad, competitive world of win-lose, retribution, and revenge, the leadership of this country has come out with a Truth and Reconciliation Commission (TRC). The way that works is quite extraordinary. It's about amnesty. It's about truth. It's about compensation, not retribution. What Mandela said was, "It's no good sweeping all this stuff up under the carpet because there's too much there. There's too much pain and suffering and anger, and too much unknown. We must get it out. We must let it flow." So day after day, this commission sits and listens to people telling stories about what happened in the apartheid era—what happened to them as blacks, what happened to policemen who were forced to do things they didn't want to do.

Another department of the TRC listens all day to people coming with amnesty abdication: "I did what was wrong." I voluntarily stood before that commission. Although my crime was not a crime of commission, it was a serious crime of omission. I should have known more about what was going on. I could have done more. When my son asked me, "Dad, what did you do?" I didn't feel good. I couldn't tell him of a single person I had hurt deliberately. But as a person in positions of considerable power and influence I had failed to be human and caring and I needed to make my confession. It was an extraordinary experience for me to rid myself of it.

I wasn't in real trouble, but I sat in the same room with people who had life sentences for terrible murders. Have you ever been in a room with convicted murderers? It's an interesting experience. Three men convicted of murdering a young, white, American woman sat on the front row; I sat right behind them on the second row. There they sat pleading for amnesty. The commissioners asked questions such as: Are you sorry? What is the full truth? To what extent was it truly politically motivated? The two accomplices were ducking and diving as many do in such painful situations: "Well, it wasn't really our fault."

The commissioners were getting increasingly impatient with them because the whole thing about amnesty is that you bring it all out. Suddenly, the man who actually drove the dagger into the young woman poured out his confession. I have never heard anything like it in my life. But more was to come. When he finished, the victim's parents got up and pardoned him. They forgave him. Then they hugged his parents, who were sitting next to him.

For a moment in our history, we are learning to live with amnesty.

We are learning to live with more than one way of dealing with things in a country that has only known win-lose. We are striving to empower people, which is not about giving people fish. It's about teaching them to fish. Additionally, we are trying to build a country that is ethical and principled. It's not doing well at the moment in that area. But you can't manage and force that kind of change. That change has to be profoundly lived. It takes time. We see it as an extraordinary challenge and opportunity to, as Gandhi said, "become the change we seek in the world."

After assuming the helm of Wooltru, I resolved to be a different kind of leader. I wanted to start giving a twist to the tail of the tiger. I wanted to teach, to affirm, to discover and draw out the uniqueness, energy, and genius inside of our people. But I had to be prepared to give up power. So I started organizing sessions with our people to talk about abundance, win-win, interdependence, synergy, community—the principles inherent within the 7 Habits. I soon found that stories of Africa, of principles they had always lived but weren't allowed to practice at work, started flowing from the hearts of our people. Can you imagine what it is like for me, as the chief executive of a business that now has thirty thousand people, to be able to take two and a half days every month, if not every two weeks, to spend with my people teaching, discovering, and empowering? Imagine what it is like for me to mix a potion of these stories coming from them, and share them throughout our business! This is how our mission reads:

> Wooltru aspires to be the core of an African "community" or uMphakathi [uMphakathi *means community. To be an* uMphakathi, *you have to work together on the inside. You have to play music of the soul to get it. You have to have agonized together*] *of diverse, focused, interdependent trading enterprises, striving towards global effectiveness through leadership, which:*

- shares and upholds a common set of admirable principles;
- respects traditional shopkeeping and trading excellence;
- embraces modern technology;
- is driven to produce substantial free cash flow;

- regards information as a key source and uses it effectively;

- above all, seeks to create an environment in which high levels of positive energy and substantial wealth are generated and shared in unique, synergistic, and open relationships with one another and with our stakeholders [most of whom are women].

We are having the time of our lives. We're coming to a deeper understanding of nature and of African culture. It is an extraordinary opportunity to share and work with people who are wiser than we are, and have been wiser for a long, long time. We are pursuing the possibility of a simpler way. If I had said to the board, "This is my menu for change," I think they would have thought I was mad. Looking back, that's exactly what I should have said. Our price-earnings ratio is now the highest in the retail sector. So this stuff works. It's not just talk. We are celebrating what, I guess, humans always knew—that families and the way families work, and that respect, joy, and admiration for difference is the thing that makes the difference; not power, not superiority, not being the master.

Colin and I were joint teaching once at a Young President's Organization International University held in Sun City, South Africa. Many in the audience were friends of Colin and others knew of his great reputation and success record. His company was the leading retailer in his industry in his country and had made tremendous upward strides in almost every way. They asked him several questions to see what the key elements were to such an astounding success. The essence of what he said was profoundly meaningful. He told his own story and related his inward struggle to reinvent his life around correct principles. He talked of the inward journey into the core of his value system; of his willingness and desire to look at it freshly and to let his conscience, his sense of right and wrong, be his guide. The real climax of his expression came when he said, "Everything began to change for me when I got apartheid out of my heart." As you may know, apartheid means "apart from." It may be on the basis of race, of social standing, educational attainment, religious affiliation, or whatever other stereotype or label might be used to separate one group from another. He indicated that when he got it out of his heart, he saw people differently. He listened to them differently. He discovered the inward resources that came from the human differences. He came to very special personal insights that eventually led him to a management style that released human potential instead of trying to control or contain it. I felt, at the time, a profound reverence for this great soul. I felt profound gratitude for the kind of inward courage it took for him to discover his true nature and the true nature of his country. And he's allowed it to express itself fully in his life, his teachings, and his leadership endeavors.

Doug Conant, President, Nabisco U.S. Foods Group

Look for three things in this story: first, the constant, personal struggle that never lets up; second, how fragile trust is—how the Emotional Bank Account, if not attended to with regular deposits, will gradually evaporate away; third, how the 7 Habits really is hard, bottom-line stuff, not just soft, touchy-feely study material.

My life in recent years has been caught somewhere between two books I keep on a shelf in my office, *Barbarians at the Gate* and *The 7 Habits of Highly Effective People*. However, this is not so much my story, as it is the story of the remarkably resilient people of Nabisco and their efforts to succeed in the face of wave after wave of significant change.

RJR Nabisco is the $25 billion company that in 1988 was the target of the world's largest hostile takeover. That leveraged buyout is the subject of *Barbarians at the Gate*, a book that chronicles the LBO feeding frenzy which took over Wall Street in the late 1980s.

Three years after RJR Nabisco was taken over by the leveraged buyout firm of KKR, who were cast as the Barbarians in the book, I joined the Nabisco U.S. Foods Group as the vice president and general manager of one of its smaller divisions. I came from simple Midwestern roots with a simple Midwestern work ethic. I developed a reputation as an executive who delivered strong performance at two large Midwestern food companies. I considered myself a principled businessperson who cared about the people I worked with. I had always tried to balance my commitment to increasing shareholder value with a genuine concern for the welfare of those who worked for and with me.

My ability to realize that balance has always been challenged in the workplace, but never more than during my seven-year tenure with Nabisco. The magnitude of the leveraged buyout created enormous pressure to perpetually produce greater returns to justify the record-setting investment. Ultimately, the demand for profit growth exceeded our capacity to produce it—creating an enormous strain on the business and on the employees.

One of the mottoes within the corporate culture was "Whatever It

Takes"—in other words, you did whatever it took (within legal, moral, and ethical bounds) to deliver the expected results in the moment, in the quarter, and in the year. Each successive quarter became the most important quarter in the company's history. You delivered and dealt with the consequences later. If you didn't deliver as expected, it was easy to feel that your career was at risk.

My challenge coming into the company was not only to deliver up to expectations every year and every quarter, but to find a way to lay a foundation for long-term success as well. The difficulty was that the company was doing things to meet short-term expectations that simply could not be sustained over time.

As I faced this new environment, I needed tools that were aligned with my own core values and that would be leverageable in this new setting. I found such tools in the 7 *Habits* I had picked up in an airport shortly before joining Nabisco. As I crafted my own Personal Mission Statement, the principles contained in the 7 Habits deeply resonated with my own core values. Looking back on it now, nearly ten years later, the vision of my life contained in my Personal Mission Statement has provided me with the inner strength necessary to weather the many storms and moments of doubt that I have encountered in both my professional and personal life.

When I arrived at Nabisco, I found an organization filled with good people who wanted to succeed. There were strong underlying business fundamentals in place. But I also found employees who were powerfully traumatized by the LBO and who were understandably suspicious of newcomers like myself. Succeeding at Nabisco would not be easy. In fact, during my early days with the company, I often wondered what I had gotten myself into. On the other hand, however, the situation energized me. That challenge was the reason I had been attracted to Nabisco in the first place. I saw an enormous opportunity to make a difference.

I certainly got the challenge I was looking for. My first assignment in Nabisco as vice president and general manager was to develop a winning business proposition and culture in the $400 million Fleischmann's division. We made great headway, delivered our financial commitments, and began to create a high-performance "Can Do" culture characterized by a remarkable degree of esprit de corps. Unfortunately, I was only in that position for nine months when I was asked to move to Nabisco's largest operating company, the $3.5 billion Nabisco Biscuit Company, as senior vice president of marketing.

As I entered the Nabisco Biscuit Company, the organization was in a painful state of disarray. The prior-year performance had been very disappointing and the marketing department, which I was to head, had experienced an extraordinarily difficult year under the previous leader, who had left the company. Clearly, we had to get both the business *and* the organization on track—and quickly! On the business front, we quickly focused the organization on a game plan that leveraged our remarkable ability to innovate with our unprecedented brand strength and our unique selling system. To get the business on track initially, we necessarily took a very hands-on, structured approach focused on delivering against a clear set of near-term priorities. Fortunately, that game plan ultimately led to the three best years of performance in the company's hundred-year history.

In many ways, that was the easy part. We also had to create a winning culture. Once again, I was most fortunate to be thrown into the breach with a group of talented people who had, only momentarily, lost their sense of direction. To get a better handle on the situation, I ordered a survey of employee attitudes using the Center for Values Research. Their expert who interprets the results is a wonderful, slightly crusty veteran of thousands of these surveys. His final report clearly stated that out of all the surveys he had ever done, ours had produced the worst results. The only way he could characterize our culture was "swamp water." He said our employees had the lowest trust levels he'd ever seen.

He was right on target, of course. I'd never encountered such a numb and distressing environment. After receiving the "swamp water" report and sharing it with my executive team, we decided that it was critical that we take a serious approach to helping us evolve from what I would call a dependent, highly reactive sea-of-victims culture to one that was highly proactive and increasingly interdependent. Encouragingly, this direction struck a chord with most of my executive team.

As we approached the end of our first year, we decided to provide 7 Habits training for everyone in our part of the organization. We did it because we were convinced that you can't just motivate people to change, you have to provide them with the tools. Looking back, it proved to be a critical step because it offered a tangible sign to all of our employees that the company (as embodied by our leadership team) did care about their personal and professional development. It spoke to them on both levels. It said that we know you are a person, as well as an employee. It also spoke to one of my core beliefs: we can't expect an employee to value the organization until we have tangibly demonstrated that the organization values that employee. Ultimately, it's that simple.

We found that we really needed to start the training with the three foundational habits. First, we started celebrating people who had a proactive mind-set [Habit 1: Be Proactive]. We began holding town hall meetings in which employees were recognized for taking initiative and displaying proactive qualities. Historically, this organization had celebrated people who put out fires, but we wanted to go beyond that. We wanted to encourage proactivity, so we rewarded and promoted people who headed off problems before they ignited, as well as those who put out the fires.

Next, we moved toward helping the organization start to focus on what was truly important. We created a team comprised of people across our organization from all levels and asked them to help us create a sense of direction (a mission) for the organization [Habit 2: Begin with the End in Mind]. We had to tackle this task pretty gingerly, though, because we were still operating in a skeptical environment where many people were still functioning in a reactive mode, questioning whether we or they could really influence the future. The skeptics viewed our approach to leadership and team building as "soft" and they questioned our "toughness." They criticized the "lovey-dovey-Covey" approach and they had the false impression that "all they want to do is hold hands and sing 'Kumbaya.'" So, we took it slow, put one foot in front of the other, and gradually built up the organization's confidence, as we delivered on our commitments and displayed disciplined mental toughness.

It took a good year to establish a more proactive mind-set, establish our mission, and begin to earn some credibility in the organization. Next, we went to work on a strategic plan to achieve our goals [Habit 3: Put First Things First]. This strategic plan needed to be different—we had to make sure we had the wherewithal to stay focused on the plan. It couldn't be like the traditional strategic plan where you developed it only for the presentation and then used it as a doorstop after the meeting. So once we developed our plan, we started building the framework of the plan into the fabric of our daily operations. We started to view the three-year plan as a twelve-quarter plan—making sure that every quarter we were on track to deliver our strategic plan commitments.

Most of this work occurred during the year following the "swamp water" report. Then we did another survey. I'll never forget the old guy's words on the tape he sent back with the analysis. "This is unbelievable," he said. "It is one of the most remarkable turnarounds I have ever seen. You have gone from swamp water to Perrier!"

The following year, we did the survey again, and the results were even better. "This is incredible," he reported. "You have gone from swamp water to Perrier to champagne!"

Without a doubt, those two and a half years in the Nabisco Biscuit Company were among the most rewarding years of my professional life. Once again, I was privileged to work with many good, caring, and committed people, who hungered to do better . . . and, together, we did.

As good as I feel about the accomplishments we've made and the tools we've tried to give people through training, my deeper satisfactions have come through my personal efforts to establish relationships with our people and to build a positive, abundant, and affirming culture.

One thing I've done over the years is "declare myself" with my people and organization each time I've moved into a new responsibility. Day one (or maybe two), I spend about an hour with each direct report and spell out what's important to me, what I believe in, and why I do the things I do. I tell them ahead of time, "I'm going to share with you some things about me, and I would be honored to know some things about you. I want to take the mystery out of this relationship as quickly as possible so we can get on with the business of doing better. Then you can start measuring me against what I tell you. I believe you'll discover very quickly on that I will act with integrity."

I've found that doing this early and in a fairly personal way with my direct reports, and then more generally in writing with the broader organization, is an incredibly powerful tool. It creates a new beginning and sets in motion a dynamic of building trust.

Another thing I've tried to do with the organization is emphasize learning and personal growth [Habit 7: Sharpen the Saw]. Over the years I have become a student of leadership and business and I have developed an extensive library on those subjects. I am constantly giving books to employees that seem relevant to their professional development. I also have an Executive Book-of-the-Month Club to whom I distribute all kinds of reading materials to stimulate thinking and growth. Fundamentally, I've come to the point of view that life is very Darwinian when it comes to professional (or personal) growth—you either grow or die, there is no in between. As for myself and our organization, we will grow or die trying.

In terms of my own personal development, I've also built a network of friends, former associates, and advisors who help me keep my thinking and my leadership development fresh and moving forward. I try to stay in touch with them regularly. I trust their caring objectivity and find it essential to my growth.

I have also learned the value of saying thank you and acknowledging people [Emotional Bank Account]. Around fifteen years ago when I was going through my one (and hopefully only) outplacement experience, my counselor challenged me to send everyone I encountered during my search a thank-you note within twenty-four hours of my interaction with them. While my track record on this front was far from perfect, I discovered it was a highly distinctive process and it paid dividends. On a more personal level, I just felt better about myself for doing it. As a result, to this day, I am constantly looking for opportunities to affirm positive behavior in the organization. Every day, we are doing thousands of things right and I believe it is critical for management to celebrate those contributions. To be sure, we are also making mistakes and we need to deal with them in an equally swift and decisive manner. Unfortunately, unless one is vigilant, it becomes easy to find the mistakes and equally easy to overlook the contributions. If a secretary goes out of their way to help me on something, I make it a point to say thank you. If I become aware that an employee has done something exceptional, I'll dash off a note to them. Whenever I become aware of someone joining the company, leaving the company, or changing jobs within the company,

I try to get off a personal note acknowledging their contributions in some way.

By writing five to ten of these notes a day, I've probably sent over ten thousand in my tenure with Nabisco, and have, once again, learned that you get phenomenal returns. But I don't do it looking for a return. I do it because it is fulfilling to me. I also do it because it is unrealistic for me to expect extraordinary effort and performance from people if I don't personally create an environment where people feel special and extraordinarily valued. As a business leader, you can never forget that your every action is being scrutinized by the organization. People watch you and they read you. They are hungry to make a personal connection with you and the greater organization, but they are also quick to judge you. That is why it is so important to declare yourself as a leader and walk the talk. If you do, you build credibility and trust; if you don't, you don't.

Even with all the progress we've made, I honestly can't say everything is perfect. After leading the Nabisco Biscuit Company marketing effort for a little over two years, I was moved to be president of the sales and integrated logistics organization, where we embarked on a massive upgrading effort which also substantially lowered our cost base. As part of the upgrading effort, we put in place a talented team of sales and logistics professionals who are continuing to lead that organization to even higher ground today. After making headway there, I was promoted to run a larger group of companies doing $3.5 billion in sales with over seven thousand top-notch employees, which is what I'm doing now. Each time, I've had to start my leadership work over again from ground zero and I've had to watch as some of the momentum I established in my former assignments took on a new direction under new leadership.

I was recently at a conference standing in front of a roomful of presidents and chief executives sharing my leadership experiences. Eventually, I began describing how I had been promoted to a position where it was increasingly difficult to have day-to-day influence on the culture of the company. Also the entire company had fallen on difficult times and we had the first CEO change in my seven-year tenure with the company. Everything we did was understandably being questioned and all of the hard work undertaken in the prior seven years was lost on the new leadership.

I went on to say that the last year had clearly been the toughest of my twenty-four-year career. We had dramatically reset the course of Nabisco. We had divested over $500 million of businesses which were strategic misfits. We had reduced head count nearly 30 percent to set the cost structure properly. We had redefined the roles and responsibilities of everyone in the organization.

From a purely business perspective, it had been a very fulfilling experience. We had made and implemented the tough decisions in a swift, decisive, and successful fashion—and we were already beginning to reap the rewards of those efforts. For the first time in my seven-year history with the company, the long-term course of Nabisco was on solid footing.

At the same time, however, it was a huge cultural change which wreaked havoc with the life of each and every employee. Friends were being let go by the company, roles were changing, and the future, at times, was uncertain. Anxiety was in the air. Through it all, we tried to honor every individual to the best of our ability but, in the end, I felt like I had cashed in every one of those ten thousand chips in the Emotional Bank Account created by writing those encouraging notes.

I described how I was beginning to doubt whether my contributions were being valued. It was unclear whether the new CEO was satisfied with my performance and I wondered how much the organization cared that I was trying to do the right things for them *and* the shareholders.

Right in the middle of my presentation, I came to a deeply disturbing realization. I was getting worn down by the enormousness of the challenge. I was becoming a victim, becoming reactive. I was starting to drift into a highly dependent state where the glass was chronically half empty. I realized that I had to start all over in proving myself and my methods. Yet I wondered if I had the courage, the strength, and the stamina to rise to the occasion yet again.

As I returned home from the conference, I reexamined my situation in depth. As I thought more about my situation I become more encouraged. Once again, the people of the Nabisco U.S. Foods Group were rising to the challenges of the day and delivering remarkable performance in the face of unprecedented change. We were growing sales and overdelivering our earnings commitment. At the same time, we were setting the table for continued success in the future. I took heart from their efforts and said to myself, "Wait a minute. We *are* doing the right things here and we *are* making a positive difference. I know it and I don't care if anybody else knows it or not. I'm just going to have to redeclare myself in this new environment and keep on keeping on."

I reminded myself that no one ever said leadership would be easy and that everyone is going to have their moments of doubt. When my moments of doubt set in, I take what I call my deep dive; I plunge back into my Personal Mission Statement and get reconnected. To that end, I have a framed copy of my mission statement on my desk and I always carry a copy in my briefcase. I make it a point to constantly be revisiting and reflecting on my values and my roles in life. In fact, I've found that my energy level almost depends on that kind of self-reflection each morning. I get up before anyone in the family is awake and I spend about thirty minutes just collecting my thoughts in a comfortable chair with a cup of coffee either in the garden or inside. Then I exercise for fifteen to thirty minutes. It's my own little way of renewing myself, getting in touch with nature and with life. In fact, the days I don't do it, I can sure feel a difference.

I've found that just as it's important to do the small things at work, I need to do the small things at home. I try to have a personal connection with each member of my family every day. I used to be in the office early every morning. Now, I stay home and try to connect with each of my children over breakfast and take at least one of them to school every day. These personal connections with them have become important to me. I also try to connect with my wife each morning. She's usually up later at night, which is her personal quiet time, so she doesn't get up as early as I do. This gives me a great chance to help her get started on her day in a warm, gentle way and then be off. I find my relationship with my wife, which is the most treasured of all my relationships, to be the one that most easily gets short shrift during the day. So, at least momentarily, we try to have a brief but meaningful connection every morning. Once I retake the plunge and have my daily victory every morning, I have renewed energy for my day.

Another step I've taken to maintain my energy and focus is to annually take a sabbatical. I go off by myself every fall for three to four days to revisit my personal mission and my professional direction. I find a supportive environment where I can escape the daily grind, get close to nature, and reflect on my life journey. It is a provocatively refreshing experience.

Professionally, my career experience with Nabisco has been challenging but rewarding. Time and again, the people in the organization have demonstrated that they have the capacity to build a principle-centered culture *and* deliver superior business results. I take heart from their efforts and I realize that I, too, have that same capacity—even if things have changed and I have to start all over.

I honestly couldn't live any other way. And, I'm starting all over again . . . and looking forward to the journey.

✳ *"Yesterday's meal does not satisfy today's hunger." If Emotional Bank Accounts are not continually attended to, particularly with the people we are working with and living around every day, inevitably yesterday's deposits will evaporate and simply will not satisfy today's need. Think of the amount of courage, patience, and persistence it took for this president to practice these principles in faith. It was like swimming upstream against very powerful currents of culture, business context, and market pressures. Idealism and pragmatism came together. Principles consistently practiced simply have to be consistently practiced again today and tomorrow. That's why it is so important to institutionalize the principles into the everyday processes, structures, and systems of an organization. Only then will the organization be freed from being dependent upon the deposits that leaders make into the Emotional Bank Account. In other words, you design the recruiting and selection system, the training and development system, the communication and decision-making system, the planning system, the information system, and the reinforcement systems of both psychic and financial compensation—all to be in harmony with the underlying principles and values built into the mission statement. Then the principle center, the soul of the organization, can be continually reinforced in its day-to-day operations. The real key is to get the 7 Habits working at the personal, the interpersonal, the managerial, and the organizational levels. There is an interactive synergy between all four levels. Creativity feeds upon itself.*

In this inspiring story, we also see an enormous amount of

Sharpen the Saw renewal activity—personally, interpersonally, and managerially. This is an amazing president who understands the importance of P and PC (performance and performance capability), the goose and the golden egg—that the essence of effectiveness is being able to get results now in a way that eventually enables getting even more in the future.

For a schedule of the 7 Habits workshops in over 300 cities and of Stephen R. Covey's public presentations, go to www.franklincovey.com/public

Pete Beaudrault, COO, Hard Rock Cafe

As you study the effects of a heart attack on this leader's life, notice
two things: first, how a crisis not only reprioritizes a person's life
and values, but also expands and deepens self-reflection and self-
awareness; and second, how this reprioritization affects not only
one's lifestyle but one's management and working style.

I have no difficulty remembering the exact time and day that I regained my perspective on life.

It was 7:00 A.M., February 25, shortly after my fortieth birthday. I'd
gone to the hospital with chest pains and the doctor told me I was
having a heart attack. I had emergency angioplasty and then six
months later I had double bypass surgery. That experience provided
me a great opportunity to reflect on my life. It really made me want to
create more balance.

Prior to my heart attack, I'd been caught up in the whirlpool. You
drive to work, you jump in the whirlpool, you get bounced around all
week, you get thrown out, and the next week you jump back in. That
was my life: seven days a week, 365 days a year. I had forfeited personal values to attain professional objectives. I had moved fifteen
times in fourteen years for the good and the glory of the company but
to the detriment of my family and my health.

When I took the time to reflect, I realized that I really had it backward, particularly when it came to my four children and my wife and
what this whole life really means. So, upon recovering from my bypass surgery, I returned to my office only long enough to pack up a
few things and to resign. Then I went looking for a less stressful place
to work.

I found it in a most improbable place: Hard Rock Cafe. The same
legendary, international restaurant chain that had just been consoli-
dated and was about to undertake one of the most ambitious expansion campaigns in its history.

I discovered that Hard Rock Cafe was not your average bear as a
restaurant operation, which is why I am now proudly the chief operating officer of Hard Rock Cafe International, which has one hundred
restaurants in thirty-four countries.

Friends Isaac Tigrett and Peter Morton opened the first Hard Rock

Cafe in London in 1971. They were Americans living in England but yearning for a hamburger and fries. Their London restaurant quickly became a favorite haunt of rock and roll musicians, many of whom donated instruments or other pieces of memorabilia that became part of the Hard Rock Cafe's signature decor. Thirteen years later, the two partners split up. Isaac opened the second Hard Rock Cafe in New York City where its reputation for attracting celebrities made it the place to see and be seen. Its success spawned expansion around the globe as well as competition from a wide array of similar theme restaurant chains such as Planet Hollywood and the House of Blues.

The culture at Hard Rock is very different from that in most organizations. We celebrate the spirit of rock and roll. We accept people for who they are and what they are. That makes it a tremendous amount of fun. Employees have traditionally been allowed to wear counterculture hairstyles and "fashion statements" that would not be allowed in more conservative restaurants. The relatively lax dress code, generous benefits, and flexible work hours have produced an unusually loyal workforce with remarkably low turnover in a business known for its fast rate of burnout. The Hard Rock chain was also among the very first commercial enterprises to openly embrace social causes, including them in its marketing and holding special events in their benefit.

When I came to Hard Rock Cafe International as vice president of operations, however, it was encountering some serious culture shock due to a merger and rapid expansion.

There I was, recovering from a heart attack and looking for more balance with a company that planned to nearly double the number of its restaurants within four or five years. I had my work cut out.

At that time, the corporate office, rather than the operators in the field, drove our culture. There were seven vice presidents and each one of them plugged into the individual restaurants at will. The poor general managers, the people most critical for the success of the organization, would be getting directions from seven different people. My goal was to invert that pyramid and make it an operations-driven company with the guests or customers and the employees at the top and the CEO at the bottom.

I saw that the rapid expansion could easily dilute and even spoil the restaurant chain's trademark dining and working environment.

Years earlier, I had been successful in applying the 7 Habits in a similar situation with another company. I introduced the Habits to Hard Rock as a way of establishing a common culture to bond all of the new employees with the existing staff, and to give them a set of guiding principles [Habit 2: Begin with the End in Mind].

But I had a far more personal reason for making the 7 Habits a centerpiece of the company. I didn't want to have another heart attack, nor did I want my employees to suffer the burnout that is endemic to the restaurant industry. I thought that an Inside-Out Approach would be a benefit to myself and everyone in the company.

I refuse to get sucked into the whirlpool again. My goal is to first succeed at home with my family and then at Hard Rock. Now, when I go home from the office, I am officially off duty. Everyone knows that I won't take or make any calls unless there is a real emergency. We tell our general managers at each store that it should be the same for them [Habit 3: Put First Things First]. At Hard Rock, my goal has been to lead by example, not to manage by dictating. I have made my family-first, work-second policy known throughout the organization because I want my employees to live with that end in mind, too.

I serve as an example of what can happen to people who get caught up in the whirlpool of work. It adds credibility to my story. People have to believe that both their personal and professional lives are marathons, not sprints. We tell everyone that our priorities are health, family, and Hard Rock, in that order. I believe that if our employees follow that philosophy we will ultimately be a better business. It takes a strong commitment to model that both at work and at home.

It is more of a challenge to keep it going at home. My ten-year-old is a first-degree black belt and I take classes with her every week. I could easily come up with a hundred reasons to skip that class, but you have to be committed.

My general manager of the Hard Rock Cafe in San Diego, Joe Baldwin, recently had his own test of faith. Just one hour before his restaurant was to stage its grand opening, Joe received a telephone call from his pregnant wife. She had gone into labor. For an instant, he was paralyzed, fearing that his staff would feel abandoned at a critical time. Instead of becoming anxious, everybody on the staff celebrated by walking Joe out to his car. They told him "Godspeed." He was just blown away by that.

Hard Rock Cafes have encouraged their employees to consider themselves part of a family. We've done that by establishing more liberal flex-work hours, benefits programs, and bonus payments. As a result, Hard Rock's employees are less likely to jump ship, and more likely to move up in the organization. Turnover among restaurant workers generally runs nearly 75 percent for management jobs and over 100 percent for hourly-wage workers. At Hard Rock Cafe, it is well below 30 percent for management and close to 60 percent for hourly workers. My management staff has worked hard to nurture its relationships with employees and customers even as the chain has expanded around the globe. The payoff has come in an industry-leading rate of low turnover, and in far less measurable but equally important ways.

Hard Rock Cafe, which often requires supervisors to make daily deposits in the Emotional Bank Accounts of their employees, also takes a proactive role with employees in need, and within the communities we serve.

In Myrtle Beach, South Carolina, a newly divorced working mother came home from a shift serving customers at the Hard Rock to find that her new apartment was not quite as threadbare as she'd left it. Her co-workers had chipped in and bought new chairs and couches so that her life would not seem so empty. It didn't, and the furniture was only a small part of the reason. She realized that her co-workers understood and cared about her.

At the Hard Rock Cafe in Maui, Hawaii, an empowered workforce has become a force unto itself. The staff put together a Christmas toy drive and a party for underprivileged children, with no management involvement. They staged the toy drive, put together a menu, invited the families, notified the press, and coordinated the entire event. The only manager involved was the one they asked to dress up like Santa Claus.

The restaurant business can grind people up, so we try to help our employees build their self-worth and their sense of belonging to a larger community. It's good for them and it is good for the company, and believe me, I know it is good for me, too.

 As the saying goes, "No one on their deathbed ever wished they had spent more time at the office." It usually takes a crisis to jerk a person

out of their unconscious, "being lived" mode into one of conscious reflection on what really matters most. Once people begin to reflect, wisdom begins to be unleashed inside, and they get hold of themselves again. In the case of this senior executive, when he both took control and became aware of and committed to the principles embodied in the 7 Habits, he slowly developed an empowering release philosophy of management. This helped form a "live and let live" culture that tapped into the deepest energies and commitment of the people in the restaurants throughout the chain.

When the leadership work of developing overall values is done first, it allows a release philosophy of management to evolve. Without a common purpose and value system, then management control is necessary to keep things together. But a control management style never taps into the deepest energies, loyalties, and creative powers of people; it enables survival only if the competitors are equally dumb. Empowered cultures behind a common vision are unbeatable.

Chris Turner, Learning Person,
Xerox Business Services

*Talk about the courage and confidence of a change agent! Notice in
the following story Chris Turner's complete belief in a release
philosophy rather than a control philosophy. She demonstrates that
the power lies within the people to figure things out, rather than with
just those at the top who make all the decisions while the rest wield
the screwdrivers.*

In 1993, I was given a unique job title and a sizable challenge. I was
appointed to be the designated "Learning Person" at Xerox Business
Services (XBS), one of the fastest growing companies in the world.

I had been with XBS nearly thirteen years at that point, and, as a
natural-born maverick, I'd made a game of working around the bureaucracy's silly rules to help it achieve its goals. When they made me
the company's change agent, they put the fox in charge of the hen-
house.

Well, they didn't exactly put me in charge. I was reporting to a
member of the president's staff, but I didn't let that stop me. The company's top executives *said* they wanted to create a greater sense of
unity and shared goals within XBS and they asked me to help them
create an entirely new organization.

Later, I'd discover that what they said they wanted, and what they
were willing to change, were two entirely different things. But at the
time I took my job title as license to change all the things I had come
to hate about bureaucratic organizations and their treatment of the
people who actually did the work and produced the profits.

My goal was to create an organization of fifteen thousand exceptional businesspeople. We assumed that everyone wanted to be an
entrepreneur within the company, and we gave them credit for having the brains and initiative to do it. I saw this as my chance also to
help create an environment where XBS'ers had the freedom to use all
of their skills, to make independent decisions, to be creative and innovative, to respond quickly and efficiently to customers' needs, and
to feel free to take risks that would benefit the organization.

My mission was to change the culture within what is essentially a virtual company. There were then more than fifteen thousand employees at XBS but only a small percentage could be found at the corporate headquarters in Rochester, New York. More than 80 percent of XBS's employees are outsourced to the offices of their client companies around the globe. They produce, manage, and distribute documents for more than four thousand clients in thirty-six nations.

The challenges of maintaining effective communication and a healthy corporate culture under such circumstances were considerable, particularly when your company is in a period of rapid growth. In the early 1990s, XBS's annual growth rate exceeded 40 percent. The inner turmoil was increasing right along with it.

Our corporation had more territorial rivalries than the Middle East. Information was hoarded. Communication was disjointed. Trust and synergy were virtually nonexistent. XBS managers in different regions would poach business in each other's territories because their compensation was based on each region's revenues and profits, not overall performance. I guess you could say the Scarcity Mentality was an organizational pattern. Most employees operated under the assumption that there was only so much business out there and they felt their jobs hinged on them grabbing as much of it as possible.

This had been going on for a while but the company had been too busy growing and producing profits for anyone to become concerned. Then, in the early 1990s, the alarms went off. Suddenly, the competition was all over us, undercutting our prices and courting our customers. XBS had to get its act together. It wasn't enough to be bigger; we had to be smarter. One of my directives was to make the company more competitive: "We must learn faster than our competition and faster than the marketplace." My job was to help create among the company's widely scattered population a sense of shared purpose [Habit 2: Begin with the End in Mind] so that they would communicate across territorial and functional boundaries for the good of the entire enterprise. Our strategy was designed to engage the entire system but it recognized that change is really a grassroots process.

One of our inspirations was Camp Lur'ning, a large gathering designed to nurture the spirit of our change strategy in a critical mass of

XBS people from a wide range of job categories. I don't believe in the old saying that change must begin from the top in an organization. I believe it comes from within, so our goal was to build momentum laterally.

After recruiting the best, brightest, and most highly motivated people, we gently immersed them in the realities of our business, presenting them with information on profit margins, the marketplace, and the influences impacting the decisions of their customers [Habit 5: Seek First to Understand, Then to Be Understood]. They also were introduced to a specially designed 7 Habits course to provide them with foundational principles and context for the other materials. But nothing was forced upon them. They had no daily schedules. No required meetings. I don't believe that chaos is good for organizations, but I do believe that at the edge of chaos is where you have that tension between control and innovation. I think you need to be on that edge because that is where you have breakthroughs and insights.

There were only three rules at Camp Lur'ning: *Take care of yourself. Take care of each other. Take care of this place.* The underlying goal was to help folks learn how to align their interests more closely with those of their customers. To that end, some XBS campers brought one or two customers to camp with them. Workshops at the five-day Camp Lur'ning encouraged employees to have fun, to seek information, and to learn in fun new ways.

Habit 5—Seek First to Understand, Then to Be Understood—was strongly but subtly incorporated into many of the programs. Many of the workshops at Camp Lur'ning were in the form of games. One called Sleuth turned XBS employees into detectives. Their challenge was to learn as much as they could about an assigned customer and then devise a solution for winning the customer's business. It was intriguing as well as rewarding to see that many teams partnered up in displays of spontaneous synergy.

Another strategy game called Keep the Change provided a fun learning experience that helped our people get into the minds of their customers, while also keeping them alert to their own company's bottom line. The genesis of this workshop began when I read a newspaper article about a bank teller left alone on a Friday night at the drive-up window in a small branch bank in a blue-collar neighborhood. On this particular night, so many people came through the drive-through to cash paychecks that the teller ran out of change. So she began rounding everything up to the next dollar. She quickly went through dollar bills, so she had to round up to fives, then tens. By the close of business, she'd rounded up her way through $200 of the bank's money. She could have gotten in a lot of trouble, but this cashier made the case that failing to meet customers' needs would have undermined the bank's long-term relationship with the community. It didn't hurt that the news media learned of her largesse and praised her for doing the right thing. In fact, the incident generated so much good publicity the bank signed up a hundred new customers the next week.

The story's message that we wove into the workshop was that when you focus on what is right for your customers, it pays off in business results. That story set the context for the board game named Keep the Change. In the simulation, you advance around the board by making decisions about customer service that influence the company's bottom line. Players keep a balance sheet and use profit-and-loss principles while playing with a timer. Another learning experience used in tandem with Keep the Change was called We're Response-able. This workshop focused on the kind of thinking and acting that inevitably leads to doing the best things for our clients [Habit 1: Be Proactive].

The Camp Lur'ning event proved so popular that after campers went home, we were swamped with requests for a second Camp Lur'ning. Since our budget was limited, we asked the division general managers if they would cover the travel costs and enrollment fees of their own employees. I had been a general manager and I know that compensation for the position *is* based on profits. Because of that, GMs are fairly cheap about paying for anything out of their own budgets. (I can say that with some authority, because as a general manager I was tight, too.)

But many of the general managers had become so convinced of the value of Camp Lur'ning that they dug into their own "pockets" and sent nearly four hundred people to the second session. One general manager dispatched eighteen people, which cost him almost $40,000. Now that was a significant expenditure, but he saw the camp as an investment that would have a manyfold return.

The specially designed classes in *The 7 Habits* and *Principle-*

Centered Leadership proved to have long-lasting and profitable returns for XBS. When the camp participants returned to their offices, it wasn't long before mission statements began appearing on cubicle walls, and the conversations among employees were marked by references to making deposits into Emotional Bank Accounts. It was an experience of self-discovery for many people. They realized that the company valued them. I had spouses come up to me after their husbands or wives had been to a session and say, "This changed my life because it changed our family."

The personal benefits reaped by employees may well have exceeded those that impacted their work, but when professionals become empowered personally, it usually leads to improved performance in their work as well. My underlying assumption in designing the change approach was that people working at XBS should be honored rather than driven. Our intent was to help people understand their roles within XBS, to appreciate the challenges of a rapidly evolving marketplace, and to become more aware of how our competitors were positioning themselves. I also thought it vital that the XBS workforce understand not only their customers, but their customers' marketplaces and competition. Instead of controlling them to get results, I believed it was better to give them the freedom to creatively seek those results in their own way.

Marc Wilson, general manager of the XBS office in Denver, is one who, quite literally, found inspiration in his work with the Habits. His own words tell it best:

> *A few years ago I was confronted with the prospect of losing $250,000 in business each month. The biggest battle of my career began when my biggest client announced a company-wide plan to lower the cost of its document-processing services in offices spread across fourteen states.*
>
> *Our contract with the client provided 20 percent of my division's gross income. Our competitors were hungry for that business and when the client put out the word that bids would be accepted, the dogfight began. Our rivals offered to slash prices on their copy machines and document services. Our products are at the high end of the market. We couldn't compete in that environment. I spent months meeting with the client's executives, trying without success to convince them to focus on*

building a high-quality partnership to serve their long-term needs, rather than focusing merely on lowering costs for the short term. But it was difficult to convince them that I was just as interested in serving their needs as my own company's.

For months I had been trying to get that idea across to our client with no luck. While I was reviewing the 7 Habits one day, an idea came to me: "What if I related the 7 Habits to two organizations instead of just an individual person?" It was kind of a magical moment. I was inspired. When I started talking to the people I worked with at XBS they had no idea what I was talking about. They were scared to death that I was off on some tangent, but it proved to be very, very effective.

The insight came just as I was preparing for a crucial two-hour presentation to top executives of this organization whose business we risked losing. More than twenty of them were to be present, with several more taking part by telephone. I threw out my original strategy for the big meeting and reworked the entire presentation around these principles of effectiveness.

I started the meeting by asking how many of those present had read or heard of the 7 Habits book. About 50 to 70 percent were familiar with it, so that made things easier. Next I asked, "What if our two organizations brought their best resources together and applied the Habits to each other's work? What if we put down our weapons and stop attacking or finding fault and instead share the same end in mind and begin with a common goal [Habit 2: Begin with the End in Mind] which is based on mutual benefit [Habit 4: Think Win-Win]? What if instead of looking for the lowest cost for supplies, you look instead for a respected partner to help you strategically and tactically change both businesses for the better?"

I talked for two hours, relating each of the Habits to organizations working synergistically. I'd been trying to sell the same concept to them for months, but now I had a framework. I was asking them to take a huge gamble and trust a single vendor, which was anathema to the way they had always viewed those relationships. They saw their vendors as predators. I was trying to recast that perception. I wanted to replace suspicion with trust. I said that they could either go on fighting with their vendors or they could decide that it was possible for both sides to benefit with neither taking advantage of the other. It was a pretty radical approach for them to take, and for me to propose, but our company had been pushing us to be more innovative and to work at building more trust with clients by finding ways to improve their businesses while growing our relationships with them.

At the end of the meeting, the highest-level representative said he thought my proposal was a very compelling, exciting, and big idea. But he added that the idea of having a contract based on trust and mutual benefit was something they had never done. I could tell they got it and that it was an appealing idea, but he was also saying that they had never done anything like that and that maybe it wasn't practical in reality.

Later, I learned that the idea of forming strategic alliances [Habit 6: Synergize] had been floating around the upper levels of the organization but they had not found a way to make it work. The Habits showed how it could be done practically. In being principled, you can figure out how to do things that have never been done before.

Two months after that meeting, our client put its copier and document processing business out for bid with a list of sixteen questions for XBS and its competitors. The first question was "How would you define a win-win relationship?" and at least half of the rest related to things I had expressed in that meeting. They also asked things like "How is the top management of your organization committed to this relationship?" When we saw the questions they wanted answered it was almost as if we had written them. From that point it was a matter of explaining in detail all the things we had in place and making our presentation.

In the end, XBS was not the lowest-priced bidder for their contract. Unlike its competitors, XBS did not make any grand promises about exactly how much it would cut costs for them. I did make one daring promise, and it definitely got their attention.

Sensing that our client's executives were having difficulty overcoming their innate distrust of vendors in general, I decided I had to do something dramatic to win their trust. It seemed like they were afraid we might be hiding something from them because our proposal sounded too good to be true, so I offered to open our books for them. I said we would share how much we paid our people assigned to their contract and what our profit margins were.

I had to get approval from the highest levels of Xerox management, but I went for it in the belief that opening our books to our client would prove our trustworthiness. I guess this was a big test of whether XBS really was serious about letting its people in the field act like entrepreneurs. I should have been more nervous, but I felt confident in using these principles as the basis of my approach. I felt this was going to be either a win-win deal or no deal [Habit 4: Think Win-Win]. It made so much sense to me that if no one else in the company understood it or if they thought I should be put away, well, then I didn't belong there anyway. It was a very gutsy, high-risk approach but it helped us distance ourselves from the competition.

It also sealed the deal that led to a long-term and mutually beneficial strategic alliance with this client—a deal that has become a model for our business. In fact, after the deal was put together, I used the same approach to land three other big contracts. Those successful campaigns contributed to my winning the Xerox Corporation's President's Award in 1994. Only twenty-five Xerox employees out of 90,000 worldwide are given the award each year.

What Marc did is a great example of doing business based on principles and trusting relationships. Our change strategy was about challenging assumptions and finding fresh approaches. His approach to renewing the contract with a major client was just that. It was also a great example of being proactive, of beginning with the end in mind, of synergizing, and of doing all the other things the Habits encourage you to do.

Now, I don't want to sound like Pollyanna here, so let me add a qualifier. As the change agent at XBS, I took a lot of heat from all over the organization. It comes with the job title.

At one point early in the process, I was asked to leave a meeting that I had put together because senior executives weren't comfortable with my presence. I nearly quit at that point. But almost exactly one year later, I was called into another meeting and asked to come to the front of the room. There, in front of most of the top executives of XBS, a vice president who had been critical of the change strategy apologized to me, saying, "You've been right all along and I wasn't." After more than a year of crashing into the structures of the old organization, that was a very healing moment for me, and it made it all worthwhile.

In 1993, the employee satisfaction level was 63 percent. At the end of 1997, it was more than 80 percent. Externally, the results of our change strategy were cited by the Malcolm Baldrige National Quality Award committee as a factor in XBS being cited for outstanding service in 1997.

XBS's CEO, Tom Dolan, has become a true champion of this whole process. He summarized our efforts well: "These principles became a way of creating an environment that empowered our people at the customer sites where being proactive is critical. Our people need to take charge and do what they feel is right for the customer. The 7 Habits help you define what is important for you and what kind of person you want to be. It is a way of enriching the whole person. I think people need to feel good about themselves before they can feel good about what they do at work every day. The principles help people put balance in their lives, which powerfully impacts the day-to-day interactions of employees."

My goal was to create a community of inquirers and learners who would dare to be innovative and to take risks in seeking solutions to their business challenges. And, by nearly any measure I know of, it worked.

⊗ *It has been my experience that many human resource professionals cease to become real change catalysts like Chris because they gradually become seduced by cultural norms and the expectations of line management, so they settle back into personnel services work. People have to have enough internal security to be thick-skinned. When people do not possess internal security, then they usually try to get it externally, aligning themselves with present norms. So while they feel approved of and their work is accepted, they cease becoming change agents.*

To change a culture is to be aware that you cannot change the culture. All you can do is set certain principles into motion, get people and principles interacting together, and continue to have faith in the outcome. The principles must also be market-friendly, customer-friendly, and people-friendly. Chris recently left XBS to establish her own consulting practice in organizational change. What a powerful contribution she will surely continue to make—now with many more organizations!

Jack Little, President and CEO, Shell Oil Company

*As you study the following story of the reinvention of a company
and transformation of a culture from the inside out, notice the nature
of the struggle the president had to deal with personally—leaving
comfort zones, taking new risks, changing deeply embedded
paradigms. You can feel the humility and the courage of this leader.
You can also sense what a shuddering, difficult, and painstaking
process it involved.*

In the mid-1980s, the oil boom ended abruptly in defiance of most
expectations. It threw the major oil companies into a decade of organizational turmoil. Crude oil that had been selling for $25 to $30 a
barrel in 1983 had fueled annual profits in the billion-dollar range for
the major oil companies. Then it fell to $15 a barrel in 1988. The price of
oil has hovered in the lower regions ever since.

Shell Oil had been aggressively hiring employees based on expectations that crude oil would be selling for around $100 a barrel by
1997. When the price declined, Shell and the rest of the oil industry
began making massive layoffs. Most figured there were two choices:
get out, or get busy finding a way to survive in an entirely new environment.

At the time, I was president of Shell's Exploration and Production
Company. I thought at first that we needed to change the structure of
our organization to react to the lower prices, when in reality we
needed to make some fundamental changes in our personal and organizational behavior patterns. Our business was being run by cultural values that were out of step and out of phase. Things were
pretty gloomy. We had several years of downsizing and our business
was really not getting any better. Our cost structure was not good. We
were fighting a huge staff morale problem. People were concerned
that we were selling our future by eliminating so many positions.
Our exploration people, who are long-range thinkers by nature, were
particularly upset and thought that we were overreacting to a short-
term phenomenon.

The leadership team was under a lot of pressure. We tried many
different things short term and none of them seemed to help. My
view was that we just had not attacked the fundamental problem.

Our organization was hierarchical, bureaucratic, and inflexible. We were applying Band-Aids to wounds that needed tourniquets, or at least several hundred stitches. So that's what led up to our transformation process.

We didn't have a road map. But I brought in Denny Taylor as manager of continuous improvement to assist me in addressing our fundamental problems. I asked him to find out what other companies were doing to reengineer. I told him to take any course, attend any conference, and see what was going on, and then to report back. Several members of our leadership team came back from a conference convinced that the 7 Habits might provide us with a foundation for building change.

Denny said at the time, "If you are going to change the culture and the environment in which this company operates, you've got to change the people within it first." And that is what we tried to do. The Habits spoke to me personally, as I'm sure they did to the other members of the leadership team. I realized there were things that I had to change in my relationship with people on the leadership team, with our employees, and with my family. Very personal things. It was difficult for me because I'm not the kind of person that particularly likes to talk about personal matters. But I got to where I could handle that, at least comfortably.

We were very much an introverted company. We had never talked openly about our feelings about people and each other and our families. That just had not been part of our normal makeup. We began to loosen up. I became more willing to share in the decision-making process. I began delegating more to people down in the organization. In doing that, I signaled that I wanted to build a different kind of organization. When we began offering the 7 Habits, it was the first time that people saw that Shell cared one way or the other how they felt, or that family considerations were important. Eventually we trained five or six thousand of our people in these principles. People began putting pictures of their families on their desks for the first time.

Now as all this was being initiated, things still weren't going very well for the company. Some questioned our sanity in doing this "soft stuff" when the business was in the tank. But I thought it was absolutely essential to deal with changing what was within us before we could start to address the fundamental problems in our organization. In reality, the soft stuff was the hard stuff.

We had empowered a large part of our organization and we had begun to build a more trusting culture. We had stripped out redundant levels and pushed authority and empowerment down, yet something was still missing.

One of the things I realized in going through the internal changes was that as a leader, I'd built a finely tuned "risk elimination machine." I had all of these layers of managers who made my job easy, but they also made it difficult for new ideas to reach the top.

I had a powerful organization with four vice presidents and sixteen general managers at that point. Between the engineering level and me there was something squeezing the life out of what we were trying to build—this strong, centrally controlled management system. That is where my personal sacrifice had to begin.

I had to give up something good to get something better. I had to eliminate that layer of very good people who made certain that I never saw any proposal requiring my approval until it had been checked, rechecked, molded, and focused so that as much as possible all of the risk was taken out of it. It was also choking what we were trying to build, so we began a six-month study of how we could change the organization from the very top. As you might expect, though, the suggestions that resulted called for only a little tweaking here and there with essentially everybody staying in the same place. I thought about that recommendation for a day and then went back to something I'd learned in the Habits: *"If you want to make small, incremental, cautious, and methodical change, then change your attitude and behavior. If you want to make quantum, significant change, revolutionary change, then change your paradigm, your frame of reference."*

At first, I hoped that the people directly under me would see the same thing without me pointing it out. I wanted them to come up with a way to eliminate the layers that were hurting our company, but they didn't. So one day I walked into a meeting of all my top executives and announced that I was going to eliminate every one of their positions. I got their attention with that.

I told them that this train is pulling out of the station. Some of you are already on the train. Some of you are right along the side about to jump on. Some of you are running behind trying to catch it. Some of you probably will never get on the train and that's okay. We will work with you and we will try to get everybody brought along but at the end of the day the train is going to leave the station and you will either be on it or you will be left behind.

I told them they would be given ample opportunity to make the change but those who refused or simply couldn't adjust would eventually be left behind. In one case I had to fire a very senior man, which is not a very comfortable sort of thing. He had been with us for a number of years. But it had to be done. That's the hardest part but you've got to do it for the organization to avoid confusion and conflict. You have to be fair to the organization and to those who are trying to make the change.

I went about it in as compassionate and caring a manner as I knew how. I tried to find places for everyone within the company. Within months, I had no immediate staff to speak of. I eliminated the risk-elimination machine. People were encouraged to become more entrepreneurial and creative and we began using our research and technology to identify new businesses for the company. In the past, our exploration people never talked to our production people and vice versa. That had to change. We had to reduce costs and develop synergy, so we broke down the walls and moved authority and accountability down to where people could act on opportunities and create new ventures much more quickly. We became one of the few oil companies to grow during this period of low oil prices.

When we began this journey we did not say, "Hey, we are going to change the structure." The original intent was to change our culture and to try, as a result, to shape a business that was more in tune with the environment and what we saw the future to be. Eliminating so much of my staff was a big risk for me. I was very nervous about it because I was exposing myself to a lot of changes without the staff support I had grown comfortable with. At the same time we took out this last level, I turned to the business unit heads and said, "Look, guys, I don't have the time to be involved in the day-to-day business. I'm not going to be calling and talking to you about what you are doing. It is your business to run. Here's the funding. Here's what we expect out of you. Call me if you need my help. I will come around periodically and we will review how things are going. But I expect you to run this business and to perform. I am here to help you if you call me. But I'm not going to be poking my nose in your business. I simply don't have the time."

They loved it, but from my standpoint, it was risky. I frankly didn't know how all this was going to work, and I certainly didn't have the backup. I simply knew it was the right thing to do. We didn't have the staff anymore at the head office to check and double-check all the numbers that came in. I tried to create more of a team-manager concept in which everybody was heard. That was a fundamental change from the way we had traditionally managed this business.

We couldn't have done this in 1991 because the trust level was not high enough. We were nowhere near mature enough in our thinking about how to work together in teams and how to depend upon one another. Over the years we had to develop respect for each other. We didn't have that in the organization before, where there was more suspicion and jealousy.

I think it's a lot better now than it was. I don't want to leave you the impression that it is perfect. Not everybody feels that way. But there are many more now who will challenge, speak out, and debate, whereas in the past it just wouldn't happen. They learned they could challenge me after the first one or two spoke out and they didn't get carried out in a body bag. In the past, there was a sense that anyone who delivered bad news would be shot. When it didn't happen, they realized we were serious about developing a new culture within the organization. We tell them that it is okay to take risks and fail, not because of sloppy work, but for legitimate business reasons. We never did that before. We want to build and we know there will be some false starts and dead ends on the way to developing good ideas that pay off.

We've had considerable success since we made these changes and I don't think it would have worked so well if we hadn't started from the inside out. By looking first within and asking our top people to change their approach, by moving from the individual to the organization, I think we ignited the flame.

⊗ *Organizations that have followed the top-down hierarchical authoritarian approach over a long period of time gradually cultivate a culture of institutionalized dependency. People get accustomed to* outside-in approaches to change and development and begin to become cynical and callused to them. Then when they begin to undergo training that focuses on inside-out, their attitude is, "This is good, but the person who really needs it is not here." But if the line leader is a good model, cultivates open communication, and builds trust, and if market forces are dynamic, changing, and threatening, the culture that emerges will begin to develop an external focus on surviving and thriving in such a market. Gradually a common sense of direction, purpose, and values emerges. Trust increases.

If the principles of responsibility, accountability, risk taking, entrepreneurship, interdependency, and alignment become built into the culture and formalized into the institutional structures and systems, a kind of moral authority around those principles forms in the culture. This deepens and strengthens the trust even more. It all becomes the foundation for releasing tremendous human potential. The business accommodates the reality of the marketplace, and all kinds of creative energy, talent, resourcefulness, and intelligence are brought to the fore to do whatever it takes to succeed in that reality.

The principles contained in the 7 Habits apply just as much at the managerial and organizational levels as they do at the personal and interpersonal levels. The principles are universal, timeless, and self-evident. Jack Little was the trim tab in this situation. A trim tab is the small rudder that moves the large rudder that moves the entire ship. When you have a monstrous, heavy, bloated, bureaucratic ship moving in one direction and the future of the market is moving in the other, a wise, courageous, and skillful trimming of the rudder begins the process of a turnaround. It usually takes up to an hour to turn around big ocean liners and usually several years for a big industrial organization. So much depends on the amount of urgency and sincere involvement people feel.

When Pearl Harbor was bombed during World War II, Admiral Yamamoto spoke wisely when he said, "I feel that all we have done is awaken a sleeping giant and filled him with a terrible resolve." Most Americans at the time subordinated their own personal interest for the greater welfare, and change occurred miraculously fast. When the culture is behind a change, there are very few sacred cows. The only sacred cows that should not be kicked are those changeless principles that ultimately govern all consequences.

Michael Bassis, President,
Olivet College

*As you read this amazing story of a college turnaround, try to
imagine the amount of internal confidence and courage of its
president. More importantly, notice the level of faith the president
had in other people. Sense his respect for them—sufficient respect to
endure the rigorous marathon process of deep, meaningful, profound,
challenging involvement with governing boards, faculty, fellow
administrators, and students. The renewal of principles represented
the spring- and headwaters of a mighty stream.*

A lot of my friends thought I was absolutely crazy to even think
about becoming president of the troubled and nearly bankrupt Olivet
College in the spring of 1993. I told them I was looking for a challenge. I found it.

Olivet was established in 1844 as something of a revolutionary
school in rural southern Michigan. It was one of the nation's first institutions of higher education open to students regardless of race,
gender, or social status. Its high-minded mission was to provide all
students with "the means of intellectual, moral, and spiritual improvement and to teach them the divine art and science of doing
good to others."

In modern times, however, Olivet College had lost its way. Like
many small colleges outside urban areas, it was hard hit by problems
related to demographics, finances, academic quality, and conflicts
within. Olivet was staggering badly as it approached its 150th anniversary in 1994. Its faculty turnover rate was nearly 40 percent. It
had low standards in student recruitment, a meager endowment, and
no national reputation. A long-term president ruled by dictate. The
faculty was underpaid, unheeded, and demoralized.

The inner turmoil had come to a head in the spring of 1992 when a
minor dispute involving a small group of black and white students
grew into a larger brawl involving about seventy people. It had not
begun as a racial incident, but it grew into one. No one was arrested
and only two students received minor injuries. But the school's reputation was dragged in the mud because the administration handled
the incident poorly. When the school's leaders refused to respond to

the legitimate feelings of black students after the brawl, many withdrew from the college.

This occurred in the middle of the national debate over the Rodney King trial. Reporters for the networks and major newspapers used it to make the point that racial tensions existed also in the heartland. Few failed to note that Olivet's charter promoted racial understanding and equal opportunity.

The incident and the negative coverage it received from CNN, the *New York Times*, and other national media led to a total breakdown. The president of the college resigned under pressure. Many alumni, community members, faculty, and students questioned the college's ability to survive.

In an effort to try and rebuild, the college trustees undertook a national search for a new president. At the time I was the executive vice president and provost at Antioch University, where I'd been involved in its successful revitalization. When I learned of the situation at Olivet, I thought it would provide me with a great opportunity to put into practice what I had learned at Antioch about leading a transformation.

I realized, of course, that I was going to need a lot of help. The school needed a revitalizing sense of shared vision [Habit 2: Begin with the End in Mind]. The first thing I did was gather the faculty together and tell them that they were going to have to take charge of the basic academic direction of the school. I gave them design criteria, some boundaries to stay within, and told them to go do it. The six criteria I set down for the school's new academic vision statement required that:

- It had to be approved by a working consensus among the faculty.

- It had to be consistent with the long-standing values of the college and emerging educational needs in society.

- It had to be responsive to issues of social justice and diversity.

- It had to adhere to principles of good practice in undergraduate education.

- It had to be implemented through a cost-effective delivery system.

- It had to be something that would generate enthusiasm and support among students, alumni, and friends.

Even with those guidelines, there was some confusion and no little resistance from a faculty accustomed to following the dictates of the past president. They thought I was going to give them marching orders or tell them exactly what to do. They weren't sure it was their job to shape the direction of the institution, but I thought it was critical for them to develop a deep sense of ownership in any revitalization effort.

Some thought I was really going to try and control it anyway and others wished I would because they didn't trust their colleagues. When I told them that there was no hidden agenda, and that we would take their proposal to the board of trustees together, they were floored.

The new faculty group became known as the Vision Commission or, in less reverent moments, "The Commish." It floundered some initially, struggling with the unaccustomed freedom and responsibilities I'd given it, but slowly the new approach took hold.

Within three months, the Olivet Vision Commission issued a one-page vision statement they titled "Education for Individual and Social Responsibility." The new vision became the foundation for the revival of the college. Interestingly, entire sections of it were taken from the college's original founding documents.

When the faculty presented the vision statement to the college's board of trustees something quite extraordinary occurred. Spontaneously, the trustees rose to their feet and gave the faculty a standing ovation. It was one of the most poignant moments I have experienced in my thirty years in higher education. It was electrifying and the faculty was astounded.

That rousing show of support gave us momentum. My next step was to ask the faculty to take their vision for the college and develop a statement of what they believed students should learn at Olivet. Several months later, they produced a list of sixteen "learning outcomes" in five key categories covering communication and reasoning skills, collaborative working skills, individual and social responsibility, and skills required in a student's chosen field.

After that plan was approved, I asked the faculty to take the next logical step. I asked them to create an entirely new curriculum based on the new vision [Habit 3: Put First Things First]. The curriculum task force members traveled the country looking at cutting-edge programs. Then they returned and devised four very different proposals that were presented to the faculty and administration at a two-day retreat in 1994.

After the first day of presentations, the faculty took a straw vote. One of the proposals received no votes; the rest of the votes were evenly split among the other three options. They were at an impasse. That evening, I hosted a picnic for all participants and their families. It was a beautiful day but many of those present were anxious over which of the remaining three proposals would be selected the next day.

Sensing the tension, I called the primary architects of the different proposals into the president's house for an informal discussion. For the first two hours, I did nothing but listen to them debate one another. Finally, I went to a flip chart that had been set up and I listed on it all the points of agreement that I'd identified within the different proposals [Habit 5: Seek First to Understand, Then to Be Understood]. As I wrote them, mouths dropped. There was quite a bit of agreement. When I put together a summary using the ideas from the various proposals, they all seemed to fit together. Suddenly, everyone began talking about how this could work [Habit 6: Synergize].

The next day, we presented our proposal fashioned from the best ideas contained in the original four options. A preliminary vote found that 90 percent of the faculty approved of it. It was a magical moment.

One of the things I did right in the whole process was to establish a set of ground rules dealing with how we should engage with one another. It wasn't so much that I dictated it, but I did model it. In the middle of the year's worth of work, I gave a speech about the difference between debate and dialogue, making the point that dialogue was a far superior method for reaching understanding and resolution. The essential difference between it and debate is that in dialogue, you are listening to understand rather than looking for ways to convince someone of your viewpoint. It was my way of trying to build understanding throughout the entire culture and it was embraced quickly and readily. It became a powerful force on campus, and a way for doing business.

We also helped to restore Olivet's long-tarnished reputation as a cutting-edge educational institution. Preparing all students to function effectively in an increasingly diverse society has become an explicit educational goal. At the heart of the new curriculum designed by the faculty is a "portfolio assessment process" in which students develop portfolios displaying their best work. The idea is to have solid evidence of demonstrated competence. In both the sophomore and senior years, students submit their portfolios for examination and they have to be approved by a faculty review committee. Students then use their portfolios when applying for jobs after graduation.

Perhaps the most significant change at Olivet is the campus-wide emphasis on both individual and social responsibility. In the spring of 1997, the college canceled classes and convened all of its administrators, faculty, and students for a day-long discussion designed to identify what it means to be a responsible member of our community. By coincidence, though an ironic one, the day we gathered marked the fifth anniversary of the racial incident that had been the catalyst for so much change at Olivet.

Since attendance wasn't required, only those who *wanted* to be there and contribute were there. Faculty, administration, and students, along with some trustees, all sat at small round tables in mixed groups in the gym. There were pads and pencils there for brainstorming. Each group was to work together and come up with their best ideas, which they would present to the whole gathering. Most groups filled several notepads with ideas. As each group explained their ideas to the body, everything was captured on large flip chart paper. The sheets were then put up on the walls, and later everyone walked around the gym with little Post-it notes and added their own ideas and insights to those already there [Habit 6: Synergize]. Here was a college community in which all stakeholders were developing standards of behavior, responsibility, and discipline! Students were amazed that they were actually taking part and having a say. They responded enthusiastically, adding their considerable energies.

After the gathering, all the large sheets of paper that included the

Post-it note ideas were displayed in the main hall so everyone in the college community—especially those who had not participated in the meeting—could see the ideas and give their input.

The set of principles that resulted from that gathering and from several weeks of refinements is now known as the Olivet College Compact. It is given to each student upon admission to the college, and it has become a sort of guiding constitution for the college and all who study and work there. Along with the school's new academic vision statement, the Compact has been cast in bronze and positioned at the main entrance to the primary academic building on campus.

The principles in the Compact are now being translated into community standards that apply equally to students, faculty, and staff and are part of the personnel processes of the college. Everyone saw the importance of integrating them. The Compact is not just fancy rhetoric to put in our catalogue or to bronze—it has real operational integrity.

In order to make certain that each new group of students commits to the values and principles in the Compact, a ceremony is held at the start of each new academic year in which the Compact is presented to a representative of the incoming class. It is a wonderful ceremony for integrating new members of the community into the spirit of all we are doing, and it is a way to make certain the Compact becomes a living document.

The entire Olivet College community of faculty, staff, and students is able to more personally integrate the principles of the Compact through open opportunities to receive training in the 7 Habits. In fact, in one of the first classes taken by all incoming freshmen, each student develops a Personal Mission Statement to articulate their vision and dreams [Habit 2: Begin with the End in Mind]. They decide what principles they want to ground both their college experience and the rest of their lives upon.

In 1996, Olivet became the first school in the nation to make an applicant's record of community service the cornerstone of its scholarship program. The Community Responsibility Scholarships are valued at up to $6,000 per year. They are seen as an important part of the college's overall effort to encourage students to assume responsibility not only for themselves, but also for the communities where they live and work.

Once again Olivet College has found itself in the national spotlight. Now, however, the school is being hailed for its emphasis on individual and social responsibility. It has been recognized by the American Council on Education and the Association of American Colleges and Universities as one of twenty-six schools nationwide for its commitment to issues of diversity and for the success of its transformation. The college has also been named to the John Templeton Foundation Honor Roll of Character Building Colleges. Over the last three years, the college has received approximately $860,000 in grants from a variety of foundations as well as from an anonymous donor. Just recently, it was one of five institutions nationwide to receive a $1 million grant from the Kellogg National Institutional Transformation Project.

Olivet College has survived, but its challenges remain considerable. Despite substantial increases in fund-raising and enrollment, including the enrollment of students of color, the school is still saddled with considerable debt from its past problems. Its infrastructure is in poor condition. It faces intense competition from other liberal arts colleges in recruiting students. And it still has some more healing to do. But I believe Olivet is on track not only to a full recovery but perhaps to achieve greatness as well.

⊗ *I've become personally involved with Michael Bassis on several occasions, including the opportunity of speaking to his campus community. I was absolutely amazed at the transformation that had taken place and the depth and breadth of the excitement throughout the institution. It is an inspiring model of organizational and cultural transformation brought about through a patient and painstaking process of deep involvement amid all kinds of internal and external obstacles.*

Faced with the very real possibility of being shut down, Olivet returned to its founding values and principles and reconstituted itself by creating a new and greater vision of its mission. The faculty and administrators learned, adapted, and committed themselves to that new vision. As we were completing this book, I learned that Michael

Bassis has accepted a new challenge as dean of the Sarasota/Manatee Campus of the University of South Florida and warden of the New College there. He told me that he is looking forward to taking the skills and perspectives that he has developed at Olivet and applying them in a wider circle.

Often, the departure of a pivotal, transformational leader from an organization still in the midst of real change can be very disruptive. But because he led a process that involved everyone, empowered people, and built principles into the college culture, he avoided the trap of many leaders of creating institutional dependency. He tapped into the power of synergy. I'm convinced that Olivet will continue on its path of growth and influence—even without him. This college is not only a model but also has the potential to be a mentoring college for others across the length and breadth of the country.

Wood Dickinson, CEO, Dickinson Theatres

*This story is an account of the transformation of a traditional,
command-and-control, low-trust business into a principle-centered,
high-trust, open-communication business. You will notice that
almost all of the defining moments that produced the most significant
results had to do with conquering private internal struggles. Notice
how those involved couldn't simply take the course of least
resistance, but had to really pause, reflect, inwardly struggle, go the
second mile, and strive to cultivate a creative orientation rather than
a problem-solving orientation.*

Dickinson Theatres, based in Mission, Kansas, was begun in 1920
by my grandfather before the first full-length talking motion picture
was created. It is one of the oldest movie theater chains in the country. When I became CEO in 1992, however, we were being challenged
on nearly every front by much larger movie chains. With more than
250 screens in Kansas, Missouri, and Oklahoma, Dickinson's is a midsize theater chain in an industry that, like many others in the 1990s,
has been swept up in wave after wave of consolidations and mergers.

To compete in this environment, our company has had to become
more responsive and innovative. To do that, we had to change from
within. As a family-owned business, we had become top-heavy. The
command-and-control model of management had made it difficult
for our store managers to respond quickly to their unique challenges.
Some of our most serious problems were at the theater level. Our
managers were being dictated to from the corporate headquarters,
who had no clue about what was going on in the individual theaters.
All of the theater managers had to be incredibly creative to work
around the system forced upon them.

As a result, morale was at an all-time low. The structures and systems in the organization were terrible. Duplicity was rampant. Staff
meetings lasted only fifteen minutes because no one would talk to
anyone else. It was a hostile environment but people were afraid to
talk about issues in the open.

In my first six months at the helm, I attempted to open up communication and to install a Total Quality management program but it
seemed to me that all of this business stuff was missing something. I

wasn't sure what it was but after a while things began to unwind for me personally, too.

My passion for the job was wavering and something was missing in life. I thought that this should be an exciting and fun time in my life, but it wasn't working out that way. My commitment to my family and my marriage is very strong and the work part of my life was becoming too all-consuming. It was having a negative impact on my marriage and my relationship with my kids. I was letting myself be pulled out of balance because of the steep learning curve I was on in trying to change the company.

In the beginning, we tried to empower our theater managers to make more decisions. They were trying but they were making a lot of bad decisions that were costing us money, so we had to pull back and rein them in and rethink how we were doing things. Our answer flew at us out of our 7 Habits training. It was the idea that trust flows from trustworthiness; it was understanding what makes someone trustworthy. That lit a fire under everybody and helped us see what our key problem was. We couldn't empower people until we trusted each other. The moment we started talking about that, it turned us around.

The new approach to management at Dickinson Theatres resulted in some striking personal transformations, as well as many unusual and rewarding business developments. One outstanding example is Andy Armstrong. Opinionated and confrontational, he questioned everything in his 7 Habits class. But after it was over, he was a changed man. He has become the most passionate advocate of these principles in the entire company and his life has changed 180 degrees.

Andy was put to a tough field test almost immediately when he was promoted to general manager of a troubled eight-screen theater in suburban Kansas City. It was a hostile environment. The staff was cliquish. They had caused a good general manager to quit. Andy went in, established new expectations for a win-win relationship, and told those who did not buy into them that they would have to leave. Within thirty days, he had changed the culture of that theater.

Andy also applied Habit 5: Seek First to Understand, Then to Be Understood to the messy problem of a perpetually dirty dumpster storage area behind his theater. It was so bad that the landlord for the strip mall was always threatening to fine us. He thought he had taken care of the problem, but then one day a letter came with a photograph

Save *on the world-renowned*
Franklin Planner™

The Franklin Planner helps more than 15 million people worldwide live more effectively. Now it can become the daily road map for your journey to professional success and personal fulfillment.

Save 15% on your purchase with this coupon.

Redeem this coupon one of three ways:
- Visit a Franklin Covey store near you
- Call 1-800-372-6839
- Shop online at www.franklincovey.com/L7

Visit us at www.franklincovey.com

Want to learn more about our workshops and other products? Visit us at franklincovey.com. In addition to information, you'll also discover interactive tools to help you build a mission statement, work less and get more done, and more easily apply the 7 Habits in your everyday life.

Save 15% on Franklin Covey's Time and Life Management Products.

To save 15% on your next purchase from Franklin Covey, please provide the following information and present this coupon at your local Franklin Covey store. You may also redeem this coupon by calling 1-800-372-6839 or by visiting our Web site, www.franklincovey.com/L7.

_____

Name

_____

Address

_____

Phone number

_____

E-mail address

By providing this information, I authorize Franklin Covey to send me information via e-mail.

 FranklinCovey™

2200 West Parkway Blvd., Salt Lake City, Utah 84119-2099, Telephone (801) 496-5000

57001

of the dumpster area in a mess and a notice that the landlord was fin-
ing us $150.

Andy called the lady who had written the letter on behalf of the
landlord. He was upset because the fine made him look bad to the
home office. But he made up his mind that he was going to be proactive and really try to create a win-win out of this conflict. Instead of
making excuses, he said he understood the pressure she was under to
get the problem cleaned up. She responded that Andy had actually
done a lot to improve the theater, but this one area was still a problem. She then offered to drop the fine because "I get the feeling that
you know exactly how I feel on this issue now."

Andy is now a full-time facilitator for us and he is no longer a general manager. His new position was created for him to do the front-
line training of the managers and teenagers who work for us. It is a
tremendous personal victory for him.

Seeking first to understand really hit home personally and professionally for me when two hearing-impaired teenagers sued our theater chain for allegedly failing to accommodate their special needs. It
was the sort of lawsuit that can seriously damage a business, particularly a family business that has prided itself on tending to the needs
and desires of its customers.

Initially, I took the lawsuit personally. I was angry because I felt
our company had long been ahead of the curve in offering to accommodate customers with special needs.

The hearing-impaired people had wanted to come in for a special
showing of a popular movie and we had agreed to bring in two sign
language interpreters for them. We thought we were bending over
backward but then they sued us because they wanted us to pay for
the interpreters. I had a reactive attitude about it at first. I felt it was
extremely unreasonable. I was frustrated particularly because we had
put equipment for the hearing-impaired in our theaters before anyone else had thought of it and we had handicapped seating long before the law required it. We do a lot of things for our customers
because we feel they are the right things to do.

But after a few days, I decided to be proactive rather than reactive.
I listened and tried to understand what the hearing-impaired teens
were eager to tell me about my business. There was this synergistic
experience that happened within me. All of a sudden, the anxiety and

frustration disappeared and I realized that these were people who simply wanted to go out and see a movie and have a good time and that there had to be a solution. I had this amazing paradigm shift. I listened to my heart. I thought, "Okay, according to Habit 5, I am supposed to see this from the other side, so let me put myself in the position of these hearing-impaired people." After doing that, I decided that there *had* to be a third alternative to either giving in to their demands or fighting them.

I wanted to find a win-win solution, so I started talking about bringing in a mediator. Since lawyers tend to beat people to death, I came up with the idea of bringing in someone to help us work out a win-win.

When the mediator walked in, there was a lot of antagonism in the room. We felt that these two kids were intimidating us with the new Americans with Disabilities Act, which calls for equal treatment for all. The teens felt they should be able to go to a movie like anyone else and that the theater should provide sign language interpreters for them under the law.

Following Plato's insight that "The beginning of wisdom is the definition of terms," the mediator began by having each side of the dispute define exactly what it wanted to achieve. He noted that when people focus on the means, it breeds contention, but when they focus on the ends, it breeds cooperation.

He instructed our people and the teenagers to each write down their ultimate goals [Habit 2: Begin with the End in Mind]. Working on flip charts at opposite sides of the room and out of view from each other, he went back and forth helping the theater chain and the teens get to their bottom lines.

When each side turned their charts around for the other to see, their end goals were almost identical. Both the teens and the theater people wanted all customers to be able to enjoy the movies, eat popcorn, drink Cokes, and pay a reasonable price for it. The major difference was that the theater owners also wanted to make a reasonable profit. After looking at both end goals, the mediator went back to the teens and asked if they would agree that the theater should make a reasonable profit, and they said yes, so that made the two end goals virtually identical. Once it was determined that both sides wanted the same thing, the stress was taken out of the process.

Suddenly, both sides found themselves on the same page. Together, they developed a mission statement that said, "We want to create a plan of action that allows all individuals to drink Coke, eat popcorn, and enjoy the movie at a reasonable price and at a reasonable profit to the theaters."

Then they began searching for ways to fulfill that mission.

We unleashed all that energy that had been wasted fighting over the problem and focused on coming up with a solution. The two sides did not magically come together, there were still points of contention, but when everyone in the room began working toward a solution the process moved along much more smoothly.

When the two teens still insisted that interpreters be provided by the theater for every movie, the interpreters helping in the mediation became participants. They informed both sides that the costs would be almost prohibitive because of the difficulties of signing for a movie in which the action often moves at a breakneck pace and many characters are speaking. They noted that it would take at least two interpreters for every movie and most would demand considerably more than $50 an hour. One estimate put Dickinson's annual cost for bringing sign language interpreters to every movie showing at $18 million.

The mediator then said that at that point we were still no closer to an agreement than we had been when the meeting started and if they couldn't move off of that demand then we were all going to leave without accomplishing anything. He urged us to start thinking more creatively. Soon we were talking about all sorts of things like subtitles, special showings, and high-tech equipment. Everybody got involved in working toward a common goal.

Still, many of the suggestions were deemed impractical or too expensive. Suddenly an idea came to me, so I made a suggestion. It was clear to me that any solution was going to cost a lot of money. I had already started three nonprofit foundations in the community and it occurred to me that perhaps a fourth one could be established to help build a reservoir of funds to help provide movies for the hearing-impaired. I offered to raise the first $10,000 myself.

When the two teens saw that offer of goodwill, everyone buckled down and started talking about other possible solutions, including one in which sign language interpreters would translate an entire movie on videotape. Then with each subsequent showing, that videotape could be shown on screens placed near the seating area. That would not violate any copyrights, but it would require special showings for the hearing-impaired. Still, it was much closer to a solution than we had been before.

With everybody scrambling to come up with ideas, we eventually formulated seven alternative solutions that each side agreed to explore [Habit 6: Synergize]. None were perfect but they all had promise. In the end, we chose to have special showings with sign language interpreters. The hearing-impaired patrons could request the special showings seventy-two hours in advance. They opted to try that for six months to see how it went and what the costs were, and then to meet again.

The bottom line was that the spirit was changed. Everybody was working together. We left as friends instead of adversaries. Even the two interpreters, who had come in with strong attitudes about not getting involved, were swept up in it. The real issue was not so much that these kids wanted to see a movie, it was that they wanted to be heard and understood, and they were.

As in the case of Andy Armstrong and the dirty dumpster dispute, the entire relationship of the two opposing sides in the lawsuit changed when both sides felt that their points were understood. It is perhaps the most powerful principle of all human interaction, this need to be understood.

⊗ *After studying this story I almost had a déjà vu because over the last thirty years of working with organizations, this story has been duplicated again and again and again. The names of the people and the specifics of the situation are all different, but the underlying problems, struggles, challenges, and solutions are almost always the same. Each situation is so unique and it does take special understanding to come up with the appropriate practices that reflect those unique realities. But at the core, people are the same and organizations are similar. They all have relationships, they all have customers and suppliers, they are all both customers and suppliers simultaneously, and the nature and quality of the relationships pretty well govern the success of the operations. Principles are universal, timeless, and self-evident, but practices are situational and specific, and therefore require special understanding.*

When the people at Dickinson Theatres got involved with their training they had to deal with specific issues that arose out of these principles and of the four basic needs of all people: the physical/economic need for survival and prosperity, the social/emotional need for good relationships with self and others, the mental need for the use and development of their talents, and the spiritual need for a sense of meaning, contribution, and integrity, meaning a principled life. Again and again you see how the Private Victory had to be won before the Public Victory could be. This took place in the illustrations of seeking first to understand, then to be understood, and of creating synergy and better feelings. The key element took place when people were willing to go the second mile, were willing to do more than others expected them to do. As soon as Dickinson himself was willing to work on and make the first investment toward creating a new nonprofit foundation to help the hearing-impaired in theaters, then those people knew they were being respected, affirmed, and understood. You can see that it took more than empathy: it took acting on that empathy. This action became the healing balm to the festering sore.

In short, the pattern is repeated again and again. People simply must pay the price individually if they are going to see the fruits in relationships and in organizational cultures.

John Noel, CEO, Noel Group

*John Noel is the human equivalent of a caterpillar transforming into
a butterfly. Notice first the influence that the scripts John received
early in life had upon him at work and at home, particularly those he
received from his father. Notice also what happens when you become
work-centered instead of principle- or value-centered. Like a pair of
glasses, you literally see everything through the work lens, and this
impacts every decision and relationship at home and at work. It also
puts you on a path of arrogance. Blind spots keep you from being
open to feedback, so you make few, if any, course corrections. Because
everything is being seen through the importance of work, family
becomes secondary, and relationships at work are exploited through a
self-justified control management philosophy.*

*As you read the story, try to mentally empathize with John. Try to
get a sense of what his life, his world, and his thinking were really
like. If you will become both emotionally and intellectually involved
in this effort, it may significantly impact the quality and quantity of
insights into your own personal life.*

I was named vice president of the international division of a large
insurance company in Stevens Point, Wisconsin, at the age of thirty-
six. I was given a great degree of responsibility and authority by my
mentor, the caring CEO who treated his employees like family members. I thought of myself as a family man, too. After all, I'd married
my high school sweetheart, Patty, and we had adopted four children
along with having two of our own biological children. But like many
driven and successful people, I'm not sure my self-image was shared
by those closest to me.

In 1985, a new CEO took over at the insurance company and I
quickly realized that this boss had an entirely different approach to
business. He reversed most of the positive things the previous CEO
had done to build relationships with his employees. He was not interested in the employees as a community. I didn't agree with his
values.

Conflicts with the new management seemed inevitable, so I faced a
difficult decision. Should I adjust to the change and stick with the relatively secure job at a company where I'd spent fifteen dedicated

years? Or should I remain true to my values and leave the company, gambling the security of my young family?

After a great deal of soul-searching, I chose to leave the company, but to take a bit of it with me. I talked to the new CEO and explained that I didn't think we were going to work well together. I said that I was going to leave, but that I wanted to purchase Travel Guard International, an insurance company that I started within the parent company. He agreed to that and after the deal was done, I moved my office and my own business into the basement at home. It was a very stressful time. I had all six kids working for me, including the youngest, Missy, who was only nine years old. They stamped policies for me. (If the customers had seen my operation they never would have done business with me!)

When I became an independent businessman I'm sure I modeled myself after my father, who had built a successful construction company even though he had only an eighth-grade education. He was a hardworking, caring person and I did the same things he'd done. I worked long hours and focused on the business just as he had. I didn't see much of him when I was growing up because he put his work before his family.

I was very successful in my focused effort to create a business and to provide security for my large family. Travel Guard International, which provides insurance through most travel agencies and tour operations in the U.S., Canada, and the U.K., quickly grew into a thriving company with annual sales of $130 million. The financial success of that enterprise spawned other businesses, including an executive vacation packaging company, a group tour company catering to health care professionals, an international emergency medical assistance company, a chain of travel agencies, and a real estate acquisition and management company.

All of these enterprises were organized under the umbrella of the Noel Group, which today has 240 employees headquartered in a seventy-five-year-old former hotel that we renovated at a cost of $4.5 million. The corporate symbol of the Noel Group is a compass needle pointing north, an image that I selected because I felt I had stayed on course with my values when I left my former employer. A large carving in the floor bearing that symbol is in the lobby of our headquarters in Stevens Point.

After a decade of hard work and considerable business success, however, I found that my twenty-six-year marriage was in trouble and my relationship with our grown children was not what I wanted it to be. All of the children had moved out of the house to attend college or begin careers, leaving Patty in an empty nest because of my frequent business travels. The isolation magnified her fears and concerns for a relationship that had lost its focus.

Speaking about this period, Patty recalled, "Our marriage was at its lowest point. We had a big family and we'd had some big problems. At work, and at home, we had become locked into crisis management as a way of life. If you take the analogy of having your ladder against the wrong wall, our ladder was on the wrong house in the wrong state and I'm not even sure if John and I even knew what ladder we were on or whether we were on the same ladder."

For me, the pressures of family and business were not only manifested in a quick-fire temper at home, but also in the office. Although I had prided myself on being a caring, fatherly employer, I had developed a tendency to confront and demean those who did not meet my expectations or demands. I would pound my fist and let loose with unjustified criticism just to manipulate people to get what I wanted from them.

Patty and I sought counseling because of our problems, but at first I was not prepared to look critically at my own behavior, let alone to seek to change it. Patty's favorite thing to say to me was, "John, we can change, we can improve our relationship." My favorite thing to say was, "Why should I change? I am happy the way I am."

My wife couldn't get through; my employees couldn't get through.

One of the things that the counselor recommended to me in an effort to put more balance in my life was *The 7 Habits of Highly Effective People.* I took the advice the way you might expect an entrepreneur to interpret it—from a business perspective. I thought the author must know something I didn't know if he could write a book that sold millions of copies, so I decided to let him influence me.

I read the book and it made a dent in my armor. I began to see a pattern of behavior that was in conflict with my self-image. When I read about Quadrant I—the area of urgent and important activities—it hit me that it was my favorite place to go. I am like a fireman in that

I respond best in times of crisis. And I was always in the crisis mode, rather than in the leadership mode. In a way, it was kind of sick behavior, but I really generate a lot of energy when I get in that mode. That is where I have strength. I'd always thought I was most effective when I was under pressure. I'd have two computers going and a phone headset on and people coming in and out of my office and I'd be energized and going full bore. But like the alcoholic who feels he is more effective when he is drunk, I was also deeply unhappy in that frame of mind.

With this first step toward increased self-awareness, I decided to explore the material further by attending a Leadership Week seminar in Utah. Making the decision to go was, in fact, a statement. However, the most significant event was Monday morning when I decided to open myself to the influence of the three instructors. I decided I would let them have me until Friday, but I could always go back to my old self. On the second day of the seminar, we were asked to record the things we wanted our loved ones to think about us on the day of our funeral. As I wrote, I broke down emotionally.

The tears started blotting the paper I was writing on and the guy next to me asked what the hell was wrong with me. I said that I was just thinking about what I wanted my kids to think of me, and I was realizing that I have not been there for them.

I wanted my children and wife to say they respected me because I gave them my time and my love. I wanted them to think of me as the best father and husband and to say that I was always there when they needed me. But then I got my 360 Degree Profile, which gave feedback from my peers and those who report to me, and it clearly told me that I was not walking my talk, and that it showed in my relationships with my family and my employees. I decided that I had lost a lot of time, but I still had the opportunity to change and to restore the balance in my life.

That night, I telephoned Patty and asked her to come to Utah immediately. Our relationship was rocky, but I felt I needed her support in my effort to change. Patty was wary. Her trust in me had deteriorated. She was suspicious of both my motives and my commitment to change. It took me three phone calls to convince her that I sincerely wanted to change.

We spent five days examining our lives, our relationships, and all of the influences and emotional baggage that were negatively affecting us. She and I read the book together in front of the fireplace, chapter by chapter, and as we read it, we'd talk about the meaning of it. There were a lot of tears and emotions but I realized the first place I had to go to free myself of this imbalance in my life was to my wife. I had to sincerely apologize to her and kind of start over and say, "This is not what we intended on doing with our lives and I am sorry about what I have done. Let's see if we can get back on track."

Patty told me it took her a while to put aside her hurt and mistrust and to see the man her husband was trying to become rather than the one he had been. "At first I couldn't believe that John could make such a transformation so quickly but I realized after a time that he was sincere. There was something different in the way he looked at me. Before he left he could see hardly anything I was doing right. It was as if almost overnight someone had taken the blinders off," she said. "He'd also always felt that he could not change himself, that he was what he was, but he learned that he could be a transition person and that he could change. We both had baggage that we had not realized we were carrying."

On the flight home, I was overcome with anxiety and fear. I had changed, but I was not sure others would believe it, or accept it. I wondered if it was too late to put my life back on course. I also feared that returning to the office and the crisis management environment might cause me to revert to my old ways. Patty was afraid for me, too.

In the first few days after returning, I spent a great deal of time unloading some of that baggage by apologizing, even to those who felt it was not necessary. It was a cleansing of sorts and a way to signal that I was willing to start anew. I guess it was my own way of trying to take responsibility.

I wrote apologies to my wife and my kids and to people at work. I realized that I had no awareness of my feelings or theirs. When I apologized, they said I was being too hard on myself, but I wasn't because I knew I had fallen far short of my own standards. I had allowed my temper to control my actions far too often. I had not listened to my children as well as I should have.

The thing I probably learned the most from the training was to seek first to understand and then to be understood. That was something I had seldom done. *My* opinion had been the one that counted in my mind. The strength of my convictions had helped me become successful in business, but it had impeded my relationships with my wife, my children, and with other people because I would not let myself be influenced by them. I could have been a better father and better boss. I regret that. I always had good values and integrity, but I could have been a better person if I had listened to others and allowed them to influence my thinking.

Several weeks after our trip, Patty and I went off by ourselves again. Our goal for this trip was to draft a mission statement that would help us focus our daily lives on the things that were most important to us. We wanted to create a clear vision, a map and plan.

Our discussion began by our asking each other a few basic questions that led to hours of soul-searching and emotional venting:

- What do you want to be?

- What character strengths do you want to have?

- What qualities do you want to develop?

- What do you want to do for the rest of your life?

- What do you want to accomplish?

- What contributions do you want to make?

- What values and principles do you want to use as a foundation for doing your best?

To help formulate answers to these questions, we did the funeral exercise together. It helped us see ourselves through the eyes of others. We discovered that there was a big difference in where we were and where we wanted to be. We wanted to close that gap. We came to see that we were like two people on a tandem bike pedaling in opposite directions. We wanted to get the bike going in one direction and we knew we might fall off and crash now and then but it would be worth it.

Once I decided that my goal was to be happy and that living the rest of my life with Patty was an integral part of my happiness, it became easy. I realized that since I own my business, I could change my lifestyle to reflect my new goals for my personal life.

We began remapping our lives. By the end of the fourth day we had put together twenty-five pages of thoughts on my laptop computer and we felt like we had accomplished so much. We were eager to get to work on narrowing it down and we had just started when the alarm went off on the laptop saying that it was out of battery power and that I had better save the document or my work would be lost. Before I could do it, it shut down and we lost all that work. It was one of those moments when you have to exercise your freedom to choose your response. I chose to say, "Tomorrow, let's go to the beach and go swimming and we'll forget we lost all that information. Then we'll come back the next day and do it again." And that is exactly what we did. The mission statement we developed and still hold is this:

> To live, to love, to laugh, to learn, and to leave a legacy for our children, relatives, friends, employees, and our global and local community through strength of purpose, in our commitment to our principles and our business success, by helping children, encouraging diversity in all areas of life, integrity of living—and all of this with our unwavering core of values being passed on to our children and grandchildren. To always have our principles and motives clear and to continually strengthen our legacy.

It has become the touchstone that we return to whenever we feel the need to realign ourselves with our values and principles.

There is this thing called "happiness," and I have to continually get in touch with that happiness. It takes some time because you meet up with obstacles that throw you into crisis mode, and you really have to go back to your mission statement and start solving problems in life by putting first things first. That is the part I sometimes lose sight of. I have to keep kicking myself in the butt to make sure I do that, not only for my personal life but for my business life, too.

My decision to restore the balance in my life has also had a substantial impact on our business. When I returned to my office after going through that first training seminar in Utah, I didn't want to go back to work. I was a changed person and thought I would probably come across as some weirdo. That part scared me, so I got the executives together and explained to them what had gone on and how I felt. I really wanted them to understand that the experience had changed my life and that it was not a short-term thing. I shared with them the 360 Degree Profile I had done in Utah. I told them about the funeral exercise and the impact it had on me. There were tears rolling down my cheeks and I'm sure the staff was wondering, "What on earth has happened to him? Should we take him to the funny farm?"

I told them that I had to make a change in my life and asked for their help. Most of them said they would. I went on to explain that the only way I thought I could hold on to this new sense of happiness was to have them go through the 7 Habits, too. I wanted them to embrace it. Luckily most did.

Within two months we had a couple trainers come in and train forty of our senior people, including all of our executives. Then they helped me decide to take the next step, which was to train everyone else in the company, including Elmer, our seventy-seven-year-old delivery guy who only works fifteen hours a week. Now we have fifteen facilitators who train all our new employees. The training has become one of the most significant benefits offered by our company. It has not only helped people in our company become much more effective on the job, it has saved marriages and helped parents raise their children. People in our community know the benefits we have derived from our commitment to these principles.

It is easy to tell people how we are going to run the company based on values; the difficult thing is to have people embrace those ideas. We found that some could not. In any business there are gossips and troublemakers who see the world as a dark place. Those people left. Some had been with me for thirteen years, but I'll tell you, our company is so much better without them. We have a happier work environment. People treat each other with respect. New employees tell me they are surprised that there is no gossip, manipulating, backbiting, or politics. I am sure some goes on, but compared to other companies there is very little because it is just not tolerated. It was difficult to see some of my friends leave the company, but they just couldn't embrace our values.

The company motto at Noel Group is "Where Our Direction Is Led By Our Values" and I attribute the success of our business to our employees' commitment to integrity and service.

Sales and profitability are, of course, parts of our objectives, but we follow our values first. Honesty and integrity are integral parts of any company's business success. The element of trust is critical in business—between owners and managers, managers and employees, employees and other employees, and customers and employees—and the fiber that holds that trust together is walking your talk, doing what you say you're going to do.

Today, I think I'm achieving balance in my life, and both my company and I are determined to focus on true north. I had business success before, but my life was out of balance. The interesting thing is that once I decided to put more balance in my life, my company became even more successful. We have quadrupled in size and I don't think that is just because of the market. I believe it is the result of all of the training my employees and I have had in these principles and their commitment to our goals of promising the best and delivering it.

Most important, however, is the impact that the new approach has had on our family.

One of the simplest, but most profound changes that my wife and I made was to turn off the television and tune in to our relationship instead. Now we talk and read and enjoy each other. We have a fuller life because our time is not dictated by outside influences. We control it.

Our children have all moved out of our home, but I talk to them ten times more now than I did before. Now when one of them calls me at the office, I drop what I'm doing. I don't care if the Queen of Sheba is sitting there for a business meeting, I take the calls from my kids. I apologize for the interruption, but I tell whoever is present that my family comes first. I've found that when you do that, you generate more respect, whether they are customers or visiting executives. They tend to see you as someone who has found a meaningful balance in life.

Patty and I feel that the greatest message in our family transformation is that you can always hope for a higher level. When we were talking about that the other day she said, "If someone had told me something like that when I was twenty, I would never have believed it. But now, not only do I believe it, I preach it. I'm always telling young couples that they should never give up on a loving relationship because it can always be better."

The decision I made on that Monday morning to give myself to those three instructors will never be rolled back. After four years of living and loving my life, there is no power that could take me from where we are . . . happy.

⊛ *John was initially open to the 7 Habits book because it was socially acceptable and might contribute to a greater business, but it immediately forced him into self-awareness. He had to stand back and examine his own life, his own scripts, his own behavior patterns, his work-centeredness, and his tendency to be driven by crisis, anger, and manipulation. His critical breakthrough occurred when self-awareness connected to his conscience as he worked on his mission statement. It became emotionally cathartic and prepared him to receive feedback from other people. This feedback enabled him to see things in a true light, which compounded his awareness of the incongruencies between deeply held values and his work style.*

Because he exercised his moral agency to choose in that moment, his awareness both deepened and expanded, and his power and freedom to choose his response to other circumstances increased. His interest in other people deepened and became much more sincere. He became not only a model, but also a mentor to many others and made certain that they participated in experiences that would help them tap into their own unique gifts.

Arrogance is the path that derails most individuals, organizations, families, and marriages. The use of all four endowments—self-awareness, conscience, imagination, and independent will—can put them back on track.

Sharing Your Story

Stories *are* a powerful source of learning, affirmation, and hope. They can open up new ideas, options, and possibilities in our lives. They illustrate principles that have universal application. Perhaps you have your own story of overcoming challenges personally, in your family, in the community, or in your work or organization. Or perhaps you've heard of one. If you would like to share your story and submit it for possible inclusion in a future volume of *Living the 7 Habits*, please send it to:

Franklin Covey Co.
Living the 7 Habits
MS 2233
466 West 4800 North
Provo, Utah 84604-4478

e-mail: stories@7habits.com
Web site: http://www.franklincovey.com
fax: 801-496-4225, attn.: *Living the 7 Habits*

Questions I Am Often Asked

Frankly, I've always been embarrassed by personal questions like some in this section. But I am asked them so often and with such interest that I've gone ahead and included them here.

The 7 Habits *was published in the summer of 1989. In the decade that's followed, what would you have liked to change, add, or subtract?*

I'm not responding lightly, but frankly, I wouldn't change anything. I might have wished to go deeper and apply the principles more widely, but I have had the opportunity to do that in some of the books published since then.

For example, the results of profiling more than 250,000 individuals trained in the 7 Habits showed that Habit 3, Put First Things First, was the Habit most neglected. So the book *First Things First* (published 1994) not only went deeper into Habits 2 and 3 but also added more substance and illustrations of all the other Habits.

The 7 Habits of Highly Effective Families applied the 7 Habits framework of thinking to building strong, happy, highly effective families.

Also, my son, Sean, applied the framework to the unique needs, interests, and challenges of teens in a very visually attractive, entertaining, and edifying way in *The 7 Habits of Highly Effective Teens*.

What have you learned about the 7 Habits since the book's publication?

I have learned or had reinforced many things. I'll briefly mention ten of them.

1. The importance of understanding the difference between principles and values. Principles are natural laws that are external to us and that ultimately control the consequences of our actions. Values are internal and subjective and represent what we feel strongest about, what guides our behavior. Hopefully we will come to *value principles*, so that we can get the results we want now in a way that enables us to get even greater results in the fu-

ture, which is how I define effectiveness. Everyone has values; even criminal gangs have values. Values govern people's behavior, but principles govern the consequences of those behaviors. Principles are independent of us. They operate regardless of our awareness of them, acceptance of them, liking of them, belief in them, or obedience to them. I have come to believe that humility is the mother of all virtues. Humility says that we are not in control, principles are in control, therefore we submit ourselves to principles. Pride says that we are in control, and since our values govern our behavior, we can simply live life our way. We may do so, but the consequences of our behavior flow from principles, not our values. Therefore we should *value principles*.

2. From experiences all over the world with this material I have come to see the *universal* nature of the principles undergirding this material. Illustrations and practices may vary and are culturally specific, but the principles are the same. I have found the principles contained in the 7 Habits in all six major world religions and have actually drawn upon quotations from sacred writings of those religions when teaching in those cultures. I have done this in the Middle East, India, Asia, South America, Europe, North America, and Africa, as well as among Native Americans and other indigenous peoples. People, men and women alike, face similar problems, have similar needs, and internally resonate with the underlying principles. There is an internal sense of the principle of justice or win-win. There is an internal moral sense of the principle of responsibility, of the principle of purpose, of integrity, of respect, of cooperation, of communication, of renewal. These are universal. But practices are not. They are situationally specific. Every culture interprets universal principles in unique ways.

3. I have come to see the organizational implications of the 7 Habits, although, in the strict technical sense, an organization does not have habits. Its culture has norms or mores or social codes, which represent habits. An organization also has established systems, processes, and procedures. These represent habits. In fact, in the last analysis, all behavior is personal. It is individual even though

it often is part of collective behavior in the form of decisions made by management regarding structure and systems, processes and practices. We have worked with thousands of organizations in most every industry and profession and have found that the basic principles contained in the 7 Habits apply and define effectiveness in all of them.

4. You can teach all 7 Habits by starting with any one Habit. And you can also teach one Habit in a way that leads to the teaching of the other six. It's like a hologram in which the whole is contained in the part and the part is contained in the whole.

5. Even though the 7 Habits represents an Inside-Out Approach, they work most successfully when you start with the outside challenge and then take the Inside-Out Approach. In other words, if you are having a relationship challenge, say, a breakdown of communication and trust, this will define the nature of the Inside-Out Approach you need in order to win the kind of Private Victory that will make it possible for you to meet the challenge of winning that Public Victory. This is the reason I often teach Habits 4, 5, and 6 before I teach Habits 1, 2, and 3.

6. Interdependence is ten times more difficult than independence. It demands so much more mental and emotional independence to think win-win when the other person is into win-lose, to seek to understand first when everything inside you cries out for understanding, and to search for a better third alternative when compromise is so much easier. In other words, to work successfully with others in creative, cooperative ways requires an enormous amount of independence, internal security, and self-mastery. Otherwise, what we call interdependency is really counter-dependency, in which people do the opposite to assert their independence, or co-dependency, in which they literally need the other person's weakness to fulfill their need and to justify their own weakness.

7. You can pretty well summarize the first three Habits with the expression "make and keep a promise." And you can pretty well

summarize the next three Habits with the expression "involve others in the problem and work out the solution together."

8. The 7 Habits represent a new language, even though they contain fewer than a dozen unique words or phrases. This new language becomes a code, a shorthand way of saying a great deal, when you say to someone, for instance, "Was that a deposit or a withdrawal?" "Is that reactive or proactive?" "Is that synergistic or a compromise?" "Is that win-win or win-lose or lose-win?" "Is that putting first things first or second things first?" "Is that beginning with the means in mind or the end in mind?" I've seen entire cultures transformed by a wide understanding of and commitment to the principles and concepts symbolized by these very special code words. Many of the stories in this book reflect this.

9. Integrity is a higher value than loyalty. Or, better put, integrity is the highest form of loyalty. Integrity means being integrated or centered on principles, not on people, organizations, or even family. You will find that the root of most issues that people are dealing with is "Is it popular (acceptable, political) or is it right?" When we prioritize being loyal to a person or group over doing what we feel to be right, we lose integrity. We may temporarily gain popularity or build loyalty, but downstream, this loss of integrity will undermine even those relationships. It's like bad-mouthing someone behind his or her back. The person you are temporarily united with through bad-mouthing someone else knows you would bad-mouth him or her under different pressures and circumstances. In a sense, the first three Habits represent integrity and the next three loyalty, but they are totally interwoven. Over time, integrity produces loyalty. If you attempt to reverse them and go for loyalty first, you will find yourself temporizing and compromising integrity. It's better to be trusted than to be liked. Ultimately, trust and respect will generally produce love.

10. Living the 7 Habits is a constant struggle for everyone. Everyone falters from time to time on each of the seven and sometimes all

seven simultaneously. They really are simple to understand but difficult to consistently practice. They are common sense, but what is common sense is not always common practice.

Which Habit do you personally have the greatest difficulty with?

Habit 5. When I am really tired and already convinced I'm right, I really don't want to listen. I may even pretend to listen. Basically I am guilty of the same thing I talk about, listening with the intent to reply, not to understand. In fact, in some sense, I struggle almost daily with all 7 Habits. I have conquered none of them. I see them more as life principles that we never really master, and as we come closer to such mastery we become more aware of really how far we have to go. It's like the more you know the more you know you don't know.

This is why I often gave my university students 50 percent of the grade for the quality of their questions and the other 50 percent for the quality of their answers to their questions. Their true level of knowledge is better revealed that way.

Similarly, the 7 Habits represent an upward cycle.

Habit 1 at a high level is vastly different from Habit 1 at a lower level. To be proactive at the beginning level may be only

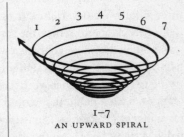

1–7
AN UPWARD SPIRAL

awareness of the space between stimulus and response. At the next level, it may involve a choice such as not getting back at or getting even with someone. At the next level, it may involve giving feedback. At the next level, it may involve asking forgiveness. At the next level, it may involve forgiving. At the next level, it may involve forgiving parents. At the next level, it may involve forgiving dead parents. At the next level, it may mean simply not taking offense.

You're the co-chairman of Franklin Covey Co. Does Franklin Covey live the 7 Habits?

We try to. To continually try to live what we teach is one of our most fundamental values. But we don't do it perfectly. Like any other business we're challenged by changing market realities and by integrating the two cultures of the former Covey Leadership Center and Franklin Quest. The merger took place in the summer of 1997. It takes time, patience, and persistence to apply the principles and the true test of our success will be in the long run. No snapshot will give an accurate picture.

Any airplane is off track much of the time but just keeps coming back to the flight plan. Eventually, it arrives at its destination. This is true with all of us as individuals, families, or organizations. The key is to have an "end in mind" and a shared commitment to constant feedback and constant course correction.

Why seven? Why not six or ten or eight or fifteen? What is so sacred about seven?

Nothing is sacred about seven; it just so happens that the three Private Victory Habits (freedom to choose, choice, action) precede the three Public Victory Habits (respect, understanding, creation) and then there is one to renew the rest and that equals seven. If there is some other desirable characteristic you would like to make into a habit, you simply put that under Habit 2 as one of the values you are trying to live by. In other words, if punctuality is a desirable trait you want to make a habit, that would be one of the values of Habit 2. So no matter what else you come up with, you put it under Habit 2, your value system. Habit 1 is the idea that you can have a value system, that you can choose your own value system. Habit 2 is what those choices or values are and Habit 3 is to live by them. So they are very basic, generic, and interconnected.

How does notoriety affect you?

It affects me in different ways. From an ego standpoint, it's flattering. From a teaching standpoint, it is humbling, but I must strongly acknowledge that I am not the author of any of these principles and deserve absolutely no recognition. I am not saying this because of a desire to be modest and humble. I am saying this because I believe it. I see myself like most of you—as a seeker of truth, of understanding. I am not a guru; I disdain being called a guru. I want no disciples. I am only trying to promote a discipleship toward principles that are already in people's hearts, so that people will live true to their consciences.

If you had it to do over again, what is the one thing you would do differently as a businessperson?

I would do more strategic, proactive recruiting and selecting. When you are buried by urgent matters and have a thousand balls in the air, it is so easy to put people who appear to have solutions into key positions. The tendency is not to look deeply into their backgrounds and patterns, not to do "due diligence," nor to carefully develop the criteria that need to be met in their particular roles or assignments. I am convinced that when recruiting and selecting are done strategically, that is, with long-term thought and proactivity, not based upon the pressures of the moment, it pays enormous long-term dividends. Someone once said, "That which we desire most earnestly we believe most easily." You really have to look deeply into both character and competence because eventually, downstream, flaws in either area will manifest themselves in both areas. I am convinced that although training and development are vital, recruiting and selection are even more vital.

If you had it to do over again, what is the one thing you would do differently as a parent?

As a parent, I wish I had spent more time in carefully developing soft, informal Win-Win Agreements with each of my children in the different phases of their lives. Because of business and travel obligations, I often indulged my children and went for lose-win too much instead of paying the price in relationship building sufficient to really develop thorough, sound Win-Win Agreements more consistently.

How is technology going to change business in the future?

I believe in the statement "When the infrastructure changes, everything rumbles," and I think technical infrastructure is central to everything. It will accelerate all good *and* bad trends. I'm also convinced that it is for this very reason that the human element becomes even more important. High tech without high touch does not work, and the more influential technology becomes, the more important the human factor that controls the technology becomes, particularly in developing a cultural commitment to criteria for the use of that technology.

Are you surprised at the universal popularity of the 7 Habits in other countries and cultures, and among people of all ages and both genders?

Yes and no. Yes, in that I had no idea that they would become a worldwide phenomenon and that a few of the words would become part of Americana. No, in the sense that the material had been tested for more than twenty-five years and I knew that it would work primarily because it is based upon principles I did not invent and therefore take no credit for.

How would you begin to teach the 7 Habits to very young children?

I think I would live by Albert Schweitzer's three basic rules for raising children: first, example; second, example; third, example. But I wouldn't go quite that far. I would say, first, example; second, build a caring and affirming relationship; and third, teach some of the simple ideas underlying the Habits in the language of children—help them gain a basic understanding and vocabulary of the 7 Habits and show them how to process their own experiences through the principles; let them identify what particular principles and Habits are being illustrated in their lives.

My boss (spouse, child, friend, etc.) really needs **The 7 Habits.** *How would you recommend I get this person to read it?*

People don't care how much you know until they know how much you care. Build a relationship of trust and openness based upon a character example of trustworthiness and then share how the 7 Habits have helped you. Simply let them see the 7 Habits in action through your life. Then, at the appropriate time, you might invite them to participate in a training program or share your book as a gift or teach some of the basic ideas when the occasion calls for it.

What is your background and how did you come to write **The 7 Habits?**

It was implicitly understood that I would follow in my father's footsteps and go into the family business. However, I found that I enjoyed teaching and training leaders even more than business. I became deeply interested and involved in the human side of organizations when I was at Harvard Business School. Later I taught business subjects at Brigham Young University and did consulting, advising, and training on the side for several years. During that time, I became interested in creating integrated leadership and management development programs around a sequential and balanced set of principles. These eventually evolved into the 7 Habits, and then, while I was applying the Habits to organizations, they evolved into the concept of principle-centered leadership. I decided to leave the university and go full-time into training executives from all different kinds of organizations. After a year of following a very carefully developed curriculum came the development of a business that has enabled us to take the material to people throughout the world.

What is your response to the people who claim to have the true formula for success?

I would say two things: First, if what they are saying is based on principles or natural laws, I want to learn from them and I commend them. Second, I would say we are probably using different words to describe the same basic principles or natural laws.

Are you really bald or do you shave your head for efficiency's sake?

Hey, listen, while you're busy blow-drying your hair, I'm out serving the customers. In fact, the first time I heard the saying "Bald is beautiful," I kicked the slats out of my crib!

Measuring the Impact

Since the publication of *The 7 Habits of Highly Effective People* more than ten years ago, much has been said and written about the Habits and how they have helped people become more effective. For this book, *Living the 7 Habits,* we reviewed literally thousands of letters received over the years from people all over the world who have written to express their appreciation for the impact of the 7 Habits upon their lives.

These stories play a very helpful and powerful role in researching and understanding the impact of the 7 Habits, but still there is much to be said for scientific research, or hard data. A complete picture and evaluation of the power of the 7 Habits includes both the hard data and the stories. So, in addition to these stories collected from letters and interviews, Franklin Covey has conducted years of research to scientifically measure the impact of the 7 Habits upon the performance of individuals, organizations, and the financial bottom line or return on investment (ROI).

That hard-data research reveals that there is a statistically significant positive impact upon all three categories after 7 Habits training occurs. For the individual, there is significant impact upon such behaviors as accepting responsibility for actions, creating more balance in all areas of life, increasing follow-up with work groups, balancing the need to focus on business results with the concerns and needs of individuals, and seeking feedback on ways to improve.

For the organization, the significant impact is evident in improved key performance results such as work habits, work climate, and service to customers and all other stakeholders.

The most profound impact for an organization is evident through ROI. Research reveals that 7 Habits training results in significant financial savings through reduced turnover and increased time savings and productivity. The bottom line is that the training pays for itself many times over.

If you are interested in specific statistical data or on how to measure the impact of training on performance in your organization, go to our Web site, www.franklincovey.com, or call the Franklin Covey Center for Research and Assessment at 1-800-331-7716, extension 64093.

About Franklin Covey Co.

Franklin Covey Co. is a 4,000-member international firm whose mission is to inspire change by igniting the power of proven principles so that people and organizations achieve what matters most. Franklin Covey's vision is to be the premier personal and organizational effectiveness firm in the world, affecting millions of lives each year and building a great enduring company—a model of what we teach.

Franklin Covey's client portfolio includes eighty-two of the Fortune 100 companies, more than two-thirds of the Fortune 500 companies, thousands of small and midsize companies, and government entities at local, state, and national levels. Franklin Covey has also created pilot partnerships with cities seeking to become principle-centered communities, and is currently teaching the 7 Habits to teachers and administrators in more than 3,500 school districts and universities nationwide and through statewide initiatives with education leaders in twenty-seven states.

Franklin Covey's approach is to teach people to teach themselves and become independent of the company. To the timeless adage by Lao Tzu, "Give a man a fish and you feed him for a day; teach him how to fish and you feed him for a lifetime," Franklin Covey adds, "Develop teachers of fishermen, and you lift all society." This empowerment process is carried out through programs conducted at facilities in the Rocky Mountains of Utah, custom consulting services, personal coaching, custom on-site training, and client-facilitated training, as well as through open enrollment workshops and speeches in more than four hundred cities in North America and forty countries worldwide.

With more than 19,000 licensed client facilitators teaching its curriculum within their organizations, Franklin Covey trains more than 750,000 participants annually. Implementation tools, including the Franklin Planner and a wide offering of audio- and videotapes, books, and computer software programs, enable clients to retain and effectively utilize concepts and skills. These and other products carefully selected and endorsed by Franklin Covey are available in more than 130 Franklin Covey stores throughout North America and in several other countries.

Products and materials are now available in thirty-two languages, and Franklin Covey's planner products are used by more than fifteen million individuals worldwide. The company has over fifteen million books in print, with more than one and a half million sold each year.

For more information on the Franklin Covey store or international office closest to you, or for a free catalogue of Franklin Covey products and programs, call or write:

Franklin Covey Co.
2200 West Parkway Boulevard
Salt Lake City, Utah 84119-2331 USA
Toll Free: 800-976-1492
Fax: 801-496-4252
International calls: 801-975-1776
web site: http://www.franklincovey.com

Franklin Covey's products and programs provide a wide range of resources for individuals, families, and business, government, non-profit, and education organizations, including:

PROGRAMS
Leadership Week
The 4 Roles of Leadership
The 7 Habits of Highly Effective People
What Matters Most Time Management
The Power Principle
Planning for Results
Presentation Advantage
Writing Advantage
Building Trust
Getting to Synergy
Rethinking Stress
Principle-Centered Community Projects

BOOKS

The 7 Habits of Highly Effective People
Principle-Centered Leadership
First Things First
Daily Reflections for Highly Effective People
First Things First Every Day
The Breakthrough Factor
To Do . . . Doing . . . Done! A Creative Approach to Managing
  Projects and Effectively Finishing What Matters Most
The Power Principle
The 10 Natural Laws of Successful Time and Life Management
The 7 Habits of Highly Effective Families
The 7 Habits of Highly Effective Teens
The Nature of Leadership
Daily Reflections for Highly Effective Teens

PRODUCTS

Franklin Planner
Collegiate Planner
Premier School Agendas
Franklin Planner software
Palm™ connected organizers
7 Habits Coach
Loving Reminders
Franklin Covey Style Guide
Priorities Magazine
On Target Project Management software
7 Habits audiotapes
Living the 7 Habits audiotapes
Principle-Centered Leadership audiotapes
First Things First audiotapes
The 7 Habits of Highly Effective Families audiotapes
How to Write a Family Mission Statement audiotapes
The Power Principle audiotapes
7 Habits Journal
Family Journal
7 Habits Teen Journal
Family and Teen workbooks

Managing Personal Change audiotapes
7 Habits Effectiveness Profile
Franklin Covey Leadership Library video workshops
7 Habits poster series

All the above terms are registered or proprietary
trademarks of Franklin Covey Co.

About the Author

Stephen R. Covey is an internationally respected leadership authority, family expert, teacher, organizational consultant, founder of the former Covey Leadership Center, and cochairman of Franklin Covey Co. He has made teaching Principle-Centered Living and Principle-Centered Leadership his life's work. He holds an M.B.A. from Harvard and a doctorate from B.Y.U., where he was a professor of organizational behavior and business management, and also served as director of university relations and assistant to the president. For more than thirty years he has taught millions of individuals and families and leaders in business, education, and government the transforming power of principles or natural laws that govern human and organizational effectiveness.

Dr. Covey is the author of several acclaimed books, including *The 7 Habits of Highly Effective People*, which has been at the top of the best-seller lists for more than ten years and was chosen by readers of *Chief Executive* magazine as the number one most influential book of the twentieth century. More than twelve million copies have been sold in thirty-two languages and seventy countries. His books *Principle-Centered Leadership* and *First Things First* are two of the best-selling business books of the decade. *The 7 Habits of Highly Effective Families* is a best-selling family book. Dr. Covey's most recent book, *The Nature of Leadership*, explores leadership principles through interviews and the lens of a camera.

Dr. Covey and other Franklin Covey authors, speakers, and spokespersons, all authorities on leadership and effectiveness, are consistently sought by radio and television stations, magazines, and newspapers throughout the world.

Among recent acknowledgments, Dr. Covey has received the Thomas More College Medallion for continuing service to humanity, the Toastmasters International Top Speaker Award, Ernst & Young and *Inc.* magazine's National Entrepreneur of the Year Lifetime Achievement Award for Entrepreneurial Leadership, and several honorary doctorates. He has also been recognized as one of *Time* magazine's twenty-five most influential Americans.

Stephen, his wife, Sandra, and their family live in the Rocky Mountains of Utah.